THE
REFERENCE
SHELF

REPRESENTATIVE

AMERICAN SPEECHES

1982–1983

edited by OWEN PETERSON
Professor, Department of Speech Communication
Louisiana State University

THE REFERENCE SHELF

Volume 55, Number 4

THE H. W. WILSON COMPANY

New York   1983

THE REFERENCE SHELF

The books in this series contain reprints of articles, excerpts from books, and addresses on current issues and social trends in the United States and other countries. There are six separately bound numbers in each volume, all of which are generally published in the same calendar year. One number is a collection of recent speeches; each of the others is devoted to a single subject and gives background information and discussion from various points of view, concluding with a comprehensive bibliography. Books in the series may be purchased individually or on subscription.

The Library of Congress cataloged this title as a serial.

Main entry under title:

Representative American speeches, 1982–1983.

(The Reference shelf ; v. 55, no. 4)
Includes index.
1. United States—Politics and government—1977–1981—Sources. 2. American oratory—20th century. I. Peterson, Owen, 1924–   . II. Series.
E872.R46   973.926   81–16070
ISBN 0-8242-0686-X   AACR2

International Standard Serial Number 0197-6928

Library of Congress Catalog Card Number 38-27962

PRINTED IN THE UNITED STATES OF AMERICA

CONTENTS

PREFACE 5

WHAT COURSE FOR THE COUNTRY?

Ronald W. Reagan. Staying the Course: State of the
    Union Address 8
Henry G. Cisneros. A Survival Strategy for America's
    Cities 24
Franklin A. Thomas. Youth Unemployment and Nation-
    al Service 43
Gary Hart. A Time for Economic Reform 55
Archibald G. Cox. The Best of Times? The Worst of
    Times? 62

THE THREAT OF NUCLEAR HOLOCAUST

Helen M. Caldicott. We Are the Curators of Life on
    Earth 72

MASS MEDIA AND PUBLIC WELFARE

David Manning White. Mass Culture: Can America Re-
    ally Afford It? 81
Michael J. O'Neill. The Power of the Press: A Problem
    for the Republic: A Challenge for Editors 97

ISSUES AND DIRECTIONS IN EDUCATION

David S. Saxon. The Place of Science and Technology in
    the Liberal Arts Curriculum 112

Jacques G. Maisonrouge. Some Education Requirements
    for the Manager of the Eighties 123
Lowell Weicker Jr. People with Ideas, Ideals, and the
    Will to Make Them Work 133
Howard R. Swearer. The Separation of Athletics and
    Academics in Our Universities 138
Lowell Weicker Jr. Prayer in Public Schools 144

DETERMINING AND PROMOTING AMERICAN FOREIGN POLICY

Walt W. Rostow. Foreign Policy: The President, Con-
    gress, and Public Opinion 152
Jeane J. Kirkpatrick. Promoting Free Elections 161

IN MEMORIAM

Albert Keller Jr. A Memorial to American Vietnam
    War Veterans 171
William Bragg Ewald Jr. A Man of Steel and Velvet
    and Peace: Dwight D. Eisenhower 174

BEGINNINGS

Thomas J. Stevenin. Now for the Hard Part 180
Walter F. Stromer. The Future Is Now: A Zest for Liv-
    ing 189

TO CREATE A BETTER SOCIETY FOR ALL

Geraldine A. Ferraro. Women in Leadership Can Make
    a Difference 198
C. Everett Koop. Violence and Public Health 207

APPENDIX: Biographical Notes 219
CUMULATIVE SPEAKER INDEX: 1980–1983 228

PREFACE

The 1982–1983 volume of *Representative American Speeches* contains a selection of significant addresses on a wide assortment of topics. Several speeches deal with persistent problems of the economy, foreign affairs, education, and the mass media. Others are concerned with more recent national issues such as youth unemployment, school prayer, intercollegiate athletics, the future of our cities, increased violence in our society, and the treatment of American Vietnam veterans.

Two elections—the 1982 congressional races and the upcoming 1984 presidential campaign—were the cause of much political speaking during the year. Of growing concern was the high cost of running for office and the increasing length of political campaigns. After the 1982 elections, *The New Republic* (N. 15, '82) observed:

> In a free society, elections are supposed to test the competing candidates' visions, their approaches to vital issues, and their qualifications for holding office. In this free society, elections increasingly are becoming first a test of the candidates' ability to raise huge amounts of money and then of their ability to spend it on slick thirty-second television commercials.

A study by the American Enterprise Institute found that the amount of money spent by all candidates for congressional seats rose from $70 million in 1974 to $185 million in 1980. By 1982, the average expenditure of a winning House candidate had doubled from two years earlier, while the average senator had spent more then two million dollars to win a seat, a 70 percent increase in two years.

What effect have these increased costs had on political oratory? Quite simply, political candidates must now spend more time raising funds and less time discussing issues. Moreover, with campaign costs skyrocketing, candidates are becoming increasingly dependent on funds from Political Action Committees (PACs), which represent special interest groups. PACs broke all records for donations in the 1982 elections, pumping more than $87 million into various candidates' campaign coffers. The pernicious effect of PACs, in the view of some observers, lies in the fact that funds are donated not so much to support good government as to reward legislative friends and punish enemies; at worst, critics charge, PACs are simply buying votes on upcoming legislation.

Even before the 1982 congressional elections were completed, the 1984 presidential campaign was already underway with seven Democrats in the race and an incumbent President deciding whether to run for a second term. The excessive length of American presidential campaigns has prompted many proposals—at least 80 separate studies in recent years—to shorten the electoral process and thereby reduce its cost. While many critics deplore the long months of campaigning, Godfrey Sperling suggests the time may not be poorly spent:

> As a number of Democrats now enter the presidential political arena, the criticism one hears is, "Why so early?" Perhaps, it is never too early for the presidential sweepstakes. Yes, it may get boring. Yes, the voters may well be tuckered out by the candidates and their rhetoric even before the 1984 presidential year begins. But the fact of the matter is that the debate over issues is a continuing process and the candidates can and often do contribute to the enlightenment that helps to make that interchange of ideas useful. . . . [If the democratic process] is to work there must be a perpetual interchange of public opinion. Thus politics, in the sense of continuing debate, must go on. It is the job of the politicians to articulate the issues. (*Christian Science Monitor*, F. 23, '83, p 24)

American public address in 1982–1983 was not free from disturbing elements. Two in particular stood out: first was the threats to free speech on university campuses in the form of attempts to prevent controversial speakers—for instance, U.S. Ambassador to the United Nations Jeane J. Kirkpatrick and former Black Panther Eldredge Cleaver—from presenting their messages to college communities. While heckling is a recognized form of free speech and is protected by the First Amendment, efforts by both students and faculties to cancel speaking invitations to Ambassador Kirkpatrick or to silence her completely by demonstrations and continuous booing were reprehensible.

The second element affecting public address was the negative campaign tactics in the 1982 congressional elections. Examples of this included a television commercial used by one Senate candidate which showed an atomic explosion paired with shots of a child pleading, "I want to go on living"—an attempt to exploit his opponent's stand against a nuclear freeze. In another commercial, the words "prostitution" and "pornography" were imposed across a large picture of a congressional candidate's face, in an effort by his opponent to brand him as soft on vice. The increase in this kind of negative political campaigning prompted several states and organizations to try to find ways to curb such misleading and damaging practices. In any event such tactics are a deplorable substitute for genuine public debate over the issues.

I could not possibly compile this anthology without the help of many people. Most important is Beth Wheeler. She has provided me with invaluable aid for three years and each year her contribution has grown.

I also appreciate the assistance of many persons who have supplied me with necessary information about the speeches, speakers, audiences, and occasions for the addresses in this year's collection. In particular, I want to thank Mary Ann Allin, Edwin Battle, Maryann Bruno, Jim Buchan, Patrick Ford, Gene Giancarlo, Diane Haddick, Solomon Hoberman, Don P. Luther, Ambassador David Newsom, Judith C. O'Neil, Ann Pellicano, Joseph Schuda, Ken Starck, Senator Ted Stevens, Richard J. Tierney, Barbara Vandegrift, and Jeff Windholz.

As usual, my colleagues at Louisiana State University have provided me with support and advice. I especially thank Waldo W. Braden, Stephen L. Cooper, Gresdna Doty, Mary Frances Hopkins, Jean Jackson, Kaylene Long, Harold Mixon, and James G. Traynham.

OWEN PETERSON

May 22, 1983
Baton Rouge, Louisiana

WHAT COURSE FOR THE COUNTRY?

STAYING THE COURSE: STATE OF THE UNION ADDRESS[1]

RONALD W. REAGAN[21]

President Ronald W. Reagan delivered his second State of the Union address to the joint houses of Congress in the chamber of the House of Representatives and, via radio and television, to the entire nation at 9 P.M. on January 26, 1983. Since his State of the Union message a year earlier (See *Representative American Speeches, 1981– 1982,* p 9), the economy had shown little improvement, unemployment had increased, the Democrats had made significant gains in the 1982 congressional elections, and his Administration's financial cuts in various social welfare programs had provoked widespread criticism. In light of these developments, the President chose to couch his address in the spirit of economic realism and bipartisan cooperation. Admitting the continued presence of serious economic difficulties, but also stressing gains during the year, Reagan appealed to the courage, patience, and strength of the American people "to stay the course."

The State of the Union address presents a formidable challenge for modern presidents. Originally designed as a means for a president to inform Congress of conditions in the country and to provide it with a projection of his plans and hopes, the address was given an additional dimension with the advent of radio and television coverage. Now a president speaks not only to the assembled senators and representatives but also, simultaneously, to the country at large. In rallying support for his programs and policies, he must strike a balance between the requirements of the two audiences.

A bit of unexpected humor was provided during the delivery of the 1983 address: Democrats, who had seen the text in advance, responded to the President with a carefully orchestrated standing ovation when he said,"We who are in government must take the lead in restoring the economy"—a phrase that contrasted sharply with earlier Reagan statements about reducing the role of government in the economy.

Response to the speech was mixed. William Safire conservative columnist for the *New York Times* and former speech-writer for Richard Nixon, wrote:

---

[1]Delivered to the joint houses of Congress in the chamber of the United States House of Representatives, Washington, D.C., at 9 P.M. on January 26, 1983.

[2] For biographical note, see Appendix.

What a disappointment. The themeless pudding called this year's State of the Union address was a series of banalities intended to ingratiate the President with his political opposition; instead, this worst of Reagan speeches invited the grinning contempt it received (i.e., the Democrats' standing ovation). . . . In all, he missed a great opportunity to be himself and to continue to try to made a difference. . . . He chose to be somebody else, or everybody else, and even his speech delivery suffered as he took up the role of Presiding Officer rather than Chief Executive. (*New York Times,* Ja. 27, '83, p 23)

Hedrick Smith, chief Washington correspondent of the *New York Times,* wrote:

Beyond the overall budget freeze, his speech lacked a single trademark such as his "New Federalism" initiative last year. . . . Nor did tonight's address reach for the rhetorical flourishes and inspirational passages of his Inaugural Address and his first State of the Union message. It was more hard-headed and businesslike.

Morton Kondracke, writing for the liberal *New Republic,* reacted more favorably, saying:

Yet another White House success—no smash, but a solid accomplishment—was a State of the Union address that managed to mollify administration opponents and skeptics while giving up next to nothing of the President's most cherished principles. (*New Republic,* F. 21, '83, p 7)

Kondracke wrote that the President himself selected the bipartisan approach, overruling some of his speechwriters.

Veteran political commentator James Reston wrote in the *New York Times,*

President Reagan is down in the polls but he's not down in the dumps. He reads a State of the Union message better than any President since Franklin Roosevelt, and like Roosevelt he pretends to be faithful to his campaign oratory while modifying it if it doesn't work. . . . His second State of the Union message is obviously different from his first. . . . What he seems to be doing now, by backing and filling, is to try to work out some kind of compromise without really admitting that he's doing so. He's talking tough but acting canny, and rather skillfully. (Ja. 26, '83, p 25)

New Yorker writer Elizabeth Drew commented on Reagan's uncharacteristically halting and defensive delivery of the speech, pointing out that he was usually confident and faultless in speaking from a broad text. She described the address as "perhaps the most difficult one the President has had to give" because "he had to proceed from unaccustomed territory—a corner," which required him "to adopt a sombre tone that is not typical of him and that he is not comfortable with." (*New Yorker,* F. 14, '83, p 102)

Ronald Reagan's speech: This solemn occasion marks the 196th time that a President of the United States has reported on the State of the Union since George Washington first did so in 1790. That is a lot of reports, but there is no shortage of new things to say about the state of the union. The very key to our success has been our ability, foremost among nations, to preserve our lasting values by making change work for us rather than against us.

I would like to talk with you this evening about what we can do together—not as Republicans and Democrats, but as Americans—to make tomorrow's America happy and prosperous at home, strong and respected abroad, and at peace in the world.

As we gather here tonight, the state of our union is strong, but our economy is troubled. For too many of our fellow citizens—farmers, steel and auto workers, lumbermen, black teenagers, and working mothers—this is a painful period. We must all do everything in our power to bring their ordeal to an end. It has fallen to us, in our time, to undo damage that was a long time in the making, and to begin the hard but necessary task of building a better future for ourselves and our children.

We have a long way to go, but thanks to the courage, patience, and strength of our people, America is on the mend.

Let me give you just one important reason why I believe this—it involves many members of this body.

Just 10 days ago, after months of debate and deadlock, the bipartisan Commission on Social Security accomplished the seemingly impossible.

Social Security, as some of us had warned for so long, faced disaster. I, myself, have been speaking about this problem for almost 30 years. As 1983 began, the system stood on the brink of bankruptcy, a double victim of our economic ills. First, a decade of rampant inflation drained its reserves as we tried to protect beneficiaries from the spiraling cost of living. Then the recession and the sudden end of inflation withered the expanding wage base and increasing revenues the system needs to support the 36 million Americans who depend on it.

When the Speaker of the House, the Senate majority leader, and I formed the bipartisan Commission on Social Security, pundits and experts predicted that party divisions and conflicting interests would prevent the commission from agreeing on a plan to save Social Security.

Well, sometimes, even here in Washington, the cynics are wrong. Through compromise and cooperation, the members of the commission overcame their differences and achieved a fair, workable plan. They proved that, when it comes to the national welfare, Americans can still pull together for the common good.

Tonight, I am especially pleased to join with the Speaker and the Senate majority leader in urging the Congress to enact this plan within the next hundred days.

There are elements in it, of course, that none of us prefers, but taken together it forms a package all of us can support. It asks for some sacrifice by all—the self-employed, beneficiaries, workers, new government employees, and the better-off among the retired—but it imposes an undue burden on none. And, in supporting it, we keep an important pledge to the American people: the integrity of the Social Security system will be preserved—and no one's payments will be reduced.

The commission's plan will do the job. Indeed, it must do the job. We owe it to today's older Americans—and today's younger workers.

So, before we go any further, I ask you to join with me in saluting the members of the commission who are here tonight, and Senate Majority Leader Howard Baker and Speaker Tip O'Neill, for a job well done.

I hope and pray the bipartisan spirit that guided you in this endeavor will inspire all of us as we face the challenges of the year ahead.

Nearly half a century ago, in this chamber, another American President, Franklin Delano Roosevelt, in his second State of the Union message, urged America to look to the future—to meet the challenge of change and the need for leadership that looks forward, not backward.

"Throughout the world," he said, "change is the order of the day. In every nation economic problems long in the making have brought crises of many kinds for which the masters of old practice and theory were unprepared."

He also reminded us that "the future lies with those wise political leaders who realize that the great public is interested more in Government than in politics."

So, let us, in these next two years—men and women of both parties and every political shade—concentrate on the long-range, bipartisan responsibilities of government, not the short-term temptations of partisan politics.

The problems we inherited were far worse than most inside and out of government had expected; the recession was deeper than most inside and out of government had predicted. Curing those problems has taken more time, and a higher toll, than any of us wanted. Unemployment is far too high. Projected federal spending—if government refuses to tighten its own belt—will be far too high and could weaken and shorten the economic recovery now underway.

This recovery will bring with it a revival of economic confidence and spending for consumer items and capital goods—the stimulus we need to restart our stalled economic engines. The American people have already stepped up their rate of saving, assuring that the funds needed to modernize our factories and improve our technology will once again flow to business and industry.

The inflationary expectations that led to a 21–1/2 percent prime rate and soaring mortgage rates two years ago are now reduced by almost half. Lenders have started to realize that double-digit inflation is no longer a way of life. So, interest rates have tumbled, paving the way for recovery in vital industries like housing and autos.

The early evidence of that recovery has started coming in. Housing starts for the fourth quarter of 1982 were up 45 percent from a year ago. And housing permits—a sure indicator of future growth—were up a whopping 60 percent.

We are witnessing an upsurge of productivity and impressive evidence that American industry will once again become competitive in markets at home and abroad—insuring more jobs and better incomes for the nation's work force.

But our confidence must also be tempered by realism and patience. Quick fixes and artificial stimulants, repeatedly applied over decades, are what brought on the inflationary disorders that we have now paid such a heavy price to cure.

The permanent recovery in employment, production, and investment we seek will not come in a sharp, short spurt. It will build carefully and steadily in the months and years ahead.

In the meantime, the challenge of government is to identify the things we can do now to ease this massive economic transition for the American people.

The federal budget is both a symptom and a cause of our economic problems. Unless we reduce the dangerous growth rate in government spending, we could face the prospect of sluggish economic growth into the indefinite future. Failure to cope with this problem now could mean as much as a trillion dollars more in national debt for every man, woman, and child in our nation.

To assure a sustained recovery, we must continue getting runaway spending under control to bring those deficits down. If we do not, the recovery will be too short, unemployment will remain too high, and we will leave an unconscionable burden of national debt for our children. That we must not do. Let us be clear about where the deficit problem comes from. Contrary to the drumbeat we have been hearing for the last few months, the deficits we face are not rooted in defense spending. Taken as a percentage of the gross national product, our defense spending happens to be only about four-fifths of what it was in 1970. Nor is the deficit, as some would have it, rooted in tax cuts. Even with our tax cuts, taxes as a fraction of gross national product remain about the same as they were in 1970.

The fact is, our deficits come from the uncontrolled growth of the budget for domestic spending. During the 1970s, the share of our national income devoted to this domestic spending increased by more than 60 percent—from 10 cents out of every dollar produced by the American people to 16 cents. In spite of all our economies and efficiencies, and without adding any new programs, basic, necessary domestic spending provided for in this year's budget will grow to almost $1 trillion over the next five years.

The deficit problem is a clear and present danger to the basic health of our republic. We need a plan to overcome this danger—a plan based on these principles:

It must be bipartisan. Conquering the deficits and putting the government's house in order will require the best efforts of all of us.

It must be fair. Just as all will share in the benefits that will come from recovery, all should share fairly in the burden of transition.

It must be prudent. The strength of our national defense must be restored so that we can pursue prosperity in peace and freedom while maintaining our commitment to the truly needy.

Finally, it must be realistic. We cannot rely on hope alone.

With these guiding principles in mind, let me outline a four-part plan to increase economic growth and reduce deficits.

First, in my Budget Message, I will recommend a federal spending freeze. I know this is strong medicine, but so far we have only cut the rate of increase in federal spending. The government has continued to spend more money each year, though not as much more as it did in the past. Taken as a whole, the budget I am proposing for the next fiscal year will increase no more than the rate of inflation—in other words, the federal government will hold the line on real spending. That is far less than many American families have had to do in these difficult times.

I will request that the proposed six-month freeze in cost-of-living adjustments recommended by the bipartisan Social Security Commission be applied to other government-related retirement programs. I will also propose a one-year freeze on a broad range of domestic spending programs, and for federal civilian and military pay and pension programs.

Second, I will ask the Congress to adopt specific measures to control the growth of the so-called "uncontrollable" spending programs. These are the automatic spending programs, such as food stamps, that cannot be simply frozen—and that have grown by over 400 percent since 1970. They are the largest single cause of the built-in or "structural" deficit problem. Our standard here will be fairness—insuring that the taxpayers' hard-earned dollars go only to the truly needy; that none of them are turned away; but that fraud and waste are stamped out. And, I am sorry to say, there is a lot of it out there. In the food stamp program alone, last year we identified almost $1.1 billion in overpayments. The taxpayers are not the only victims of this kind of abuse; the truly needy suffer as funds intended for them are taken by the greedy. For everyone's sake, we must put an end to such waste and corruption.

Third, I will adjust our program to restore America's defenses by proposing $55 billion in defense savings over the next five years. These are savings recommended to me by the Secretary of Defense, who has assured me they can be safely achieved and will not diminish our ability to negotiate arms reductions or endanger America's security. We will not gamble with our national survival.

Fourth, because we must insure reduction and eventual elimination of deficits over the next several years, I will propose a stand-by tax limited to no more than 1 percent of the gross national product to start in fiscal 1986. It would last no more than three years and would start only if the Congress has first approved our spending freeze and budget control program. You could say that this is an insurance policy for the future—a remedy that will be at hand if needed, but only resorted to if absolutely necessary.

In the meantime, we will continue to study ways to simplify the tax code and make it more fair for all Americans. This is a goal that every American who has ever struggled with a tax form can understand.

At the same time, however, I will oppose any efforts to undo the basic tax reforms we have already enacted—including the 10 percent tax break coming to taxpayers this July and the tax indexing which will protect all Americans from inflationary bracket creep in the years ahead.

I realize that this four-part plan is easier to describe than it will be to enact. But the looming deficits that hang over us—and over America's future—must be reduced. The path I have outlined is fair, balanced, and realistic. If enacted, it will insure a steady decline in deficits, aiming toward a balanced budget by the end of the decade. It is the only path that will lead to a strong, sustained recovery.

Let us follow that path together.

No domestic challenge is more crucial than providing stable, permanent jobs for all Americans who want to work. The recovery will provide jobs for most, but others will need special help and training for new skills. Shortly, I will submit to the Congress the Employment Act of 1983 designed to get at the special problems of the long-term unemployed as well as young people trying to enter the job market. I will propose extending unemployment benefits, including special incentives to employers who hire the long-term unemployed, providing programs for displaced workers, and helping federally funded and state-administered unemployment insurance programs provide workers with training and relocation assistance. Finally, our proposal will include new incentives for summer youth employment to help young people get a start in the job market.

We must offer both short-term help and long-term help for our unemployed. I hope we can work together on this, as we did last year in enacting the landmark Job Training Partnership Act. Regulatory reform legislation, a responsible clean air act and passage of Enterprise Zone legislation will also create new incentives for jobs and opportunity.

One out of every five jobs in our country depends on trade. So, I will propose a broader strategy in the field of international trade—one that increases the openness of our trading system and is fairer to America's farmers and workers in the world marketplace. We must have adequate export financing to sell American products overseas. I will ask for new negotiating authority to remove barriers and get more of our products into foreign markets. We must strengthen the organization of our trade agencies and make changes in our domestic laws and international trade policy to promote free trade and the increased flow of American goods, services and investments.

Our trade position can also be improved by making our port system more efficient. Better, more active harbors translate into stable jobs in our coal fields, railroads, trucking industry and ports. After two years of debate, it is time for us to get together and enact a port modernization bill.

Education, training and retraining are fundamental to our success as are research, development and productivity. Labor, management and government at all levels can and must participate in improving these tools of growth. Tax policy, regulatory practices and government programs all need constant re-evaluation in terms of our competitiveness. Every American has a role, and a stake, in international trade.

We Americans are still the world's technological leader in most fields. We must keep that edge, and to do so we need to begin renewing the basics—starting with our educational system. While we grew complacent, others have acted. Japan, with a population only about half the size of ours, graduates from its universities more engineers than we do. If a child does not receive adequate math and science teaching by the age of 16, he or she has lost the chance to be a scientist or engineer.

We must join together—parents, teachers, grassroots groups, organized labor and the business community—to revitalize American education by setting a standard of excellence

In 1983, we seek four major education goals:

A quality education initiative to encourage a substantial upgrading of math and science instruction through block grants to the states.

Establishment of education savings accounts that will give middle- and lower-income families an incentive to save for their children's college education and, at the same time, encourage a real increase in savings for economic growth.

Passage of tuition tax credits for parents who want to send their children to private or religiously affiliated schools.

A constitutional amendment to permit voluntary school prayer; God never should have been expelled from America's classrooms.

Our commitment to fairness means that we must assure legal and economic equity for women, and eliminate, once and for all, all traces of unjust discrimination against women from the U.S. Code. We will not tolerate wage discrimination based on sex and we intend to strengthen enforcement of child support laws to insure that single parents, most of whom are women, do not suffer unfair financial hardship. We will also take action to remedy inequities in pensions. These initiatives will be joined by others to continue our efforts to promote equity for women.

Also in the area of fairness and equity, we will ask for extension of the Civil Rights Commission, which is due to expire this year. The commission is an important part of the ongoing struggle for justice in America, and we strongly support its reauthorization. Effective enforcement of our nation's fair housing laws is also essential to insuring equal opportunity. In the year ahead, we will work to strengthen enforcement of fair housing laws for all Americans.

The time has also come for major reform of our criminal justice statutes and acceleration of the drive against organized crime and drug trafficking. It is high time we make our cities safe again. This Administration hereby declares all-out war on big-time organized crime and the drug racketeers who are poisoning our young people. We will also implement recommendations of our Task Force on Victims of Crime, which will report to me this week.

American agriculture, the envy of the world, has become the victim of its own successes. With one farmer now producing enough food to feed himself and 77 other people, America is confronted with record surplus crops and commodity prices below the cost of production. We must strive, through innovations like the payment-in-kind "crop swap" approach, and an aggressive export policy, to restore health and vitality to rural America. Meanwhile, I have instructed the Department of Agriculture to work individually with farmers with debt problems to help them through these tough times.

Over the past year, our Task Force on Private Sector Initiatives has successfully forged a working partnership involving leaders of business, labor, education and government to address the training needs of American workers. Thanks to the task force, private sector initiatives are now under way in all 50 states of the Union and thousands of working people have been helped in making the shift from dead-end jobs and low-demand skills to the growth areas of high technology and the service economy. Additionally, a major effort will be focused on encouraging the expansion of private community child care. The new advisory council on private sector initiatives will carry on and extend this vital work of encouraging private initiative in 1983.

In the coming year we will also act to improve the quality of life for Americans by curbing the skyrocketing cost of health care that is becoming an unbearable financial burden for so many. And we will submit legislation to provide catastrophic illness insurance coverage for older Americans.

I will also shortly submit a comprehensive federalism proposal that will continue our efforts to restore to states and local governments their roles as dynamic laboratories of change in a creative democracy.

During the next several weeks, I will send to the Congress a series of detailed proposals on these and other topics and look forward to working with you on the development of these initiatives.

So far, I have concentrated mainly on the problems posed by the future. But in almost every home and workplace in America, we are already witnessing reason for great hope—the first flowering of the man-made miracles of high technology, a field pioneered and still led by our country.

To many of us now, computers, silicon chips, data processing, cybernetics and all the other innovations of the dawning high technology age are as mystifying as the working of the combustion engine must have been when the first Model T rattled down Main Street U.S.A.

But, as surely as America's pioneer spirit made us the industrial giant of the 20th century, the same pioneer spirit today is opening up another vast frontier of opportunity—the frontier of high technology. In conquering this frontier we cannot write off our traditional industries, but we must develop the skills and industries that will make us a pioneer of tomorrow. This Administration is committed to keeping America the technological leader of the world now and into the 21st century.

Let us turn briefly to the international arena. America's leadership role in the world came to us because of our own strength and because of the values which guide us as a society: free elections, a free press, freedom of religious choice, free trade unions, and, above all, freedom for the individual and rejection of the arbitrary power of the state. These values are the bedrock of our strength. They unite us in a stewardship of peace and freedom with our allies and friends in NATO, in Asia, in Latin America and elsewhere. They are also the values which in the recent past some among us had begun to doubt and view with a cynical eye.

Fortunately, we and our allies have rediscovered the strength of our common democratic values. And we are applying them as the cornerstone of a comprehensive strategy for peace with freedom. In London last year, I announced the commitment of the United States to developing the infrastructure of democracy throughout the world. We intend to pursue this democratic initiative vigorously. The future belongs not to governments and ideologies which oppress their peoples but to democratic systems of self-government which encourage individual initiative and guarantee personal freedom.

But our strategy for peace with freedom must also be based on strength—economic strength and military strength. A strong American economy is essential to the well-being and security of our friends and allies. The restoration of a strong, healthy American economy has been and remains one of the central pillars of our foreign policy. The progress I have been able to report to you tonight will, I know, be as warmly welcomed by the rest of the free world as it is by the American people.

We must also recognize that our own economic well-being is inextricably linked to the world economy. We export over 20 percent of our industrial production, and 40 percent of our farmland produces for export. We will continue to work loosely with the industrialized democracies of Europe and Japan and with the International Monetary Fund to ensure it has adequate resources to help bring the world economy back to strong, noninflationary growth. As the leader of the West and as a country that has become great and rich because of economic freedom, America must be an unrelenting advocate of free trade. As some nations are tempted to turn to protectionism, our strategy cannot be to follow them but to lead the way toward freer trade. To this end, in May of this year, America will host an economic summit meeting in Williamsburg, Virginia.

As we begin our third year, we have put in place a defense program that redeems the neglect of the past decade. We have developed a realistic military strategy to deter threats to the peace, and to protect our freedom if deterrence fails. Our armed forces are finally properly paid, after years of neglect, are well-trained, and becoming better equipped and supplied—and the American uniform is once more worn with pride. Most of the major systems needed for modernizing our defenses are already under way and we will be addressing one key system—the MX missile—in consultation with the Congress in a few months.

America's foreign policy is once again based on bipartisanship—on realism, strength, full partnership and consultation with our allies, and constructive negotiation with potential adversaries. From the Middle East to southern Africa to Geneva, American diplomats are taking the initiative to make peace and lower arms levels. We should be proud of our role as peacemakers.

In the Middle East last year, the United States played the major role in ending the tragic fighting in Lebanon, and negotiated the withdrawal of the P.L.O. from Beirut.

Last September, I outlined principles to carry on the peace process begun so promisingly at Camp David. All the people of the Middle East should know that, in the year ahead, we will not flag in our efforts to build on that foundation to bring them the blessings of peace.

In Central America and the Caribbean Basin, we are likewise engaged in a partnership for peace, prosperity and democracy. Final passage of the remaining portions of our Caribbean Basin Initiative, which passed the House last year, is one of this Administration's top legislative priorities for 1983.

The security and economic assistance policies of this Administration, in Latin America and elsewhere, are based on realism and represent a critical investment in the future of the human race. This undertaking is a joint responsibility of the executive and legislative branches, and I am counting on the cooperation and statesmanship of the Congress to help us meet this essential foreign policy goal.

At the heart of our strategy for peace is our relationshilp with the Soviet Union.

The past year was a change in Soviet leadership. We are prepared for a positive change in Soviet-American relations. But the Soviet Union must show, by deeds as well as words, a sincere commitment to respect the rights and sovereignty of the family of nations. Responsible members of the world community do not threaten or invade their neighbors and they restrain their allies from aggression.

For our part, we are vigorously pursuing arms reductions negotiations with the Soviet Union. Supported by our allies, we have put forward draft agreements proposing significant weapons reductions to equal and verifiable lower levels. We insist on an equal balance of forces. And, given the overwhelming evidence of Soviet violations of international treaties concerning chemical and biological weapons, we also insist that any agreement we sign can and will be verifiable.

In the case of intermediate-range nuclear forces, we have proposed the complete elimination of the entire class of land-based missiles. We are also prepared to carefully explore serious Soviet proposals. At the same time, let me emphasize that allied steadfastness remains a key to achieving arms reductions.

With firmness and dedication, we will continue to negotiate. Deep down, the Soviets must know it is in their interest as well as ours to prevent a wasteful arms race. And once they recognize our unshakeable resolve to maintain adequate deterrence, they will have every reason to join us in the search for greater security and major arms reductions. When that moment comes—we will have taken an important step toward a more peaceful future for all the world's people.

A very wise man, Bernard Baruch, once said that America has never forgotten the nobler things that brought her into being and that light her path. Our country is a special place because we Americans have always been sustained, through good times and bad, by a noble vision—a vision not only of what the world around us is today, but of what we, as a free people, can make it be tomorrow.

We are realists; we solve our problems instead of ignoring them, no matter how loud the chorus of despair around us.

But we are also idealists, for it was an ideal that brought our ancestors to these shores from every corner of the world.

Right now we need both realism and idealism. Millions of our neighbors are without work. It is up to us to see they are not without hope. This is a task for all of us. And may I say Americans have rallied to this cause proving once again that we are the most generous people on Earth.

We who are in government must take the lead in restoring the economy. The single thing that can start the wheels of industry turning again is further reduction of interest rates. Another one or two points can mean tens of thousands of jobs. Right now, with inflation as low as it is, 3.9 percent, there is room for interest rates to come down.

Only fear prevents their reduction. A lender, as we know, must charge an interest rate that recovers the depreciated value of the dollars loaned. That depreciation is of course, the amount of inflation. Today, interest rates are based on fear that government will resort to measures, as it has in the past, that will send inflation zooming again.

We who serve here in this capital must erase that fear by making it absolutely clear that we will not stop fighting inflation; that, together, we will do only those things that will lead to lasting economic growth.

Yes, the problems confronting us are large and forbidding. And, certainly, no one can or should minimize the plight of millions of our friends and neighbors who are living in the bleak emptiness of unemployment. But we must and can give them good reason to be hopeful.

Back over the years, citizens like ourselves have gathered within these walls when our nation was threatened; sometimes when its very existence was at stake. Always, with courage and common sense they met the crises of their time and lived to see a stronger, better and more prosperous country.

The present situation is no worse and in fact is not as bad as some of those they faced. Time and again, they proved that there is nothing we Americans cannot achieve as free men and women.

Yes, we still have problems—plenty of them. But it is just plain wrong—unjust of our country and unjust to our people—to let those problems stand in the way of the most important truth of all: America is on the mend.

We owe it to the unfortunate to be aware of their plight and to help them in every way we can. No one can quarrel with that— we must and do have compassion for all the victims of this economic crisis. But the big story about America today is the way that those extraordinary "ordinary" Americans who never make the headlines and will never be interviewed—are laying the foundation, not just for recovery from our present problems, but for a better tomorrow for all our people.

From coast to coast, on the job and in classrooms and laboratories, at new construction sites and in churches and community groups, neighbors are helping neighbors. And they've already begun the building, the research, the work and the giving that will make our country great again.

I believe this because I believe in them—in the strength of their hearts and minds, in the commitment each of them brings to their daily lives, be they high or humble. The challenge for us in government is to be worthy of them—to make government a help, not a hindrance to our people in the challenging but promising days ahead.

If we do that, if we care what our children and our children's children will say of us, if we want them one day to be thankful for what we did here in these temples of freedom, we will work together to make America better for our having been here—not just in this year, or in this decade, but in the next century and beyond.

A SURVIVAL STRATEGY FOR AMERICA'S CITIES[1]

HENRY G. CISNEROS[22]

The members of the City Club of New York and their guests, including government officials, scholars, and civic activists, gather yearly to hear a distinguished student of public affairs present ideas for the betterment of life in the cities at the Richard S. Childs Lecture in Municipal Administration. Mr. Childs, a member of the City Club for seventy-one years and its president for twelve years, was best known for two major creative achievements in public administration: the city manager system, now

[1]The 1982 Richard S. Childs Lecture in Municipal Administration, delivered to the City Club of New York in a conference room at noon on February 26, 1982.

[2] For biographical note, see Appendix.

used in more than 1800 cities, and the short ballot. The lectureship in his honor was established shortly before his death in 1978.

Selection of the Childs lecturer is made by a committee of club officers, university administrators and professors, and civic leaders from a list of nominations by members. The committee chose Henry C. Cisneros, mayor of San Antonio, Texas for the fourth lecture. Mayor Cisneros was well qualified with two master's degrees—one in urban and regional planning from Texas A & M University and the other in public administration from Harvard—and a Ph.D. in public administration from George Washington University. The son of Mexican immigrants, Cisneros served two terms as a councilman in San Antonio, the largest American city with a majority Hispanic population, before becoming in 1981 its first Mexican-American mayor since 1842. Although only 34 years old, Cisneros also had experience working with city managers and national city organizations as well as teaching at the University of Texas at San Antonio.

Mayor Cisneros delivered the lecture at approximately 1 P.M. at a luncheon held in a dining room of the City University of New York Graduate Center on February 26, 1982. Preceding the speech, an award was given to a club trustee and the mayor was introduced by the chairman of the selection committee. In attendance were approximately 80 member of the club—businessmen, civic leaders, and professionals—and a few journalists. The speech was aired live over radio station WNYC and taped for rebroadcast on cable television. *USA Today* magazine and the newsletter of the Council on Urban Economic Development later reprinted the speech in full and the *Nation's Cities* newspaper ran it in abbreviated form.

Journalist Ken Auletta, who was present, observed,

> Mayor Cisneros is worth listening to because, despite his Ph.D. and Eastern education, despite his liberal credentials and the fact that he is, at 34, only this nation's second Hispanic mayor, he is mayor of the 10th largest city and a progressive who has found success in the Sunbelt. (New York *Daily News,* Mr. 7, '82)

Syndicated columnist Richard Reeves, who also heard the lecture, described it as "one of the more thoughtful speeches I have heard from a politician," and wrote:

> Cisneros reported on the civil war in America, the new one between East and West. This Westerner, son of immigrants from Mexico, surprisingly took the Eastern side . . . no, he took the national side, the American side,

> I wanted people here to understand that in many places they are seen as the enemy," he said after the lecture. "I hear statements every day in my city that would make you think there was a civil war. I had

to search for what I really believed in to give this lecture. I realized
that I believe we are a nation. . . . Are we just 50 states? No, first
I'm an American. (Reeves, *Charlotte Observor*, Mr. 5, '82, p 19A)

Reeves observed, "it was very refreshing to hear a Western politician
thinking about some of those things from a national perspective. Actually,
it is almost always refreshing to hear that any politician anywhere is
thinking." He prophesied, "I suspect that, sooner rather than later, many
more Americans will be hearing from Henry Cisneros."

Henry Cisneros' speech: America's cities are the windows through
which the world looks at American society. It is true that at various moments each of us in our own way, for our own reasons,
would define things that we are proud of about America—the
level of our culture, the advancement of our science, the fairness
of our democracy—by citing examples from technology or art or
music, from architecture, or from business accomplishments. But
the fact remains that the most comprehensive and the likeliest
measure of American society is found at a glance in the American
cities.

The cities are the focal point of American life today because
they are the integrating mechanism for all the essential dynamics
of our modern society, the point of convergence for those dynamics: the quest for justice and the dialogue by which we find opportunities for people. People who seek a place on the American
ladder of opportunity come to the cities from other countries. New
art forms are presented at the galleries and the museums of the
great cities. New communication technologies are developed in the
cities, such as the paperless office and cable television innovations.
There is experimentation and research in the great centers of
learning. And when the cure for cancer is found, it is likely to be
found in one of the medical centers of a great American city. New
forms of architecture are proposed. The search for a better quality
of life and for ways in which people can live together goes on in
the neighborhood movement sweeping virtually all of America's
large cities.

The role of the city as an integrating mechanism for such essential dynamics is particularly true with respect to the economic
life of the nation. Cities are key entities in the economic life of

America. They are economic factors in several important ways. First, because when you look at the origins and the histories of the city, they are generally the result of economic decisions and common sense. Secondly, because the daily mechanics of the functioning of cities and their change and development are economic in nature. And thirdly, because the role they will play in the future of American society involves the national economic future.

Let us look briefly at each of these economic aspects of the cities—first at their origins, as a result of essentially economic facts and decisions. The concept of the city came with the first European colonists, both to the Northeast and, though less well-chronicled, to the Southwest. At the risk of over-simplification, North American Indians had generally lived " . . . in nature, rather than building upon it. . . . But the plans of the various companies that settled the English colonies in North America envisioned the establishment of tight little villages and commercial centers," creating requirements for specialized skills of craftsmen. Thus, as we learn from a letter written by John Smith to the English sponsors of the Jamestown Colony: "When you send again, I entreat you rather send but thirty carpenters, husband-men, gardeners, fishermen, blacksmiths, masons, and diggers up of roots and trees . . . for except we be able to lodge them and feed them, the most would consume the wants of necessaries before they can be made good for anything."

The product of those craftsmen—patterns of skill specialization and the concentration of people in the villages—was that the colonies by 1690 were actually more urbanized than England itself. A higher percentage of the early colonists lived in cities than the percentage of people living in cities in England at the time. And the communities that led the urban settlement were six seaports, commercial centers successful because of natural harbor facilities that made possible the chief economic activity of the colonies, trading the produce of the hinterland for the finished products of Europe.

They were Boston and Newport in New England. Boston, where the barrenness of the countryside forced the town to develop as a trading and shipbuilding center, was a city which urban historians describe as having had a " . . . metropolitan form of economy that was essentially modern, . . . " before Boston was a generation old. By 1700, Boston's capacity as a seaport and the size of its fleet ranked third in the English-speaking world, surpassed only by London and Bristol. But the city faced various economic crises and so had to make economic adjustments to survive:

—When the Revolutionary War ruptured their favored trading status with England, Boston's merchants had to develop entirely new markers in heretofore unfamiliar parts of the world.

—When the War of 1812 once again threatened trade, a few enterprising businessmen founded the textile and shoe manufacturing industries.

—When the economy of the hinterland began to grow and the westward expansion created a need for banking and investment, the city began to grow as a financial center.

—When, by the 1950s, the balance of national power had shifted rapidly to the West and the textile industries had moved South, then it was a growth spurt of defense-related, scientific and technological research that prepared the base for the recovery that Boston is experiencing today.

But going back to the beginning of the Colonial Era, the leaders in the Middle Colonies were New York, Philadelphia, and later Baltimore. New York was blessed with a magnificent deep water harbor, with more fertile soil than was the case in New England, and with easy access to even more extensive rich farming areas by way of the Hudson River. Later in 1825, the completion of the Erie Canal so stimulated New York as a trade center that its supremacy was established and has lasted to the present. New York grew from 60,000 people in 1800 to over one million in 1860. In that year, only London and Paris were larger in the world. New York handled one-third of the nation's imports and two-thirds of its exports.

In the Southern colonies, the leader was Charleston. It formed an early commercial base trading rice, Indigo, and skins, and by the mid-1700s, it had an economic system in which one-half of the participants were slaves.

At roughly the same time in the southwestern United States, Spanish missionaries and the captains of military expeditions were founding missions and naming fortresses. They built hundreds of missions, forts, and administrative centers in the 1700s.

But the difference between centers that never worked, such as La Bahia and Los Adaes in Texas and, on the other hand, places with such recognizable names as Los Angeles, San Francisco, Santa Fe, and San Antonio is that the latter group caught on as economic enterprises. My city, San Antonio, for example, in 1730 was a mission, a military garrison, and a home to some thirty families of Spanish settlers from the Canary Islands. Twenty years later, it was an active trading center, a crossroads for materials and livestock, the center of fertile farmlands, and well on its way toward becoming the most important city in early Texas.

Later cities came into existence and have grown with new technologies and new economic circumstances. The midwestern railroad center of Chicago, for example, grew from 4,000 at the time of its incorporation in 1833 to one million in 1890. In the 1820s, the "Queen of the West," Cincinnati, expanded with trade and travel made possible by the steamboat. The center of the nation's breadbasket, Kansas City, expanded upon its role as the meeting point for cattle drives and rail lines and as the market place for grain farmers and their buyers. The capital of the "Rocky Mountain Empire," Denver, grew from a frontier trading post to the financial and communication headquarters of an energy-rich region that extends today from the northern New Mexico border to the Edmonton and Calgary regions of Canada. The petroleum-driven phenomenon which is modern Houston exists today because its leaders carved a ship channel from an east Texas bayou, built upon the discovery of oil in the nearby countryside, attracted a national space center, and pushed the city into a role as the world headquarters of oil technology. The desert technology center of Phoenix has jumped into the top ten among U.S. cities in the last decade, a jump that has coincided with the development of an economic base in which 38 percent of all the manufacturing jobs are in computers or electronics.

But perhaps the American city best prepared economically for the 21st century is Dallas. Its early role was as a highway crossroads. It built upon that, continually diversifying, balancing, and strengthening that role. Today it is a transport focal point, a financial capital, a high technology manufacturing center, a distribution node and the heart of a communications network for the entire Southwest.

Cities are created and they grow, or they stagnate, based on economic sense: based on economic decisions which take into account the sweep of economic history and economic trends that confront the nation. We tend to forget that reality. We see cities in many other ways—as the places where we live, as the places where people congregate, as social centers—in so many different ways and we forget that the origins of cities generally stem from economic decisions and economic common sense. Cities grow or stagnate depending on realities that relate to the adequacy of infrastructure, the adequacy of transportation, or the maturation and change in the makeup of the national economy as is occurring at the present.

But cities are also economic entities in the daily dynamics of their change and functioning. Consider briefly the all too familiar ways in which economic phenomena buffet and batter cities today. In times of cyclical turndown in the national economy, it is the cities that are hurt the worst: their economies the hardest hit, their tax bases reduced most, their social services expenditure requirements the hardest pressed. When demand is weak, production is usually curtailed first or stopped altogether at the oldest plants, which tend to be located in the central cities. As a result, at the peak of the 1975 recession when national unemployment peaked at 8.5 percent, the rate in the cities was 9.6 percent and in the central city poverty areas it was more than 15 percent. Even worse disparities exist in the recession we are experiencing today.

The other side of the economic roller coaster, inflation, also batters the cities with particular severity. The costs of goods and services purchased by city government tend to rise faster than consumer prices. From 1972 to 1977, for example, when the consumer price index rose by about 48.6 percent, the costs of purchases by state and local governments rose by well over 50 percent. But the real losses to cities from the inflationary spiral can be seen only by comparing the inflation in required expenditures—the package of goods that the city has to buy—with the slower rise in revenues available to meet those expenditures. The fact is that city revenues do not keep pace with the escalating costs because, " . . . although sales and income taxes rise automatically with inflation, the property tax, which is the mainstay of local finance must be readjusted through conscious reassessments. Such reassessments generally occur only at specific intervals and are politically difficult to accomplish during periods of high inflation. The result is that cities lose purchasing power faster than the rest of society. Atlanta, for example, in a recent two-year period lost 16.6 percent of the value of its revenue by experiencing an effective property tax rate decline of 14 percent."

Still another effect of national economic problems for cities is the range of issues that come under the heading of structural changes in the U.S. economy. Structural changes, such as the decline of specific industry sectors, have created patterns of regional advantage and disadvantage, population shifts and industrial migration. The story of population and job loss in central cities is all too familiar. Today's news carries the story that 137,000 General Motors workers are now "on furlough." The implications are clear for Detroit, Akron, Toledo, South Bend, and all of those other cities where GM plants are located or where the factories exist that make automobile tires, windshields, ball bearings, and engine parts.

The conclusion is clear: cities are daily buffeted by economic realities to a degree that the economic assault is the dominant fact of life for city governments.

Let us talk about the economic future of the cities in America. There is an immediate temptation to point to the need for a national urban policy. As we review national urban problems, the natural response for one searching for solutions is to look for national solutions. A person such as myself, a mayor of a growing southwestern city, observing the current economic circumstances in the nation and in the cities, tries to draw conclusions about a national urban policy. But that is a very difficult thing to do, because the differences across the cities and the regions of this country are great. Yet I do think it is possible to make two points about the relationship between the cities and the nation, perhaps as a basis for national policy.

The first is obvious and is often stated: that the health of the cities requires as a precondition a prosperous national economy. The second point is less well understood, but I believe it needs to be developed as part of our basic understanding of the workings

of our society: that to attain a prosperous national economy, one
that is able to deal with ideals of American society, requires the
general health of a balanced system of cities. I see the role of the
cities not as incidental beneficiaries or unintended victims of economic trends but instead as fundamental building blocks for the
national economy—and building blocks for the social ideals of
United States society. It is a two-sided coin.

Let us examine the two sides of that coin separately. First, the
health of the cities requires as a precondition a prosperous national economy. I have already stated some of the elements of my case:

—When national unemployment is up, it is higher in the cities by as
much as 5 percent.

—When inflation is high, it affects the package of city expenditures
worse.

—When inflation is up, it outstrips the revenue-producing power of such
basic taxes as the property tax.

—When interest rates are high, cities must pay more for public debt, the
need for which cannot be postponed because replacement or expansion
of such critical public requirements such as sewer systems or water services cannot long be delayed.

—When recession induces plant closings, they occur first in the cities and
often it is the city plants which remain closed even after cyclical recov-
eries.

—When the national savings rate declines and capital business reinvestment in modernization is unavailable, it is the productivity of older city-
based plants which suffer by comparison with newer facilities.

Although these facts tend to be true for cities all across the nation, some people would argue that the health of every city in fact
does not depend upon national prosperity; that it is possible to
have some, in fact, many city economies, remain strong even in a
severe national recession by virtue of prosperous regional or local
conditions. As evidence, one could cite the fact that Oklahoma City
today, to pick but one example of a dynamic Sunbelt city, had an
unemployment rate of only 3 percent through much of 1981 and
that about 15 percent more new jobs were created in the oil business, agriculture, retailing, and real estate. Nearly similar statistics could be cited for Phoenix, Denver, Tampa, Jacksonville,

Tulsa, Houston, Dallas, San Diego, San Jose, San Antonio, Austin, or Tucson. And there is frankly a great temptation to cite such successes as indication of what is possible and write off the problems of the northeastern and north central cities. That temptation has found expression in the implicit thrust of a national commission's recommendation that citizens from depressed areas should "vote with their feet" and pursue opportunities elsewhere. Such feelings are reinforced by Sunbelt convictions that in previous periods of our national history, the regions that are today's losers—the depressed cities—were heavy-handed oppressors of the rest of the nation. There is a sense that this is a period of reckoning for the eastern bankers, the railroad barons, the steel producers, and the so-called eastern establishment politicians who held such a stranglehold on the machinery of production, the raw materials, and the capital so badly needed to fully develop the South, the West, and the Southwest in earlier periods of our history. And if calling these feelings "revenge" is too strong, then there is at least a sense that much of the North's problems are of its own making, the products of profligate spending by big city political organizations, of out-of-control labor unions, or of overpromising that assumes dimensions of a political-economic ethic.

Such feelings are most certainly out there and they run deeply through the currents of the public consciousness in the Southwest and throughout the South. And so they become an element of making those public policies that are to deal with vastly different conditions and trends across the regions and the cities of our country. Whether those convictions have basis in fact or not is not nearly so important as that they are the shared convictions of many citizens west of the Mississippi; therefore, in the modern political arena they find expression more and more in public policy.

And yet despite the fact that there are those temptations to split the nation along lines that divide growing regions from mature regions, the fact remains that we are a nation. First and foremost we are one nation. One has to question whether escalating the competition for advantage between regions is the best way to behave as a nation. We have to ask whether it is possible under those circumstances to hold together any semblance of a national consensus on how we deal with the poor, the old, the unskilled and those for whom social justice is still a dream. I read in national policy statements today a clear preference for policies which would encourage unbridled competition between regions. Implicit in those policies is the hope that somehow as the migration out of declining areas reaches a sufficient momentum, the market mechanism will right some of the wrongs; there will be corrections to costs, wages and governmental organization in the northeast. But there are critical questions we have to ask ourselves: "What is the human price that will be paid as those who are the least mobile in our society suffer from that kind of competition?" "Is such an intense interregional competition the best way to meet the challenges of an international environment in which we have to behave more as a nation than ever before?"

But that begins to address the other side of the coin, so let us forget sentimentality or ideals or the subjective value of national cohesiveness and talk instead just of economic benefits. The other side of that coin is this: to attain a prosperous national economy which is able to sustain an open society requires the health of a balanced system of cities across the country. Consider these facts:

—When structural unemployment in the central cities rises from inattention, each increase of one percent in the national umemployment rate adds $25 billion to the national deficit in a combination of decreased tax payments and increased benefits entitlements.

—When cities are unable to meet the cost of building roads, bridges, ports or sewer systems, there are bottlenecks and inefficiencies that affect the national economic prosperity.

—When central city schools are no longer able to train youngsters and prepare them for technological jobs, the nation pays a price in manpower shortages and gaps in the technical skills base needed for reindustrialization.

—When racial strife becomes one of the dominant features of urban life, the nation sustains a high crime rate and must live with alienation and division.

—When the cities are characterized by deterioration and when the urban landscape is a picture of decline and despair, then I believe there occurs a psychological change of mood such that national optimism is replaced by national pessimism.

All of this suggests that policies which promote or reward regional abandonment are damaging, both to the cities and to the larger national economy. It suggests that a national policy whose essential thrust is to "Let them vote with their feet," leaving behind pockets of despair for the least mobile citizens of the society, is flawed both for the cities and for the national economy. It suggests that because of the nature of American society today, to make national economic policy is to make national urban policy. And the best national urban policy is one that integrates the problems of the cities into national economic policymaking. These two great interests of national policy need to be considered.

What does it mean to think of them concurrently? What should we expect of a national economic policy that relates to urban areas? What is the overarching framework for a federal economic role in the cities? What are the principles or basic elements of such an approach? I would like today to suggest three elements.

The first element would be to create a sense of integration of the concerns of the cities into national economic thinking. This is a delicate area because it deals with a kind of cooperation that we have not had in our nation. But it parallels the spirit that the national government, the cities and business need to foster in order to create the framework that best enables business to prosper and create jobs in the long run, drawing lightly as it does from the Japanese concern for "long run vision." Actually that term is a nickname for one of the most important divisions of the Japanese Ministry of International Trade and Industry. We need to think not in terms of subsidy, control, guidance, or supervision of business but in terms of creating the conditions for business that are necessary to realize long-term visions and infuse in that process some sense of the high stakes for the survival of the cities. In the Japanese case, an organization which serves as a clearinghouse for several ministries, the Economic Planning Agency, avoids attempting to manage the economy but it does " . . . provide targets reflecting long-term trends and specifying what would be necessary for balanced national development. It is, in effect, a point of communication, coordinating estimates of future growth made by governmental branches and by the business community. It helps draw attention to various needs and helps shape the thinking about what is required for a certain level of growth."

The Ministry of International Trade and Industry itself shows initiatives beyond what has been considered acceptable in our economy. Ministry of International Trade and Industry officials try to " . . . push the pace of modernization ahead of market forces by setting high standards for modernization of plants and equipment and by promoting means to shore up companies that lack the capital to meet those standards. They point out areas where resources need to be concentrated in order to keep Japan competitive internationally in the future. MITI officials consider it their responsibility to assist companies and declining industries to merge or go out of business while encouraging new ones to move into the localities and employ the personnel who were laid off."

A key aspect to this entire process in Japan is that its success cannot in general be attributed to statutory powers or authorities, which would be resisted. "Overwhelmingly, the success of the Ministry is derived not from rules or regulations but from its efforts at administrative guidance and from the voluntary cooperation of the business community."

It is a cooperation which derives from a spirit that conveys a genuine interest in the welfare of the companies, from a high degree of competence and professionalism, and from constant formal and informal discussions within industrial sectors.

This spirit of cooperation applied to our case, to our economy, would seek " . . . to create an understanding that a partnership of business and government is a necessary condition for achieving individual and social objectives, . . . " prominent among them the need to rebuild the central cities.

Cooperation has been tried before. "Every U.S. administration since that of Calvin Coolidge has established tribunals composed of government, business, and occasionally labor with responsibility for the economic development of particular industries. Herbert Hoover, as Secretary of Commerce, sought industry-wide associations to rationalize production and increase productivity. Similar notions underlay Franklin Roosevelt's National Recovery Administration and the various business-government boards responsible for production during World War II. More recently, the Carter Administration set up tripartite boards to develop policy for the steel, auto and coal industries."

But those efforts have been hampered by bureaucratic disorganization, characterized by fragmentation which prevents promoting the idea of a "big picture" approach to the revitalization and reinvestment efforts, and by a philosophical resistance to understand and cooperate on the supply and production side of the economy at the level of regions and geographic areas. In addition, the traditional adversary relationship between government and business is so engrained that it prevents meaningful cooperation, and many of the people who have the greatest stake in the policies—for example, representatives of cities—have not been included. They could help assure that cooperative government-business efforts stay on track toward success instead of being torn apart by defenders of the status quo.

But there is one effort which is interesting as a demonstration of how close cooperation genuinely committed to building a prosperous industrial sector can succeed and prevent a great deal of human misery. In 1977, the American shoe industry was being driven out of business by imports. Employment had been cut down from 230,000 to 165,000 jobs in less than a decade. Production had dropped from 640 millions pairs of shoes to 400 million, while imports had doubled from 175 million to 370 million. In the face of demands for import barriers and tariffs, the Carter Administration, in an effort spearheaded by Under Secretary of Commerce Sidney Harman, embarked on an effort to overcome the gaps in information and the competition between U.S. Departments of Labor and Commerce in providing assistance to the nation's shoe producers. In contrast to mounting efforts to shore up the shoe industry in Europe, officials in the United States had neglected the creation of early warning forecasting systems for anticipating structural adjustment problems.

The program, coordinated by Under Secretary Harman, with the Department of Labor, was more than just an effort to speed up standard adjustment assistance to a dying industry. It innovated assistance for the industry's self-help by improving the quality and volume of private technical expertise provided to companies. Domestic retailers and manufacturers were brought together to identify market trends and style changes. An export promotion program was developed. The Office of Science and Technology was directed to work on new technologies, the first government-industry program to develop a new generation of technology in a nondefense field. By pointing out this kind of direction, the program showed results within six months. Half of the 150 companies eligible for help applied for it. Imports were dropping as a result of marketing agreements that staved off the need for strict import quotas. Employment and production began rising. Some companies began to report record sales and earnings and by 1978, Commerce Department statistics showed that America's shoe exports had increased by 28 percent. That is not to say that the shoe industry does not remain a troubled one nor is it to say that the program that Harman instituted continues. With his departure, enthusiasm and interest in the program diminished. However, the pilot program did bring some results: the revitalization of essentially sound firms and the conversion to other manufacturing fields or firms that would never have been competitive in the industry. The pilot program helped bolster the strong and facilitated conversion of the weak. Harman considers the approach a contrast to the policies that we are normally more ready to employ but which have often failed, such as imposing quotas on imports. Such reactions do not solve the inherent problems of the industry involved.

While the Harman experiment with U.S. shoe firms is novel by U.S. standards, it is one that is approached more regularly by our allies and competitors. Germany under Economics Minister Carl Schiller, for example, designed a four-fold framework to guide the government's assistance to private firms in ailing industries. Those guidelines were the following:

—One, that the entire sector, not just some firms, must be in difficulty.

—Two, that the actual restructuring program chosen be the decision of the private firms.

—Three, that the government's role be only to trigger self-help efforts to restore the sector's competitiveness.

—Four, that the aids be both temporary and result in competitiveness and efficiency.

In practice, the German program has involved targeted depreciation allowances, has encouraged industrial innovation, and has set up voluntary agreements among firms in a sector to provide breathing space for testing new production methods.

In summary, I believe that a first principle of national urban policy must be to begin to institutionalize the forms of cooperation which I believe are going to be more necessary in the economy of the future.

A second principle, and perhaps a specific outcome of the cooperation which I have just described, is investment in public infrastructure. Many of the investments necessary to the continued health of the U.S. economy—ports, bridges, and disposal sites—are public goods; they need to be provided by government. Yet, " . . . investment in infrastructure by government has been declining, from $38.6 billion to 1965 to less than $31 billion in 1977, a drop of 21 percent measured in constant 1972 dollars. As a percentage of GNP, infrastructure investment declined from 4.1 percent in 1965 to 2.3 percent in 1977, a drop of 44 percent."

Now to make the picture even bleaker, President Reagan's "New Federalism" proposals would turn over to state and city governments complete financing responsibility for such essential economic development infrastructure as roads and highways, airports, sewer systems, and disposal facilities. Keep in mind that these responsibilities will be turned over to the same levels of government which will shoulder even more human services burdens and education costs. I would suggest that in "sorting out" which programs the Administration is going to send back as the responsibility of the states, that it set up a test for what should not be included. In my view, a key test for what ought to remain funded from federal resources would result from an identification of those infrastructural programs that are required for dealing with the problems of the national economy as it affects the cities in both a short-term cyclical sense, and in the longer term sense that involves structural blockages caused by declining infrastructure. That would be the public investment element of a true supply side strategy to revitalize U.S. industry and help the cities at the same time. And it ought to be considered as a principle in reviewing the New Federalism proposals which would send programs back without economic rationale, to state and local governments.

The third principle which I would suggest be part of national urban policy would be recognition that if indeed we are to load responsibilities on local government, then we must give local government more capacity and resources. It is a characteristic of our intergovernmental development that all over this country there are dying cities at the center of metropolitan areas that are, in fact, essentially healthy. The truth of the matter is that there are no devices in our present system for relatively healthy metropolitan areas to participate in solving the problems of the central cities. And while there exists no means for mandating such participation, it is advisable to begin to think of ways to provide incentives for regional solutions. We should look at umbrella levels of financing and of providing services that make sense on a regional basis. It may be useful to consider, for example, a system of federal tax credits to citizens in metropolitan areas which have taken the initiative to finance central city problems on a metropolitan-wide basis, such as the Dayton Housing Plan or the public works and water works services more commonly delivered on a metropolitan basis. Citizens under such metropolitan systems would then be paying taxes or service fees to an umbrella metropolitan organization, but would receive credit on their federal income taxes for having set up such metropolitan service that would help unburden the central cities.

I have described three principles which I hope will be discussed as elements of national urban policy as it merges with the considerations of national economic policy. But fundamentally the economic future of the cities is going to rest with the cities themselves. Those cities that know what they want and where they are going are the ones that are going to be more successful. Even in the declining regions of the nation, those cities which have set goals, devised strategies for how to achieve those goals, and generated the organizational discipline to make the machinery of city government work for economic objectives will be better off. An example is Baltimore and the clear sense of direction that Mayor William Schaffer has provided. Recognizing that such direction can be effective, I would like to highlight five themes which I think will be important to any city administration that is trying to develop an economic strategy.

First, cities must understand their essential economic origins and must understand the role that the shifts in the American economy portend for them. Against that backdrop, city leaders must think hard in order to understand what it is they really want to accomplish. In our case in San Antonio, the driving goal is to raise the incomes of a large percentage of the population living below the national median. Our short-term strategy to achieve that goal involves the development of a high technology sector that is first labor intensive, but that builds the base for developing jobs. Those jobs will have long career ladders and higher skills requirements and provide channels for this generation, and certainly the next, to climb out of poverty and underemployed circumstances. Dallas, on the other hand, has different goals, as befits a city at a very different stage of life and with a much higher income level. The Dallas strategy is not raising incomes per se, but preparing the city for national leadership in the 21st century. As a result, its leaders are making infrastructural decisions today that will build the communications complex which will assure Dallas' role as the communication capital of the Southwest. Houston leaders understand that to remain a growth city for the long run they must deal with serious traffic congestion, and so they have embarked upon a $16 billion program integrating mass transit, highways, and double-decked expressways. The long and short of it is that a city has to make explicit what it's trying to accomplish in an economic sense and then must express in clear terms how it intends to go about it. Secondly, cities have to organize themselves for economic development. That means creating a municipal organization that has entrepreneurial qualities. We believe we have created such an entrepreneurial team in San Antonio. In fact, we have gone beyond that to create an economic agenda which allows us to filter policy discussions in seemingly unrelated areas through the screen of its significance for the economic future of our community.

The third theme which I believe cities will have to master is an understanding of what it means to create a climate in which the private sector can produce jobs. We in San Antonio have developed what we refer to as our "two-fisted" approach to job creation. The first "fist" is understanding, in practical commonsense terms, what it actually takes to create jobs. That kind of recognition is expressed in the most recent issue of your newsletter, *The Gadfly*, in which Ed Logue of the South Bronx development effort is quoted as saying: "The fundamental need in the South Bronx is to create jobs." The second fist of our strategy is to make sure that the jobs occur in ways and in locations such that the poorest of the society can benefit.

The fourth theme to which I believe cities will have to be attentive involves the "building blocks" of the national economy of the future. That means stressing education for high technology, technical-vocational programs, and engineering curricula offered in the central cities, motivating central city youth to gravitate toward technological jobs. This is critically important. I say this because I believe that the divisions in our society have the potential to be deeper and more serious than even the present racial division, as national technological development separates those who are technologically illiterate from those who are technologically competent. That is not a line which can be crossed via affirmative action programs; it is a line that can be crossed only by investing in the educational system and early technological training for youngsters in the central cities.

The fifth and final point I would make today is that I believe a component of local policies must be a tangible optimism that fuels our relentless effort to invest in the future. The surest way to perpetuate the cycle of decline in depressed regions and to create conditions of eventual decline in the regions that are presently growing would be to slow down or hold back the process of investment in infrastructure.

Ladies and gentlemen, I am grateful to you for the opportunity to be here. I am personally optimistic about the American city. I believe in it as a key institution of our society. While other institutions will play a part in the important national task of integrating our society, of creating opportunities, and of finding justice, I believe the best hope for attaining those national ideals is the American city.

YOUTH UNEMPLOYMENT AND NATIONAL SERVICE[1]

Franklin A. Thomas[23]

The Economic Club of Detroit, founded in 1934, has a membership that comprises prominent men and women from all walks of life, but particularly from business, government, labor, and the professions. The club's weekly luncheon meetings usually feature an address by a guest lecturer. The speaker at the March 7, 1983, meeting was Franklin A. Thomas, president of the Ford Foundation.

Mr. Thomas, who is an attorney, was born in the Bedford Stuyvesant section of Brooklyn. Three decades later be became president of the Bedford Stuyvesant Restoration Corporation established to restore his old neighborhood, which had become a national symbol of urban decay. After serving as Deputy Police Commissioner of New York City and as Assistant U. S. Attorney for the Southern District of New York, he became president of the Ford Foundation in June of 1979.

Speaking in Detroit, a city particularly hard hit by the recession and high unemployment, to an audience deeply concerned about the economic welfare of their city, Thomas proposed the creation of a national service for youth aged 16 to 22. Emphasizing the need for such a program, he noted that,

> Virtually every industrial country is now burdened with unprecedented rates of unemployment, especially among young people. In our country the affliction appeared earlier than elsewhere. It has been intensified by disastrous rates of unemployment among inner-city minority youth. . . . Over a long stretch of years, whatever the adult unemployment rate has been, the rate of youth unemployment has been at least twice as high. And whatever the unemployment rate of white youth, the unemployment rate of black youth has been at least twice as high.

The speech is an example of John Dewey's reflective thought process for problem solving. Thomas began by showing the seriousness of the problem, examined its causes, and sought to show why various attempts to solve it had failed. He then presented his proposed solution—national service—and explained how it would work and why he believed it to be desirable.

[31]Delivered to the Economic Club of Detroit at 12:45 P.M., March 7, 1983, in a banquet room in Cobo Hall, Detroit.

[2] For biographical note, see Appendix.

Mr. Thomas presented his speech to approximately 255 members of the Economic Club in a banquet room in Cobo Hall after the luncheon. The presiding officer at the meeting was the Right Reverend H. Coleman McGehee Jr., bishop of the Episcopal Diocese of Michigan.

Franklin Thomas's speech: I want to speak today about two subjects, one that is familiar to you and another that deserves to be. The first concerns the worsening problem of youth unemployment. The second is related to the first but embraces a broader set of issues. It examines the case for the adoption of a system of national service.

Virtually every industrial country is now burdened with unprecedented rates of unemployment, especially among young people. In our country the affliction appeared earlier than elsewhere. It has been intensified by disastrous rates of unemployment among inner-city minority youth.

The measures of youth unemployment seem to be governed by what might be called "the two-times rule." Over a long stretch of years, whatever the adult unemployment rate has been, the rate of youth unemployment has been at least twice as high. And whatever the unemployment rate of white youth, the unemployment rate of black youth has been at least twice as high. The source of the problem is not just a weakened economy and severe recession. It is a structural problem as well. The discouraging statistics show up in good times as well as in bad, and they get more discouraging all the time.

No one in Detroit needs to be told that structural unemployment is also reaching deeply into the adult labor force, and not only into the ranks of the blue-collar worker. No caring person would claim that the frustrations of unemployed teenagers, most of whom live with parents and many of whom seek only part-time work, are anything like the shattering blows of protracted unemployment on adult workers. Nothing can be more demoralizing than the specter of displaced jobs, obsolete skills, uprooted homes, and disintegrated families. Yet, viewed across a lifetime, the consequences to the young of insufficient career opportunities are equally destructive. Without such opportunities, life chances are diminished and a dismayingly large number of young people are condemned to a lifetime of haphazard employment and marginal earnings. And, as Reverend Leon Sullivan told you so forcefully at an earlier meeting, in the minority ghettos where residents have the greatest cause to fear for their persons and their property, youth unemployment, by no coincidence, is most concentrated.

The incidence of structural unemployment—a term commonly used to describe a mismatch between the skills of workers and the requirements of available jobs—is evidenced by ever rising average levels of unemployment for adults as well as youth, and males as well as females. Successive business cycles have been accompanied by higher rates of unemployment at both the peak and the bottom. Looking across the decades, the youth unemployment rate has climbed from 14 percent in the 1960s to 17 percent in the 1970s to upwards of 20 percent so far in the 1980s. Indeed, the progression has been more rapid than for adults and the historical multiplier of two is now something over three.

The trauma of youth unemployment is no longer uniquely American. Western Europe is undergoing a similar experience. In the Common Market countries over the past three years, 42 percent of the 12 million unemployed have been below 25 years old.

But compounding America's problem is the tragic circumstance of black youth. To be sure, an overwhelming majority of unemployed youth—something like 70 percent—are white, not black. But the other 30 percent are black even though blacks make up only 15 percent of the general population. Worse yet, in the 1960s, black youth and white youth were employed roughly in proportion to their numbers in the population. By the end of the 1970s, while the rate of white employment came down only slightly, the rate of black employment declined by 19 percent.

We need not linger long over the explanations for the problem of structural youth unemployment. You've probably heard them all. An important one is the extraordinary bulge in the birth rates during the fifties and sixties that later produced a significant mismatch between the supply and demand for labor. Second, are the industrial and technological changes in the American economy that resulted in a decrease in the number of traditional entry-level jobs. Third has been geographic shifts in production, which moved manufacturing out of the inner city into the suburbs and then across the oceans to other countries. Fourth has been the onslaught of foreign competition. Fifth is the rise in productivity, which gives us more goods and services with fewer hands. Sixth is the growth of female participation in the formal labor force, the dramatic entry of older women who, driven by economic necessity, swelled the ranks of those seeking paid employment and thus absorbed some of the opportunities that might have been available to the young. Additional job competition came from new waves of legal and illegal immigrants.

The nation's responses to youth unemployment have been numerous and varied. Starting in the late fifties, when the problem of youth unemployment first came to public notice, our nation launched a long succession of remedial programs, so many, in fact, that only a handful of labor experts can describe them all. But most of us know their essence. One series was directed toward job training and job creation in the private and public sectors. Another series encouraged continued school attendance and sought to improve reading, writing, and number skills. There were special programs targeted on the severely disadvantaged, on ex-offenders, on teenage mothers, and on many other subsets of the population. Although only a few of the programs have been thoroughly evaluated, we know that along with some frequently exaggerated failures there have been some programs that yielded fair to good results. Much of value has been learned that should add to the effectiveness of future programs.

Yet, for all these efforts, youth unemployment continued its upward trend. And who knows that better than you here in Detroit, where so many youth have no hope of a job and where the school dropout rate is so extraordinarily high? A deep yearning has been growing for more comprehensive answers, for some fundamental changes in the way youth make the difficult transition from school to career and from adolescence to adulthood.

One major reform that has been periodically advanced is the adoption of a system of national service. I want to elaborate on that concept. But first a caveat. Whatever the potential benefits of national service—and they are, as I will try to show, very considerable—I do not regard it, taken by itself, as a direct or specific cure for youth unemployment. France and West Germany have had national service systems for many years, but have not escaped the high youth unemployment rates I cited earlier. There is little doubt that a system of national service could have many desirable consequences for the economic future of the young. But those gains would be of a general nature and a by-product of fulfilling other national and individual needs. In my judgment, there is no way to produce enough jobs to go around except through a high rate of economic growth. And there is no effective cure for inadequate skills, inadequate education, and inadequate motivation except through adequate programs aimed at each of these problems.

National service has been defined as "an idea which recognizes that individuals can and should contribute to the larger society and that society should be structured to . . . encourage such activity." It rests on a belief that contributed service is a vital part of citizenship, an act that can help bind us together as a people, accomplish needed tasks, and provide for individual growth and improvement.

Proposals for national service come in many varieties, but nearly all seek to address one or more of three critical national needs. One is to provide for national security and the commom defense. The second is the need to provide opportunities for young people to help solve social and environmental problems. The third has to do with the personal improvement I just spoke of. Given a well-designed system, a period of service could open new perspectives for the young, new windows on the world, and new choices for bettering themselves as workers and citizens.

Indeed, for the earliest proponent of national service—the eminent American philosopher William James—nation-building and character-building were the primary virtues of such service. In an oft-quoted essay published in 1910, he saw it as a means of mobilizing the willingness of citizens to serve their country, a willingness that is generally called upon only at times of external danger. To James, national service was the institutional embodiment of the moral principle that every individual owes something to the larger community.

The 1960s endowed the concept of national service with another dimension, one that concerns the principle of social equity. The youth rebellion and the anti-Vietnam protests of that era resulted in widespread resistance to military conscription, manifested by no small measure of draft evasion and a very large measure of draft avoidance. Middle-class and educated youth often found escape routes not open to or sought by working-class or disadvantaged youth. So, while one part of a generation was mired in a far-off jungle, exposed to death or injury, the greater number lived in safety and comfort. If William James was right in saying that democratic society requires sacrifice, a just society requires that sacrifice be more equally shared. If the military is to claim one part of the pool of young people, fairness dictates that others should serve too. In other ways, perhaps, but serve *somehow*.

The sixties revealed some of those ways. If the antiwar marches and campus sit-ins of that era mobilized the idealism and energy of youth in one direction, the civil rights movement, the Peace Corps, VISTA, and other programs to combat injustice and poverty mobilized it in another, and demonstrated the principle that by serving others, one could also serve oneself.

Thus, the constituency for a system of national service expanded as particular interest groups began to see it as the means to achieve particular objectives. For some, it was seen as a way of addressing social needs. For others, the attraction was greater military capability. Some minority leaders saw it as a way to help the disadvantaged, and some environmentalists saw it as a way to reclaim the land. National service was endorsed by political leaders, educators, civil rights leaders, by official commissions and by private study groups. However, because each constituency has tended to give primacy to its own objectives, no irresistible political coalition for the establishment of a national service program has yet been formed. Various interest groups—some in Congress, some private—have proposed various kinds of systems, but few of them have been mutually compatible.

All of the numerous models of national service can be classified according to five criteria.

One is whether a given plan is totally mandatory, totally voluntary, or somewhere in between.

Second is the degree to which the model calls for universal or selective registration: that is, whether it is intended to include every person of a specified age without regard to sex, education, or socioeconomic status or whether it is to be limited to designated groups.

Third is the question of scale: how many of those registered would actually be asked to serve? To give you a sense of the numbers, about 4 million youth are now turning eighteen years old each year. Of these, the armed forces enlist about 400,000. That leaves up to 3.6 million theoretically available from that age cohort alone for a wide range of other kinds of service.

Fourth is the emphasis to be placed on personal improvement and development, that is the extent to which the system would provide schooling, training, and guidance as well as meaningful work.

Last are the questions of costs and management. How much of a net burden would a given plan add to the national budget and how would a comprehensive program be administered?

Each of the models so far proposed varies in terms of these five criteria. Let me offer three illustrations that mix the specifications in different ways. Number one might be called the maximum or military model, because enlistment would be mandatory and universal and because first priority would be given to the armed forces. This plan calls for the registration of all persons reaching a prescribed age, say eighteen years old. Every registrant would be required to serve, say, up to two years in a civilian capacity or, alternatively, to enlist for up to two years in the military. Should the armed forces fail to enlist a sufficient number of persons with the right attributes, it could draft the remainder by lottery from the civilian-service pool. Such maximum or military models allow for various exemptions and usually allow the military option to be discharged with shorter periods of active service and longer periods in the reserves. As a bonus for military service there are extra rewards in the form of G.I. bills and the like. Because national service, under this model, would be mandatory, stipends for both civilian and military enlistments could be kept low and military costs thus sharply reduced.

A second model goes to the opposite extreme. Under it, service would be voluntary and limited. Young people would not be required to register. There would be, however, a substantial expansion of such familiar programs as the Job Corps, VISTA, the Peace Corps, and the youth components of CETA. The assumption underlying this limited model is that there are large numbers of youths who want to perform a useful community service and who do not need to be coerced into doing so. What is necessary is a sufficient number of well-organized opportunities. There is no explicit relationship to military needs. Indeed, this model is just on the threshold of the national service concept.

Most proposals fall into the third category: intermediate plans that minimize coercion and maximize incentives. Such plans tend to be universal in coverage, relatively large in scale, and are attentive to military needs. Though registration would be mandatory, actual enrollment into national service would be by inducement rather than by conscription. Stipends would be set at or just below the minimum wage and there would be, further, a schedule of generous mustering-out bonuses. Other inducements would include both in-service and post-service educational subsidies, eligibility for preferential housing loans, and bonus points on civil service examinations. Such intermediate models propose a scale of between one and four million enrollees.

For many people, the national security goals of national service are paramount; they have little interest in any plan that fails to satisfy such goals. The U.S. ended the draft in 1972; since then, we have relied on volunteers to fill the 2.1 million positions in the armed forces. The all-voluntary force has suffered from many serious problems. First is the high unit cost of recruitment. It is estimated that the Department of Defense spends $2500 per individual for the recruitment process and the enlistment bonus alone, and military personnel now receive wages and benefits that approach civilian scales. Because military compensation systems are hierarchical, the higher the pay levels at the bottom, the higher they are at the top. Compensation costs now account for a high proportion—nearly half—of the total defense budget, so high that they may limit our national security options by competing with other military outlays. The compensation budget could grow heavier if the future supply of potential recruits diminishes, and Census Bureau data predict that this will indeed occur.

Second is a set of issues related to the quality of personnel. The military prefers individuals with a high school education or more because such people tend to do better with today's sophisticated military equipment. They also tend to have better staying power;

80 percent of them make it through a three-year enlistment compared to 60 percent for non-high school graduates. But in 1980, more than one-third of all army recruits were non-high school graduates.

Then there is the troublesome issue of racial imbalance. Just as was the case during the Vietnam era, blacks and other minorities still comprise a much greater percentage of the armed forces than they do of the general population. This is especially so in the combat forces. To many, that is an undemocratic situation. An army whose soldiers come disproportionately from disadvantaged groups—whether "voluntarily" or not—violates our sense of fairness.

Most models of national service presume the existence of large numbers of unmet, important social and environmental tasks that a large number of youth could perform. The key word is important; digging and filling holes or similar make-work tasks would be fatal to the integrity of the national service idea. Everyone's favorite model is the Civilian Conservation Corps of the New Deal years. The CCC was among the most acclaimed inventions of the thirties and was, in some respects, a precursor of national service. It drew millions of poor youth from farms and cities—youth very much like the disadvantaged young people of today—fed them, sheltered them, looked after their health and other basic needs, and, while doing so, reforested America. The CCC not only planted over 2 billion trees covering 21 million acres—about half the trees ever planted in America—it built 46,000 bridges, 126,000 miles of roads, 62,000 buildings other than CCC camp buildings, restored 4,000 historic structures, built almost a million miles of fence, laid 89,000 miles of telephone line, and cleared 69,000 miles of fire breaks. In addition, the CCC developed 800 new state parks, spent 12 million man-hours preventing and fighting forest fires, and introduced erosion control measures to 40 million acres of farmland.

Are there, in fact, enough productive jobs today for national service members to undertake without displacing other workers? In the past year or two, the problems of America's decaying infrastructure—roads, bridges, and transportation systems—have been a lead story in the media and and the basis of all kinds of job legislation in the Congress. The proponents of national service generally do *not* see it as a work force for reconstructing or rehabilitating all aspects of that infrastructure. The changes that have occurred since the thirties, including the rise of organized labor, must be taken into account. But according to recent estimates, even if tasks in the public works sector are excluded from the national service mandate (except for some maintenance tasks), there would still be no lack of assignable tasks for national service workers to perform. In 1978, the Urban Institute published a study of America's job-creation potential. This study identified and catalogued more than 200 types of organized activity that could be undertaken or expanded by national service workers without significant displacement of other workers. In only 100 of these activities, the Institute reported a potential total of 3 million jobs. Other experts have put the total at over 4 million jobs. In short, even if we were to adopt a maximum-scale national service model, the labor demand would equal the labor supply.

What kinds of jobs? The Urban Institute's researchers indicated that a substantial part of the total—about one million jobs—would be in education: in classroom and teacher assistance, student counseling and tutoring, and maintenance of facilities. Health and hospital services, clinics, and nursing homes would account for another 900,000 jobs. Social services such as day care and care of the elderly would account for another 500,000. Environmental needs would add 800,000 jobs, of which 500,000 would be in conservation. Police and fire protection were estimated, in 1978, to account for 300,000 jobs, but that number is probably low, as there is an ever-growing need for citizen patrols and arson-watchers in urban neighborhoods. Finally, an estimated 400,000 jobs would be in libraries, museums, cultural facilities, and miscellaneous other areas.

What is the potential for some cost reimbursement from employers? There is reason to believe that many or most of the hospitals and school systems that would seek national service enrollees could provide food and lodging and possibly part of any stipends. There are two advantages in a reimbursement formula. First, it would obviously reduce the federal budgetary burdens of a national service system. Second, it would act as a safeguard against

make-work. It's worth noting, however, that with or without reimbursement, and whether or not national service results in any
tangible, short-term economic gains, the nation would gain from
any and all worthwhile work performed. The CCC was a significant expense in the federal budgets of the thirties and produced
few short-term gains. But the subsequent value of the trees planted by the CCC was enormous.

Finally, we come to the potential of national service for individual development. Many staunch supporters of the concept believe that young people would come to regard national service not
as an unwelcome burden but as an interval for personal exploration and growth. They recall with fondness the best years of VIS-
TA, the Peace Corps, and the civil rights movement, when young
people from a diversity of backgrounds volunteered with enthusiasm for a diversity of assignments in a diversity of places. The
alumni of those activities generally report that they were better
persons when they came out than when they went in. In later
years, those periods of service were proudly inscribed on job re-
sumes. Employers and admission deans have respected that entry,
as have I and many of you.

None of us can now say to what extent similar attitudes prevail
among today's youth. Nor can we be sure of how well national
service would function for street-corner youth with backgrounds
of truancy, drug abuse, and crime. Evaluations of the Job Corps,
which enrolled large numbers of the disadvantaged, indicate that
most participants have benefited by their experience as measured
by improved work-readiness and job attitudes. According to several surveys of Job Corps alumni, those who remained in the Job
Corps for more than three months gained significantly in self-
esteem, in willingness to accept authority, and in ways of using
leisure time. In my view, it is essential that any program of national service be accompanied by strong programs in remedial education, counseling, and social service. And because, for the
disadvantaged, personal development depends so often on a
change of social environment, it is also my belief that an effective
national service program should include substantial opportunities
for people to obtain training and to carry out assignments while
living away from home.

No one believes that national service will work magic on all its enrollees. Service in the armed forces has not done so, despite considerable efforts in remedial education and similar compensatory programs. Such programs have had only mixed success, as evidenced by persistent disciplinary problems and a high incidence of less-than-honorable discharges. But the record also shows that a successful period of service has been a pivotal factor in the efforts of many youth to carve out rewarding careers and a life in the mainstream of society.

The concept of national service has critics as well as supporters. Some of the criticism comes from those who are opposed on moral or legal grounds to any kind of mandatory plan. Some object to the complexity of such a large undertaking and others are troubled by its potential cost. Whatever the arguments pro or con, one thing is clear: the implementation of a large-scale national service program would constitute a major reform. And that reform will be greatly facilitated if it is preceded by a period of comprehensive research, thoughtful planning, and informed public debate. In support of that public debate, the Ford Foundation recently made a substantial grant to a private study group to assess several models of national service, measuring each against criteria of individual and social needs and operational and administrative feasibility. The final report, to be ready at the end of the year, will estimate the likely costs and benefits of national service—to labor markets, to rural and urban communities, to the armed forces, and to the employment, earnings, and attitudes of young people themselves.

National service is a compelling concept that merits a place near the top of the national agenda. Security needs may make the concept an urgent one. But the idea would have sweep and power even for a society unthreatened by external enemies and without armies. In its fullest expression national service can be an institution of historic importance to America's youth—and to America's future.

A TIME FOR ECONOMIC REFORM[1]

GARY HART[2]

By mid-1982, the race for the Democratic nomination for the presidency was well under way. Contenders were already trying to win support in a variety of ways. One of these hopefuls was Senator Gary Hart of Colorado. David F. Salisbury described Hart's efforts as follows:

> Through voluminous position papers, speeches to groups like the Los Angeles World Affairs Council presented in a dry, almost academic style, and activities such as the organization of a recent "summit meeting" of promising young politicians from several Western countries, Hart has been trying to stake out the high ground as a liberal idea man. The thrust of his thinking, Hart explains, "is to seek nonbureaucratic and nonprogrammatic ways to achieve the ends which liberalism has had the government do in the past 50 years." (*Christian Science Monitor,* F. 18, '83, p 14)

Although young—45 years old—Hart, a former divinity school student, is not lacking in political campaign experience. Twelve years earlier he left his Denver law practice to direct George McGovern's 1972 successful attempt to gain the Democratic presidential nomination.

During his initial campaigning, Senator Hart delivered a speech at the White Center for Law and Government at the University of Notre Dame on October 13. Stating that he was going to discuss economics, a subject that was very controversial and not accidentally called "dismal," the speaker surprised his listeners by declaring, "I want to look at economics, not as an economist or lawyer, but as a divinity school graduate." Hart's topic actually was broader than economics; it dealt with what he called "statecraft," which he defined thus:

> Statecraft is not a fancy new theory—as "supply side" economics once was. We've seen what happens to those theories. Rather, it's an attempt to make national policies sensitive to deeper motivations than the desire for a paycheck. It's an attempt to confront the question: What does it profit a society to conquer inflation, reduce interest rates, and create new jobs, if we don't enjoy what we have or what we are doing or sense some greater national purpose?

[1]Delivered in the auditorium of Memorial Library, University of Notre Dame, South Bend, Indiana, at 2. P.M. on October 13, 1982.

[2] For biographical note, see Appendix.

Hart delivered his speech at 2 P.M. in the auditorium of Memorial Library where the talk was open to the entire student body and attracted approximately 200 people, mostly students, with a few faculty and local people.

Hart's personality and manner of speaking are described in various ways by reporters and columnists. Louise Sweeney put it this way:

> He is the tall guy with auburn hair over there by the door, the quiet man who listens a lot, nods, smiles like a cowboy facing into the sun, then speaks softly. When he speaks it's liable to sound more like the brave-new world ideas of a think-tank than "The Last Hurrah" of traditional politics. . . . He's not a person who makes a speech just to hear his own voice. (*Christian Science Monitor,* D. 8, '82, p B2)

Some commented on "his Robert Redford-style good looks" and "his quality of detachment, of heeding the voice inside his head." Others described him "a loner" and as possessing "a crackling, ironic wit, paired with a driving determination."

On February 17, 1983, Hart announced his candidacy for the Democratic presidential nomination.

Gary Hart's speech: Today, I want to ask you to join me in considering a new way of thinking about a subject which is very controversial—and not accidentally called "dismal": economics. I'm still wrestling with the ideas I'll offer today. They are in a very early, formative stage, and they are tentative. There may even be some false leads among them, and some may be obscure. And as a politician, there is some hazard in launching out on this uncharted course. But as a citizen, I feel I must. For, as a nation, we must think anew.

We all know this country faces very serious economic problems—problems so serious that people are wondering about our whole economic structure, wondering whether we may be facing a collapse like that in the 1930s. I don't think that will happen. But the American people are increasingly uneasy about the possibility. And, despite the recent rise in the stock market, the current realities are grim enough: unemployment is over pre-World War II levels; interest rates, though falling, remain high; business investment is lethargic; and the Federal deficit still looms ominously over it all.

We need some answers to these problems, and in other forums I have talked about some potential answers. But I don't intend to talk about them here. I don't intend to because, as serious as these challenges are, they may only be the surface of the problem, like the bark of a great tree. Today, I want to try to penetrate the bark. I want to examine the core of the tree to see if there may be some deeper, more fundamental deficiencies. I want to look at economics, not as an economist or lawyer, but as a divinity school graduate.

Such an examination might start with the realization that, in a larger, social sense, all economic policies have been failing for at least a century and possibly longer. Time and time again, nations have succeeded economically—both in growth and equitable distribution of wealth—only to find social dissatisfaction growing, not diminishing.

The economic success of the Victorian period in Europe bred enormous dissatisfaction in every social class, leading to massive internal instability. In America, the economic success of the 1950s was followed by the widespread social turmoil of the 1960s. And the dissatisfaction was led by many of those who had benefitted most from the economic gains.

Something fundamental has gone wrong; success does not succeed. "More" is not enough. The science of producing and getting more is not sufficient as a guiding principle for a great nation.

It's time for an economic reform movement—a movement with the goal of going to the heart of the nature of society and of human behavior. The best place to start may be with a bit of history.

Before the Industrial Revolution, Western societies were characterized by a high degree of stability over long stretches of time. People were born, lived, and died in the same village or town, among the same neighbors, often following a family craft or profession. This stability, a stability spanning generations, created many rewarding *general* relationships.

But industrialism shattered traditional society. With its demand for physical and social mobility, its disruption of agrarian societies, its segregation of home life from life at work, its mixing of people from different origins, and its lack of concern for anything other than quantitative output, it substituted *functional* relationships for general relationships. Now we see some people only at home, others only at work. We move frequently; the extended family has become obsolete. Children live in a different world from that of their parents. As a result, while industrialism has brought material wealth, it has also brought impoverishment of the individual and collective spirit.

But industrialism did give rise to the modern discipline of economics—the consideration of production, consumption, and distribution of goods and services as matters of state policy. Economics in its modern sense was born along with industrialism in the 18th century. It defined us as economic creatures—creatures driven almost exclusively by material wants, who make rational decisions, in the words of the 19th century economist Stanley Jevons, "to satisfy (our) wants to the utmost with the least effort."

Unfortunately for economics, "economic man" does not exist.

In 1967, Robert Kennedy wrote: "The gross national product measures neither our wit nor our courage, neither our wisdom nor our learning, neither our compassion nor our devotion of country. It measures everything, in short, except that which makes life worthwhile; and it can tell us everything about America—except whether we are proud to be Americans."

We are not defined by our possessions. Our vision reaches beyond the material plane. The quantitative instruments of economics cannot circumscribe the human spirit.

The desire for goodness—the search for truth—the love of beauty—all soar above the narrow bounds of materialism. Of course, without economic prosperity, we cannot meet the most basic needs of our own people and others throughout the world. But prosperity does not provide purpose. It is not—of itself—a worthwhile vision.

Tennyson wrote: "Thou hast made us, we know not why. We think we were not made to die." And he might have added in this Industrial Age: "We think we were not made merely to possess, or to be governed only by the static measure of a discipline confined to the principles of production and consumption."

As the Industrial Age evolves, the discipline it produced—economics—is increasingly looked to for new theories to keep the giant engine running. And, increasingly, we sense economics alone cannot do this. To use the language of economists, traditional economics is necessary but simply not sufficient.

What would be sufficient? Perhaps we need, in the words of Theodore Roszak, "a nobler economics that is not afraid to discuss spirit and conscience, moral purpose and the meaning of life, an economics that aims to educate and elevate people, not merely to measure their low-grade behavior." In a sense, an economics of such richness and depth would be so different from economics as we know it today that perhaps a new term is needed. Certainly, we need a broader term than economics to describe the overall foundation for government and public policy. The term I suggest is "statecraft."

Statecraft is not a fancy new theory—as "supply side" economics once was. We've seen what happens to those theories. Rather, it's an attempt to make national policies sensitive to deeper motivations than the desire for a paycheck. It's an attempt to confront the question: what does it profit a society to conquer inflation, reduce interest rates, and create new jobs, if we don't enjoy what we have or what we are doing or sense some greater national purpose?

A definition of statecraft must start by identifying human aspirations that go beyond material needs. I would suggest four as a starting point:

A sense of purpose and vision, a perspective on our existence in time and place and on our direction as individuals and as a nation;

Opportunity for creativity;

Opportunity for individual growth, for continuing and recurring education and exposure to information and experience;

And automony or individuality—the need to be able to shape our lives, as individuals and as communities, within the context of our constitutional liberties.

To give us a chance to achieve these needs—and to give some content to the notion of statecraft—we must weave certain themes into public policy:

First, decentralization, since human growth can be best achieved within small units: local control in politics, in social issues, and the business world must be central.

Second, community. To have richness instead of isolation in our personal lives, we must allow communities to grow. Economic policies—public or private—which shatter communities are destructive to the human spirit, however "efficient" they may be.

Third, a manageable pace of change. Future historians may wonder if the 20th century drove itself to collective madness with its desperate velocity of change. Continuity must be given a chance to grow between generations. We must control the pace of change, rather than letting it control us. Technology must adapt to human realities, not vice versa.

Fourth, we must question modernity's most sacred cow: the notion that you can't "turn back the clock." Of course, in many areas we wouldn't want to return to past practices, but in too many cases we have lost the ability to value what we had in the past. A look backward can give us a reference point. Historically, many great movements forward have been attempts to return to the past—the Renaissance being an example.

Fifth, we must give more thought to aesthetics. Anyone who lives with the architectural monstrosities in our cities or the "Vegas strips" that foul our towns and suburbs knows aesthetics is important. John Ruskin's attempt to blend economics and aesthetics may not have been the blind alley most classical economists think it to be.

Sixth, we must give greater consideration to the act of producing. We focus too much on the product, rather than the process. But can we expect our society to be successful if most people's jobs reward them only with a paycheck? The Medieval guilds may have known something we have forgotten: the reward of a job well done, a job that gives reign to creativity, that requires real skill, may be as important as the company's bottom line. In fact, it may even increase the bottom line. Giving workers a greater voice in their workplace may yield more gains in productivity than replacing them with robots.

Finally, we must think differently about education. This is perhaps the most important component of all. Ortega y Gasset, in his classic, *The Revolt of the Masses,* warned that 20th century man was becoming a technologically competent barbarian. We can punch the buttons on our machines, but we cannot see ourselves or our world in any context, because we have not been educated. Education is not training, though training is also valuable. Education is essentially the classical education, intended to give us understanding of our culture and our values. It is rooted in history and literature and religion, the only sources for understanding these things. It teaches us mathematics and science—not to make us technicians, but to teach us to think logically. It must be revived—first, among our educators. Without it, we cannot hope for a society that does more than lurch blindly from crisis to crisis, unable to see where it has been, and thus know where it can go.

As we evolve the qualities which constitute statecraft, what should we seek to do with them? Our principal task is to relate them to the technology, wealth, and growth which should remain part of our social order. The task is not to overthrow technology or growth, but to use them within the framework of this new discipline—to drive them and control them, rather than being driven and controlled by them. One might say, our task is to civilize them.

And so, a great nation must have a great framework by which it is to govern itself. Industrial economics—with its one dimensional "economic man"—is simply insufficient. As Robert Kennedy said: "We will find neither national purpose nor personal satisfaction in a mere continuation of economic progress, in an endless amassing of worldly goods. We cannot measure national spirit by the Dow-Jones Average, nor national achievement by the gross national product."

Tracing modern economics back through political economics to its conceptual roots, we find it was Aristotle, after all, who urged that economics be considered a department of ethics. I can see it now—an endowed chair of ethical economics right here at Notre Dame.

The idea of statecraft—or something like it—must provide the framework and foundation for government in the years to come. The policies that guide and shape our nation must spring from the wealth of human aspirations, not just from narrow materialism. Only in this way can we hope to free the American character, to offer it a chance for renewal and new growth, to forge the national purpose necessary for true world leadership.

This undertaking must engage the best in all of us—not just in Washington—but in South Bend and in Denver and all across this nation. For we must all become, in Walter Lippman's words, "the custodians of the nation's ideals, of the belief it cherishes, of its permanent hopes, of the faith which makes a nation out of a mere aggregate of individuals."

THE BEST OF TIMES? THE WORST OF TIMES?[1]

ARCHIBALD G. COX[25]

Using Charles Dickens' famous opening words to *A Tale of Two Cities* as his theme—"It was the best of times, it was the worst of times"—Professor Archibald G. Cox of the Harvard Law School sought to reassure the 1982 graduating seniors of Vassar College that in spite of adversity there was reason for hope and joy.

Professor Cox brought to the occasion a very high degree of credibility. Although he had previously held important government posts, Cox first became well known to the general public when he was appointed special prosecutor, to investigate the Watergate scandal and its connections with the White House. His subsequent dismissal by President Richard Nixon, in what became known as the "Saturday night massacre," won him national respect as a man of courage and integrity. His appointment as Carl M. Loeb University Professor at Harvard in 1976 further enhanced his reputation. At the time he delivered this address, he was also president of Common Cause, a nonpartisan citizens' lobby created in 1970 and widely respected for its efforts in promoting governmental reforms, including "accountability" by elected officials.

Among the problems discussed by Cox, and of particular concern to him, was the high cost of political campaigns and the influence of special interest political action committees in determining the outcome of elections. "A Congressman must raise $500,000 every two years in order to keep his seat," he said, pointing out that more and more financing was coming from special interest groups who expect legislative support for their interests in return for contributions. Almost a year after Professor Cox's address, the Federal Elections Commission reported that political action committees broke all records for fund-raising and spending during

---

[51]Commencement address at Vassar College, Poughkeepsie, New York, in the Outdoor Amphitheatre at 10 A.M., May 23, 1982.
    [2] For biographical note, see Appendix.

the 1982 elections by pumping more than $87 million into candidates' campaign chests.

The commencement exercises at Vassar College took place on the rainy morning of May 23, 1982, in the outdoor theater. The audience of 3,200 included the senior class, their parents and friends, trustees, faculty, and administrators. The exercises began with a welcome from Vassar President Virginia Smith, which was followed by remarks from the senior class president. Then, Mary Draper Janney, a member of the Board of Trustees, introduced the speaker. Maryann Bruno, assistant press secretary of Vassar, noted that in spite of the rain, "Mr. Cox was undaunted as was his audience. He said it would have been a shame to hold graduation inside and that it often rained on Harvard graduations." Umbrellas and plastic garbage bags kept some of the audience dry. Professor Cox added,

> Actually, much of my prepared Vassar text was omitted. It poured rain that morning just as I began to speak, and out of mercy for the audience I shortened my remarks in ways that I cannot recall.

Therefore, in reading Cox's speech, one should keep in mind that it is not a transcript of exactly what he said and that in any case the audience's attention was probably considerably distracted by the rain.

Archibald Cox's speech: May I first take a moment to congratulate the Class of 1982 and to say that I am honored and pleased by the invitation to share in your Commencement.

Honored, for any number of reasons but chiefly because the old especially value the good opinion of the young.

A little puzzled because if four years of professorial lecturers have failed to do the trick, what can one more professor do in the last few minutes. Dare I add even a Harvard professor?

Pleased, too, because I enjoy ceremonial occasions which look to the future. The ceremony links the past to the future. The link gives the best proof that there is a future, bright and exciting; it is proof of the continuity of change.

Some may think it odd to describe the immediate future as bright and exciting. Even a sanguine disposition might characterize the present in Charles Dickens' ambivalent words: "It was the best of times, it was the worst of times."

The worst of times because our vaunted industrial power is unable to keep up with foreign competition? Because the government bureaucracy is massive, wasteful, and unfeeling? Because jobs are growing scarcer and the only alternative offered is inflation? Because Congress is fragmented and inept? Because those in the corridors of power show scant recognition of the urgent need to act now to prevent nuclear destruction of western civilization?

Granting all this and more, granting—nay, emphasizing—that all times are a mixed bag, still I would emphasize "the best of times." Say, "the worst of times?" No, "The best of times." Let me put it to you directly as a colleague put it to me when I asked him what I should say in a commencement address. He replied, "Can you think of a better time to be alive?"

Can you?

I think first of the Hellenic age. The Athenians breathed freedom and had a nobler view of man than ours, even though they also faced grief, death and sorrow without papering over the facts of their condition. But the citizens of Athens built their state upon the backs of slaves, and Sparta as well as Athens lay in Greece.

The Elizabethan age, perhaps? Those were years of boisterous confidence and extraordinary creativity. They were also years of disease, poverty, ignorance, and extraordinary cruelty. Men were hanged for scores of petty crimes. The populace turned out in joy to see men burned, spitted alive, or drawn and quartered. You may say that we kill more efficiently on a larger scale now, but at least we have grown squeamish and kill from a distance; and we do it only when we can call it war.

Perhaps you would wish to live with the Founding Fathers. That was another extraordinary age. A contemporary described Jefferson as "a gentleman of 32 [years], who could calculate an eclipse, survey an estate, tie an artery, plan an edifice, try a cause, break a horse, dance the minuet, and play the violin." Two years later he wrote the Declaration of Independence. I think I would like to have lived in that age *if* I could have been Thomas Jefferson, or even John Adams or Alexander Hamilton. But suppose that I was not Jefferson but Jefferson's slave, or an indentured servant, or an impressed seaman, or a woman dying alone in childbirth in a sod hut in a remote forest clearing to the west.

I think that if I had to draw lots as to whom I would be, I would rather draw my lot today.

One central challenge of our day is much like that which faced the Founding Fathers. Can we govern ourselves? Can we keep ours—in Daniel Webster's words—"a government made for the people, made by the people, and answerable to the people."

The question is the same but the problem is different. There are 70 times as many of us as in 1800. The institutions and procedures which enabled three million people to govern themselves will not suffice for two hundred million. Government has a new and very different role than when Emerson could say that the government which governs least governs best. Harnessing the power unlocked by science and technology required vast aggregations of wealth and human organization. To prevent abuse by the giant enterprises, and to protect those who can no longer help themselves, we expanded the activities of government and made it big and central. The new functons of government will not disappear, despite the nostalgia of some members of the present Administration, even though it is equally imperative that we abandon the notion that for every ill there is a governmental remedy, that to solve a problem we have only to enact another law or appropriate another billion dollars.

Because of the change, Washington became the forum in which business corporations, labor unions, farm federations and other organized groups, contend for tax breaks, regulatory advantage, subsidies, rich government contracts, and other benefits with all the selfishness and ambition, and, all too often, with the ruthlessness and deceit, which once characterized the market place. The common purpose—the awareness that long-term good results only from the progress of the whole enterprise—gets lost in grabbing for short-term, selfish advantage.

Two examples of the vast gulf between the common sense of the people and the politics of Washington will suffice.

The selling ground wave of support for an immediate freeze on the build-up of nuclear arms demonstrates the people's awareness of the overriding necessity for immediate action to reduce the threat of mutual self-destruction—a risk to which those in power are remarkably insensitive. Yet the event—the swelling ground wave and resulting shift in the Administration's public posture—also makes plain that as citizens we can work our will and force reduction if we have the energy and staying power not to become enmeshed in the enormous technical complexities but to keep building political pressure to achieve some form of prompt and meaningful reduction as the one essential act.

Similarly, there is little doubt of the public commitment to protection of the environment in which we live. Yet appropriations for EPA are cut, enforcement lags, and Congress has not yet renewed the Clean Air Act.

What to do? Where to begin?

Shortly after I became Chairman of Common Cause, a stranger came up to me at a large public dinner to say: "You have assumed an awesome responsibility." I must have looked as baffled as I felt. "You and Common Cause," he explained. "In another few years the government of the United States will be regularly bought and sold at auction. I know because I'm buying it." The man went on to identify himself as an official of a trade association with a large Political Action Committee engaged in making campaign contributions to candidates for the U. S. Senate and House of Representatives who would promote his association's special interests. Last week Richard Bolling, Chairman of the House Rules Committee and a profound student of government with 34 years of experience in Congress, called present campaign financing a "perversion of the system that threatens the future of democracy." A Congressman must raise $500,000 every two years in order to keep his seat.

Much of the money comes from the ever larger financial contributions of special interests, corporate, and labor union Political Action Committees. [From 1974–1982, PAC contributions went from $12.5 million to $80 million.]

As the role of money rises, so increases the obligation of the successful candidate to those who supply the means of victory. Each PAC targets its contributions to reach the chairman and members of the congressional committees and subcommittees with jurisdiction to affect the particular PAC's selfish concerns. One of the largest corporate PAC's in 1980 was maintained by Grumman, a defense and aerospace manufacturer. The *New York Times* reported that "In races for Congress, the (Grumman PAC's) list reads like a 'Who's Who' of the House and Senate

Armed Services and Appropriations Committees." Apparently Grumman shared the view of Justin Dart, president Reagan's friend and the chief executive of Dart Industries, another company which maintains a large PAC. "Dialogue with politicians is a fine thing," Mr. Dart explained, "but with a little money they hear you better." The members of the Armed Services and Appropriations Committees who received Grumman PAC contributions are regularly called upon not only for how much to spend on weapons' systems but to choose between Grumman products and those of competitors.

Consider another example. In recent months the House and Senate Committees have been considering a bill to renew the Clean Air Act amidst heavy pressure to weaken the safeguards of the environment. Ninety-three corporations found in violation of the Clean Air Act standards during 1982 contributed through their PAC's $729,715 to members of these committees during 1980 and 1981—$184,655 during 1981 alone, a non-election year but the year in which the recipients were deliberating whether to weaken the Clean Air Act. This March, a twenty-member House subcommittee voted to weaken the present law. The twelve-member majority who consistently voted for weakening the present law had received $288,000 from the PAC's of businesses subject to the Act—an average of $24,886 apiece. The eight-member minority supporting environmental protection received a total of $20,325, an average of $2,541 apiece. "Dialogue with politicians is a fine thing," Justin Dart had said, "but with a little money they hear you better."

We should not forget the power of PAC's without direct corporate and labor union backing. In 1981, the National Chairman of Senator Helms' NCPAC wrote Congressman Neal:

> If you will make a public statement in support of the President's tax cut package and state that you intend to vote for it, we will withdraw all [independent, hostile] radio and newspaper ads planned in your district. In addition, we will be glad to run radio and newspaper ads applauding you for your vote to lower taxes.

1983 will be a critical year. Will you help to muster the public pressure to excise this cancer or will you acknowledge that the dream has died, that government of, by, and for the people is to become government of money, by, and for money? The most constructive reform would be to extend to House and Senate races the system of public financing now applicable to Presidential campaigns. Short of that, a bill limiting the amount of money any PAC can give to a House or Senate candidate and limiting the total amount a candidate may accept from all PAC's together would go far to contain the evil.

You ask, "What can one person do on this and the other enormously complex issues of modern government?" I am constantly surprised how much difference a relatively few individuals can make.

Recently, Senator Dole of Kansas broke away from the Administration's position on the Voting Rights Bill to propose new language for an important amendment strengthening and renewing the Voting Rights Act. He appears to have broken a log jam that threatened the entire Act. While he deserves much individual credit, the important point is that no little impetus came from the voters back home in Kansas who took the trouble to write letters, to telephone or to call upon him in person because they knew that his was the key vote in the Senate Judiciary Committee. The number was not really large, just enough who cared. The number who energized the activists was even smaller, but their work made the difference.

Similarly, I am repeatedly struck by the endless opportunities an individual has to help to shape events on a local or even a national scale, unless not satisfied by anything less than a public pinnacle. I think of Bruce Terris, a young man just a few years out of law school, who wrote the bulk of the brief in the first of the "one person, one vote" cases that Chief Justice Warren ranked the foremost of his years on the Supreme Court, even above Brown vs. Board of Education. I think too of Florence Rubin, neither office holder or elected representative, whose dedicated assistance aided by a few fellow members of the League of Women Voters induced a reluctant Massachusetts Legislature to enact court reforms overdue for decades.

Surely you will think of other examples in your home communities.

And so I hope that you will take from here, along with knowledge, training and variety of skills, a strong sense of citizenship in the larger political enterprise of which we are all inescapably part. John Adams described our parts when he wrote home to Abigail from the Continental Congress in Philadelphia in July, 1776, erring only, and to Abigail's annoyance, in speaking of sons and not of daughters!

I must study politics and war that my sons my have liberty to study mathematics and philosophy, geography, natural history and naval architecture, navigation, commerce and agriculture, in order to give their children a right to study painting, poetry, music, architecture, statuary, tapestry, and porcelain.

Notice the emphasis upon the study of politics. The Founders were practical politicians but they knew that the way we shape our governmental institutions governs the substantive results. Note, too, the sense of personal responsibility for, and confidence in a continuing adventure, the commitment to a future, ever-nobler but never perfect flowering of the human spirit.

It is harder than it was in the past to preserve the sense of personal responsibility for the common enterprise and the confidence in its ultimate perfection. Our numbers and the complexity of society obscure the first. The failures of foreign policy, inflation, and now depression have dispelled the endless resources for easy success. Ironically, our past successes try rather than lift our spirits. In the beginning, misfortune and suffering were as inexorable as sowing and reaping or birth and death. Should the plague come, should the crops fail, still one could say with the psalmists that the judgments of the Lord are true and righteous altogether. Now, most of the western world has largely defeated three of the Four Horsemen of the Apocalypse—ignorance, poverty, and disease. Now, the sense of inevitability is gone. Men and women feel that men and women are in charge, and they are in charge as never in all history—men and women with their limitations and faults and their perversity.

It takes honesty and courage to face these facts. It is to the credit of present generations that we have the honesty and courage to look in the mirror and see ourselves as we are. The mistake would be to suppose that we are the first to face these perceptions.

The danger is that we become obsessed by our failings, lose perspective, and forget the progress made and the true nature of the enterprise bequeathed to us. It is the fashion in some circles to forget Prometheus' reach and see only his chains. But those who take the long view of human experience know that there were other societies no less honest than ours in facing all the ugliness, cruelty, and complexity of life, and, worst of all, the sheer indifference, but which also held a brighter, nobler view of man and had the courage to pursue their vision.

The Hellenes knew the bitter taste of tragedy. They also knew joy and beauty. The Founding Fathers had no illusions about human weakness, indifference, and propensity for evil. They did not use Pogo's words, "we have met the enemy and he is us," but their religion taught them the same truth in the language of original sin. Like the Hellenes they faced themselves and still had the greater insight to perceive the nobler potential of man and the greater courage to commit themselves to the shared pursuit of that vision even though they knew that neither they nor their children nor their childrens's children would ever wholly achieve it.

Youth measures in only one direction, we are told, from things as they are to an ideal of what things ought to be; while the old measure things as they are against the past they remember. I hope that you will never become patient about the gap between what is and what ought to be. Yet, I hope that you will have acquired from your years at Vassar a sense of perspective and awareness that the one indestructible human quality is the ability of men and women to do things for the first time, to do what has never been done before. The scientist does not know the truth he seeks; he or she lacks assurance that there is a truth, yet knows that by putting one foot before the other, despite false starts and blind alleys, a little progress is achieved. The humanists know that participants in the human adventure have never had proof that there is a goal, but they also know if we look back towards our remote forbears, we can catch glimpses of the bright potential for nobility in men and women and perhaps can see that mankind, despite its capacity for evil, has by reason, trust and forbearance learned to walk a little straighter. The scientist and humanist both reveal the power of creativity—the unique human ability to break from the past and to learn and do in common enterprise what he has never learned or done before.

Perhaps then, if you compare where we are with where we have been, as well as with where we ought to be, you will conclude that even if you cannot bring about the millennium, still you and I, and all of us can help each other to learn to walk a little straighter.

I can give you no assurance even of that, but I can and do promise you joy in the endeavor.

THE THREAT OF NUCLEAR HOLOCAUST

WE ARE THE CURATORS OF LIFE ON EARTH[1]

Helen M. Caldicott[2]

An important development in 1982–1983 was a surge of support in this country and Europe for an immediate freeze of the production and deployment of nuclear weapons by the United States and the Soviet Union. The 1982 publication of Jonathan Schell's *The Fate of the Earth,* first in *The New Yorker* and later as a book, focused attention on the danger of nuclear extinction, as no other work had done. In addition, support for a nuclear freeze expressed by such prominent foreign policy and defense experts as Robert S. McNamara, McGeorge Bundy, and George F. Kennan gave the movement respectability. (For additional background information, see also George McGovern's speech, "The Arms Race vs. the Human Race," in *Representative American Speeches, 1981–1982,* p 25–32.)

The anti-nuclear movement burgeoned: new organizations were formed, rallies were held, polls were taken, referenda were held in eight states, and the House of Representatives passed a resolution for a nuclear freeze. Scientists and doctors joined the movement through such organizations as the Boston-based Physicians for Social Responsibility, whose president, Dr. Helen M. Caldicott, had managed to increase its membership from ten to 30,000 in the years from 1979 to 1982, with 180 chapters in fifty states. And giving up her practice to travel and speak, the forty-three year old Australian pediatrician is said by some to be most effective in gaining support for a nuclear freeze. One reporter observed:

> In New England churches and Midwestern Grange halls, in high school auditoriums and before the US Congress in Washington, she confronts her listeners with graphic descriptions of the physical consequences of nuclear war, using blackboard diagrams to explain the capabilities of MX missiles and the effects of radioactive isotopes. She wants to educate, to raise moral questions, to crack through her listeners' defenses, and make them cry if necessary to get them feeling. (Manuel, *Christian Science Monitor,* D. 28, '82, p 18)

[1]Delivered to the National Press Club in an interim ballroom at 1 P.M., February 25, 1983. Also broadcast on 260 National Public Radio stations and carried live or on a delayed basis on 1400 cable outlets of the Cable Satellite Public Affairs Network.

[2] For biographical note, see Appendix.

Journalist Jack Carroll described Dr. Caldicott's speaking as "compelling, exact, direct, and sober. And terrifying." At the same time, he criticized her for being too emotional and sensational:

> Her approach, however, is what has brought her to national attention. Combining medical expertise, oratorical powers, and maternal concern, she stumps across the country forcing upon audiences the horrors of nuclear war. . . . Her rhetoric is inflammatory and draws upon rabble-rousing techniques which critics have blasted as sensational and melodramatic rather than level-headed (but) . . . those who listen and hear are moved. (Baton Rouge *State-Times,* N. 29, '82. p 10)

On February 25, 1983, Dr. Caldicott addressed the National Press Club in Washington, D.C., at a luncheon. She spoke in a temporary ballroom of the club (while its regular facilities were undergoing renovation) to approximately 220 members, guests, and representatives of the working press. The speech began promptly at 1 P.M., and afterwards Dr. Caldicott responded to written questions until 2 P.M.

Interest was heightened by an announcement that morning that the United States Justice Department had ruled that the Canadian film, "If You Love This Planet," based on an anti-nuclear speech by Dr. Caldicott, was propaganda. This action prompted Senator Edward M. Kennedy to notify the club that morning that he wished to introduce the speaker. (The film was later nominated for, and eventually won, an Academy Award.)

In addition to being broadcast over 260 NRP stations, Dr. Caldicott's speech was carried either live or on a delayed basis on more than 1400 cable outlets of the Cable Satellite Public Affairs Network, C-SPAN.

Helen Caldicott's speech: In 1980, less than 26 percent of the voting American public elected Ronald Reagan as President. Recent Harris polls show that 66 percent of the public feels that President Reagan is doing an unsatisfactory job on arms control, 57 percent believe that America is at least as strong as the Soviet Union, 75 percent want a bilateral nuclear weapons freeze, and 80 percent favor bilateral reductions, 90 percent would favor a multi-lateral freeze and 91 percent multi-lateral reductions in nuclear weapons.

Among the strongest supporters for these proposals are Republicans, conservatives, and people who voted for Ronald Reagan.

This represents almost a total mandate from the American people, people who are becoming increasingly knowledgeable about nuclear weapon strategies. They watch this Administration's policies with alarm. Yet, how does the President respond to this mandate? He produces two sets of proposals: INF [Intermediate Nuclear Force] and START [Strategic Arms Reduction Talks], which are designed by the nature of the numerical advantage they give to the U.S. to fail. The INF proposals do not account for the British, French, or Chinese nuclear weapons nor the American forward-based systems on bombers and submarines designated to NATO. Mr. Reagan's zero option is a call for partial unilateral disarmament on the part of the Soviet Union. The START proposal calls for dismantling of more than half the Soviet land-based strategic nuclear weapons (75 percent of which are land-based), while the U.S. can actually add a few more weapons to its 25 percent ratio of land-based nuclear weapons (50 percent of which are on relatively invulnerable submarines and 25 percent in bombers). Bombs on intercontinental airplanes are not included, nor are 8,000 cruise missiles about to be produced and deployed.

He has initiated a $65 million public relations program to convince the American and European public that more nuclear weapons are good for them, while the Arms Control and Disarmament Agency—responsible for all the negotiations on arms control—has an annual budget of only $20 million. This will only act as a catalyst to the cynical, well-informed European public, and also I suggest to the increasingly well-informed American public.

While the President talks about deep reductions, he is, in fact, planning to build 17,000 more hydrogen bombs, including the small strategic sea-launched cruise missile, unverifiable by National Technical Means, which signals the end of arms control agreements; the extremely accurate and rapid Pershing II missile, which could well instigate a Soviet Launch-On-Warning system where computers initiate nuclear war; MX and D5 Trident II missiles, which were designed with the accuracy and reliability the Administration feels it needs for a first-strike, so-called "winnable" war. Such a nuclear war is described in the Pentagon's Five-Year "Defense Guidance," which calls for preparations for a protracted nuclear war to be fought over a period of six months, at the end of which time the U.S. will "prevail." That is, the U.S. will have more nuclear warheads than the Soviet Union. The "guidance" also calls for decapitation of the Soviet leadership by Pershing II missiles (leaders who could only "control" such a war if alive); for guerrilla warfare in eastern Europe; for anti-satellite and anti-submarine warfare; and for economic warfare with the Soviet Union.

The President's past advisor, Eugene Rostow, said that "We are living in a pre-war and not a post-war world," and his new nominee to head the Arms Control and Disarmament Agency, Kenneth Adelman, calls arms control a "sham," and said that one reason not to rush into talks is "that in a democracy these negotiations tend to discourage money for defense programs."

The Administration plans to spend $2.2 trillion, including cost over-runs on defense in the next five years, while programs for health care, Medicaid, health insurance are cut, and WIC [Welfare and Institutions Code] programs which supply milk for infants and pre-natal and post-natal care for poor women are dismantled. The national infant mortality rate is now 12.8 per 1,000; in Washington, D.C., 22.8, with whites at 8 and blacks at 28 per thousand. The world's most affluent nation now ranks 11th in the world in infant mortality. The world spends $600 billion a year or $1 million a minute on the arms race, while two-thirds of the world's children are malnourished and starving. The economy of this country is in disrepair, a large cause being the cost-plus-exorbitantly expensive dead-end defense industry. More than half the country's scientists and engineers are funded by the Defense Department. The brilliant technological expertise which once made this country so powerful economically is systematically being diverted towards weapons technology, while Japan and West Germany, with virtually no war budgets, forge ahead in their economies, relatively speaking.

The people of this country are now understanding the magnitude of the problem. They are beginning to realize that there is no "defense" against nuclear weapons; that the Department of Defense is a misnomer and should probably be accorded its original title of Department of War.

Physicians, along with many others, have produced this enormous popular mandate to end the arms race. The people now understand that there may very likely be no long-term biological or social survival after a nuclear war, and that nuclear war cannot be "limited" or "protracted."

Conversely, the Administration seems to believe in post-nuclear war survivability, otherwise, there can be no rationale for these new weapon systems. I would suggest that T. K. Jones, Deputy Under-Secretary of Defense, who said, "If there are enough shovels to go around, we are all going to make it," and others, have not studied the scientific literature on long-term survivability.

Recently the Royal Swedish Academy of Sciences investigated the medical and ecological consequences of a conservative nuclear war scenario, using only one-half the total 1985 megatonnage of the super-powers. Targeting involved all cities and towns with populations greater than 100,000 in U.S., Canada, east and west Europe, USSR, Japan, North and South Korea, Vietnam, Australia, South Africa, and Cuba, and cities of more than 500,000 in India, China, Pakistan, and the rest of Southeast Asia.

Of the 1.3 billion urban population in the northern hemisphere, 750 million would be killed immediately from blast alone, and 350 million severely injured. Fire and fall-out will kill hundreds of millions more. An attack only on the nuclear reactors in Europe and the U.S. would render uninhabitable by normal radiation standards for years or even decades both these continents.

Many millions of survivors would die from epidemics of cholera, typhoid, dysentery, tuberculosis, rabies, polio, Black Plague, and hepatitis. These diseases would be spread by proliferating radiation-resistant insect vectors (cockroaches, flies, lice and fleas) from animal and human corpses to the living. Birds which normally eat the insects will be killed from fall-out. Survivors will be susceptible to disease as fall-out and starvation compromise their immune systems, and antibiotics and medical care will be virtually non-existent.

By conservative estimates, 5.4-12.8 million will die of fatal cancers, 17-31 million will be sterile, and 6.4-16.3 million children will be born genetically defective. (These calculations were made only for a 7-day radiation dose. A 25- year dose would incur millions more cases of disease.)

A summer attack could spark forest and grass fires, which could cover the U.S. A thick layer of particulate and photochemical smog from forest, oil and gas fires could blanket the northern hemisphere, reducing noon-day sun by a factor of 2-150.

Massive reductions of stratospheric ozone could cause increased solar UV [ultraviolet] light to damage most unprotected human and animal eyes; induce lethal sunburn within an hour to exposed people; increase the incidence of skin cancer, melanomas, and vitamin D toxicity in the northern and southern hemisphere survivors; destroy large populations of phytoplankton in the ocean, which create oxygen to replace the ozone layer. The increased UV light could also kill most microorganisms which constitute the base of the pyramid of life at which man stands at the apex.

Severe famine induced by smog, UV damage, cooling of the earth, absent fertilizers, insecticides, machinery and manpower would catalyze the effects of disease and would kill hundreds of millions in the Third World. Cooling of the earth by 1-2 degrees Fahrenheit could induce another Ice Age. Rain water and surface water and most food will be contaminated with radio-active isotopes. Survivors may well be psychotic with grief, acutely anxious, or so severely depressed that the drive for survival and reproduction may disappear. If these known and unknown global effects reacted in a synergistic fashion, it is possible that most planetary life would be extinguished.

The 19th century German pathologist, Rudolph Virchow, said, "Medicine is a social science, and politics is medicine writ large." In the past, physicians have worked with politicians to practice preventive medicine—to eliminate small-pox, control maleria, and immunize our children.

Nuclear war is the ultimate medical issue. PSR [Physicians for Social Responsibility] has effectively educated the public about the medical dangers of nuclear war. It must now help to prescribe the therapy. Prevention of nuclear war can only be accomplished through the democratic political process.

PSR will, therefore, encourage passage of bilateral nuclear weapons freeze resolutions in the House and Senate, will support passage of a comprehensive test-ban treaty, and will discourage authorization and appropriation for the new destabilizing weapons and delivery systems—the MX, D5-Trident II Missile, Pershing II, sea-launched and advanced cruise missile. This is not unilateralism. There now exists a position of strategic parity between the two super-powers. Russia has said if these new weapons are produced she, too, will build them. Therefore, the window of opportunity for obtaining a freeze remains open, at the most, 1-2 more years.

The freeze movement has only just begun. It will become the dominant topic of the presidential and congressional campaigns. But what beyond the freeze? There are still 50,000 nuclear weapons and only 1,000-2,000 "worth-while" targets in either super-power. Every day we live on borrowed time. Do the politicians, Pentagon officials, scientists, and military industrial complex understand this?

The children do. Recently, the American Psychiatric Association studied 1,000 adolescents in Boston, and to their horror found the majority don't believe they will live to adulthood, have babies, or get jobs. One little girl recently said at a conference, "Nobody likes to be given a broken gift. This is how we feel about our future." The parents do. The polls reflect this. The women do, illustrated by the gender gap in the polls. Women and men with nurturing vision are the driving force in this movement. They provide a unique contribution. They comprehend the genesis of life and, also, understand the concept of conflict resolution. Negotiating from the "position of strength" never produces resolution, only destruction of relationships.

How many leaders of the world really emotionally understand what they are doing? They are people who are caught in pre-nuclear thinking. Einstein said, "The splitting of the atom has changed everything save man's mode of thinking, thus we drift towards unparalleled catastrophe."

How many leaders of the world have witnessed the explosion of a hydrogen bomb, felt the intense heat, and seen battleships disappear in the ocean like splinters? How many have witnessed the miracle of the birth of a baby? How many have helped a child to die and supported the parents in their grief?

The American people are realizing the only pragmatic way to break the psychic numbing of politicians is to threaten their political survival. Americans are organizing in towns and cities throughout the country to elect a President and Congress in 1984, committed to rapid bilateral nuclear disarmament.

We live on a gravely threatened planet and face an acute clinical emergency. Time is of the essence. As we move towards disarmament, we must not forget that the cause of the illness is not the weapons per se, but the relationship of the superpowers. This can be solved only by moral initiatives and a climate of good will. Recent history demonstrates such a move with a hegemonic Communist superpower, which has not always respected human rights. Nuclear-armed China, once such a despised and bitter enemy, was made an ally by a conservative Republican president.

After the Cuban missile crisis, President Kennedy initiated conciliatory moves with the Soviet Union. He stopped atmospheric testing. They responded. They stopped production of strategic bombers. A hotline was established. The Russians were so pleased with these moves they called it "The Policy of Mutual Example." Tensions between the superpowers reached an all-time low. The whole world breathed a sigh of relief and then deeply mourned his death.

President Reagan could also be perceived by posterity as a great statesman, if he took the moral initiative and made the first move towards the Soviet Union. For example, he could offer them a much-wanted Most-Favored Nation status in trade. Should Russia and America become friends, the weapons would become anachronistic overnight.

America is the greatest democracy on earth. Because the Russian people don't have a democracy, we have double the responsibility to prevent nuclear war. Americans are wonderful, kind, loving people, who desperately want to do the right thing. America built and used the first nuclear weapon. It has led the arms race. It can and will lead the world to salvation and survival.

To this end and on behalf of humanity, I make this call today. Mr. President, you have given us a Five-Year Plan for massive rearmament with a goal of nuclear war fighting capability. We call upon you to respond to the people's needs, and give us a five-year plan for disarmament with a goal of nuclear war prevention.

We call upon you to negotiate a U.S.-Soviet freeze within one year.

We call upon you to achieve a 50 percent bilateral cut in all nuclear weapons and delivery systems in the next two years.

We call upon you to achieve a bilateral two-thirds reduction of the remainder in the following two years.

The vast majority of Americans want not only a freeze, but also reduction.

It is your patriotic duty to preserve this country. Four billion human beings live neither in America nor Russia and they, too, desperately want to survive.

We are the curators of life on earth. The decisions we make in the next two years may determine the future of God's creation.

MASS MEDIA AND PUBLIC WELFARE

MASS CULTURE: CAN AMERICA REALLY AFFORD IT?[1]

DAVID MANNING WHITE[2]

In 1957, David Manning White with his coauthor Bernard Rosenberg, published *Mass Culture,* the best-selling book that introduced that term to the world. At the time, the authors were optimistic about the role that mass media eventually would play in our lives. Manning wrote in the *Saturday Review of Literature,* "I see a hopeful picture of our future as we go into the era of extended leisure that Americans will share in the next decade or two," envisioning the day when mass media would edify us and enhance our lives.

Twenty-five years later, at the annual Murray lecture at the University of Iowa on September 29, 1982, White had changed his mind:

> *Mea culpa!* I was wrong in thinking that if the opportunities to use the mass media to gradually improve the quality of our cultural life were present that the public would readily avail themselves. Today the *Saturday Review* is defunct, while during these same 25 years magazines like *Playboy* and *Penthouse* enabled such wily entrepreneurs as Hugh Hefner and Robert Guicione to fabricate veritable empires.

Defining mass culture as a "multi-faceted process by which most Americans decide what they buy, what style of clothes they wear, what they eat, and certainly how they spend their leisure hours or otherwise acculturate themselves in a mass society," he pointed out that the average American spends nearly half his waking hours in some involvement with the mass media. Whereas in the 1950s, White could tell his audience that they could not find a more optimistic champion of the beneficial potential of the mass media, now he said, "I must be candid with you at the outset and tell you what I feel tonight: the price mass culture in America is exacting from contemporary society is one that we cannot afford." He then proceeded with a scathing indictment of American mass media in which he condemned them for violence, pornography, and immorality.

---

[1] The annual Murray lecture delivered at 7:30 P.M. on September 29, 1982, in a lecture room in the Iowa Philosophy-English Building at the University of Iowa, Iowa City, Iowa.

[2] For biographical note, see Appendix.

White was invited to return to the campus where he had earned his Ph.D. degree to receive a plaque and speak in observance of his election to the University of Iowa Hall of Fame in the School of Journalism and Mass Communication. Recently retired from Virginia Commonwealth University, he was being honored for his contribution to academic scholarship, journalism, and mass communications as a reporter, consultant, and educator.

The speech, delivered in a classroom in the Iowa English-Philosophy Building, took place at 7:30 P.M. before an audience of about 125 people made up of students, faculty, and interested members of the community. It received front-page coverage in the university newspaper, *the Daily Iowan,* was the feature of articles in the *Des Moines Register* and the *University of Iowa Spectator,* and was carried by WSUI radio and a cable television station.

David White's speech: It is hard for me to realize that twenty-five years have passed since Bernard Rosenberg and I unleashed the book we called *Mass Culture* into the great American marketplace of public discussion. But apparently it was an issue whose time had come, for only six months after its publication the lead editorial in the vaunted London *Times* dealt with the debate that Rosenberg and I had stirred up. Today the term *mass culture* is used almost generically to delineate the effects of the mass media upon the vast majority of people in modern society. It has even found its way into the fabric of our everyday language as evidenced by its inclusion in some recent dictionaries.

Actually, in its totality mass culture is a multi-faceted process by which most Americans decide what they buy, what style of clothes they wear, what they eat, and certainly how they spend their leisure hours or otherwise acculturate themselves in a mass society. The bottom line is that the average American spends *nearly half the waking hours of his or her life* in some involvement with the mass media. Of the 16 waking hours, four are spent in front of a television set, 30 minutes or so reading a newspaper, and another 15 minutes with one or more of the 10,000 magazines published in this country, and about 2 and a half hours listening to radio (much of this while driving to and from work). Add an occasional excursion to a movie theater, or reading a paperback thriller or a Harlequin romance, while playing one of the millions of record albums or tapes we Americans buy each year, and the average comes to about eight hours a day. Keep in mind that the purveyors of mass culture do especially well during those 60 allegedly *free* hours from Friday at 5 P.M. until 7 A.M. on Monday, when we get ready for another working week.

As William Shakespeare so aptly observed in *Antony and Cleopatra,* "When such a spacious mirror's set before him, his needs must see himself." The mass media provides this "spacious mirror," which we enter in some ineluctable way. Yet, as the poet Rainer Maria Rilke so aptly perceived, we become part of the mirror just as the mirror simultaneously becomes ingrained in our personal lifestyle.

The question I would like to pose to you this evening is one over which I have literally agonized for a number of years. I hope you will not believe that I am engaging in rhetorical hyperbole when I ask you to at least consider whether the price that America has to pay for its mass acculturation is more than we can afford.

In the mid-1950s when I began to formulate my thoughts on popular culture you would have to look far to find a more sanguine champion of the power of the mass media. I believed then that the media had barely begun in their potential to enhance, even edify, the lives of the American people.

However, the developing patterns of the mass culture in this country over the past quarter century has led me to gradually change my opinions. So, I must be candid with you at the outset and tell you what I feel tonight: the price mass culture in America is exacting from contemporary society is one that we *cannot* afford.

Having said this, let me make it clear that I am not about to launch an *ad hominem* attack, a la Spiro Agnew, against the mass media. In addition to teaching various aspects of mass communications from 1946 until this past May, at one time or another during my lifetime I have worked as a newspaper reporter and editorial writer, as an editor on several magazines, as a news commentator both on radio and television, for several years as a cinema and drama critic for the Group W radio network, as well as in several phases of book publishing. From the time I started as a high-school stringer on the Davenport *Democrat* 50 years ago this month until last Friday when I completed an assignment for a new magazine on my recent trip to the People's Republic of China, my life has been intimately involved with the mass media in America.

So, if I appear to express certain strong caveats about the mass media, I assure you they are not spoken in petulant anger. The anxieties I am sharing with you this evening have been marinating for quite a long time. For years I didn't want to acknowledge these convictions even to myself, for as one who was steeped in Jeffersonian libertarianism I believed that the First Amendment was the alpha and omega of American freedoms. I still cherish Jefferson's wisdom in placing the First Amendment at the head of our Bill of Rights. But in recent years I think that too many cynical, casuistic lawyers have twisted the letter, not to mention the spirit of the First Amendment.

When I say that we ought to calculate the cost of our mass culture, I am not merely talking about the price we pay in dollars. Not that the amount of money we expend upon the artifacts and products of the mass media is insignificant.

You might be somewhat surprised to learn what proportion of our national income is spent on entertaining ourselves. If you include the money spent on beer and other alcoholic beverages, this past year we Americans spent in excess of $250 billion dollars in search of Lotus Land. And that's even more than the frightful annual budget we've adopted to build up our military posture.

I recognize, of course, that the horrendous rate of inflation which has plagued this country for several years hasn't spared the costs of producing mass media products. But this did not stop me from wincing when I had to pay $1.50 for this week's copy of *Time* magazine at the airport when I flew out here a couple of days ago. Is it worth the 10 or 15 times (as much) it cost when I first started to read *Time*?

And some in this audience may remember when we saw movies like "The Tale of Two Cities" for 35 cents, with that incomparable Ronald Colman playing Sidney Carton. When I was an impoverished graduate student here in Iowa City in the early 1940s I somehow managed to go to the Englert Theater once or twice a month to see memorable movies like Gary Cooper in "Sergeant York," even though 35 cents took a big bite out of my meager resources. Today, if the Englert has kept pace with the inflated cost of movies in Richmond, Virginia, where I now live, the price of admission is about ten times as much. And Sidney Carton has been replaced by Pink Floyd. On a recent Saturday night I saw a line of adolescents cueing up to see a rerun of a piece of violently malevolent bilge called "The Texas Chain Saw Murder" and it almost brought tears to my eyes as I remembered actors like Paul Muni and the dignity he brought to such films as "Juarez" or the "Life of Emile Zola."

I'm not really placated when I'm informed by the media moguls that I'm actually only paying about a half of what it costs to produce my daily newspaper or the current copy of *Time*. But they assure us that without advertisers picking up the lion's share of the tab they'd all be out of business.

Personally, I've never been quite convinced by the old argument that advertising doesn't cost me, the consumer, anything, or that in fact it may even save me money. How do they figure it accomplishes this? Well, first by creating mass sales, which thereby stimulates mass production. This, according to this slick paradigm, lowers the unit price of the product, so that whatever is spent on advertising is more than made up by the lowered price of the merchandise.

It sounds pretty convincing, but don't forget that the promulgators of this line of reasoning are in the persuasion business. Even they must find a rationale for explaining the virtually exponential rise of advertising costs in the past quarter century.

Again, let me recall the days when I was a struggling graduate assistant at this university and made the magnificent salary of $40 a month (but got my tuition free). In 1940 the total amount spent for advertising in the United States was something less than $2.5 billion; the amount spent this past year may exceed 50 billion. In any case, 15 to 20 times as much is being spent for advertising in the United States today than 40 years ago.

My anxiety about the inordinate cost of advertising extends far beyond its synthetic artificiality. Frankly, I doubt the worth of a system that thrives only when the people who live in a country are perceived as mere potential consumers, the statistical targets for cynical marketing strategists.

Perhaps Marshall McLuhan was right when he said that advertising is the cave art of modern civilization, although like many of McLuhan's brilliant epigrams I'm not quite sure what he meant. But I find no ambiguity in Arnold Toynbee's argument that advertising creates false images which in turn breed false souls.

We are exposed to some 1500 advertising messages every day of the year, urging us to buy something, anything, whether we truly need it or not. By this constant bombardment of product propaganda we are made to feel that our lives have been less than successful if we do not possess all the goodies that are being hawked.

If our young ladies do not use a wide variety of cosmetics and hair lotions and body perfumes they are excoriated by their peers and relegated to a life of barren spinsterhood; at the same time our young men are being assured by the Madison Avenue magicians that unless they drink Miller Light or Budweiser that they are not real red-blooded American boys.

As for us older citizens, the preeminent image that the advertising fraternity presents of us is of a bunch of goodnatured ninnies who cannot start the day without taking a couple of laxatives, or cementing our dentures to our gums, or looking frantically in the medicine cabinet for a cure-all for our chronic hemorrhoids. In the world of mass advertising everyone has to fit a stereotype and heaven protect those who dare to question the wisdom of the account executive!

Granted that such machinations may be good for gigantic advertising agencies like J. Walter Thompson or McCann and Erickson whose billings amount to more than three our four billion dollars annually, but I'm not convinced that this unremitting barrage of materialistic messages incessantly beguiling us to buy the latest gadgetry, to be the prettiest, the sexiest, or the most conspicuously affluent has been beneficial to the American pysche or *soul*, if you wish.

Some of you, I'm sure, might say that I am being too severe in my criticism of advertising as a significant component in the malaise that has crept into our society. Perhaps I am confusing the egg for the chicken, or is it the chicken for the egg? The fact is that we seem to have locked ourselves into an economic *schema* that demands ever-expanding production; this, in turn, requires an ever-expanding population which *ipso facto* will become the ever-expanding consumers who keep the system going.

While financial gurus like Louis Rukeyser watch the gross national product as if it were devised on a stone tablet on Mount Sinai, the majority of us Americans are still playing some kind of chain-letter pyramid game.

There has to be a sounder approach to the economic cycle than endlessly consuming more and more, but if there is the media of mass culture, which rely on advertising for their lifeblood, they do not want to discover it.

In not very subtle ways the media continually tell us that if we want a happy life in this country we must acquire a plethora of wealth and material goods. The trouble with this message is that less than *one percent* of the people in this country ever acquire enough money to stop in their inordinate quest for it; for the rest it is an elusive, alluring brass ring that the mass media continually AFFIRM is the alpha and omega of life.

By the year 2000, unless heaven forbid our entire system collapses, the gross national product of this country may exceed three trillion dollars. Unfortunately, I have also seen extrapolations of the amount we will be spending then on advertising, and my source is no less than *Advertising Age,* the industry's weekly bible. Would you believe 250 billion dollars! What in the world will we be producing of such lasting value that it will cost 125,000 times more than Thomas Jefferson paid for the Louisiana Purchase!

Will it be the $50 million dollars we spend during one single day each January to pay homage to the smart entrepreneurs who dreamed up the Super Bowl? If the game itself is usually an anticlimax after the millions of words of hype the press has freely given it, well, that's tough turkey.

Maybe we'll be spared Super Sunday this year because the owners and the players can't agree on how to divvy up the more than two billion dollars recently negotiated in television rights. It reminds me of the Episcopal bishop who wondered if the American public had rewritten the Lord's Prayer to read something like: "Our football, which art on television, Hallowed by thy Game; Thy fullback run, thy pass be flung in Miami as it is in Dallas."

I can't help wondering what Jefferson would have thought about a basketball player named Moses Malone who has just signed a contract with the Philadelphia 76ers for $13.2 million dollars. This rather fair sum of money is only $10 million less than Mr. Jefferson paid for all of the land from the Mississippi River (including Iowa) to the Rockies, and to earn this Mr. Malone will provide his athletic services for the next six years. Thirteen million dollars! That's probably more than the total salaries of all the presidents of the United States from Jefferson to Ronald Reagan.

Twenty-five years ago, in an article I wrote for the then thriving *Saturday Review* I was extremely optimistic about the role the mass media could and would play in our leisure time. As a matter of fact I waxed so enthusiastically about the future, that I wrote the following line: "I see a hopeful picture of our future as we go into the era of extended leisure that Americans will share in the next decade or two, because I see substantial amelioration in the uses of our mass media."

Mea culpa! I was wrong in thinking that if the opportunities to use the mass media to gradually improve the quality of our cultural life were present that the public would readily avail themselves. Today the *Saturday Review* is defunct, while during these same 25 years magazines like *Playboy* and *Penthouse* enabled such wily entrepreneurs as Hugh Hefner and Robert Guicione to fabricate veritable empires.

For example, thanks to the profit of his *Penthouse,* a couple of years ago Mr. Guicione invested $20 million dollars in producing a movie called "Caligula," which for sadistic violence and orgiastic pornography is without a peer. Far from having one redeeming social value, this film can only be viewed by those with a very strong stomach. That Mr. Guicione would attract such gifted actors as Malcolm McDowell and Peter O'Toole to this miscegenation of a film only gives added meaning to the term "filthy lucre."

Norman Cousins, one of America's most distinguished men of letters was editor and guiding spirit of the late *Saturday Review* for three or four decades. Small wonder, then, when he was recently interviewed on National Public Radio on the demise of the *Review* he said we have come into a period of great sleaziness in our popular culture, one in which Gresham's Law is applying more and more to those endeavors which try to stand up against a tidal wave of cheapness and vulgarity.

What saddens me is that the same printing press that can spew out the slimiest soft core pornography of a Harold Robbins can also print the artistic likes of a Saul Bellow, a Bernard Malamud or John Gardner. But let an unknown author who could potentially become the Bellow or Malamud of the next generation try to get his or her first novel published today and you'll find a very frustrated artist. If a John Irving, who learned so much of his craft here at Iowa's famed Writer's Workshop, offered his first novel today he probably would get a polite kiss-off with a deprecating letter about the precarious financial condition of book publishing today. In fact, the big publishing houses in New York are running so scared these days that about the only books they seem willing to take a chance on are sexual how-to-do it manuals and diet books. Even that small segment of the American population that actually buys new hard-cover books seems predominantly concerned with the excessive layers of fat which surround their abdomens or their indomitable search for the ultimate orgasm.

A few weeks ago I talked with my editor at a major New York publishing house and proposed a new book idea. Since this particular house has published seven of my books during the last 20 years, none of which lost any money, I am not exactly an unknown author to them.

"David," my long-time editor (and friend, too, I think) said to me, "about the only title I can get through the sales and marketing people who have the dominant say-so in any new book we undertake is *How to Make Love to a Rhinoceros for the C.I.A. and Lose 20 Pounds in a Month.* The sorrowful thing is that the joke he was making had more truth than fantasy in it.

One of my greatest anxieties about mass culture in this country is that it has led most Americans into an incessant quest for escapism, a kind of narcotization of the senses, a process which in the case of television has been accomplished in less than two generations.

In all honesty, aren't most of the programs offered on television, that endless array of soap operas, sitcoms, quiz shows, cops and crime stories, not to mention those late night talk shows in which the same round of celebrities preen themselves and hype their latest record or movie amidst a stifling self-adulation—isn't it all a monument to boredom and superficiality! The moguls of television programming know it, but as long as the Great American Public is watching they couldn't care an iota.

I wonder if these moguls could even have begun to surmise the seductive power of the television set in the late 1940s; indeed, could they have believed in their wildest dreams that it would take only a few years to acculturate this entire country into a nation of videots.

The 28-hours a week that the majority of American adults sit inertly in front of their TV sets amounts to 1456 hours a year, or about a quarter of their waking hours. This means that if our addiction to television continues unabated (and there are no signs that its popularity has decreased) that a one-year child, whose life-expectancy will exceed 75 years will spent at least 110,000 hours of his or her life in front of the tube. And if my arithmetic is correct, that amounts to 12 total years of your precious child's life (I mean 24 hours times 365 days of a year) as an acquiescent member of the *tubeoisie,* willingly chained to our contemporary version of Plato's cave.

But does allowing a fantasy life to usurp a tremendous share of our hard-sought leisure hours really help millions of Americans who are predominantly unhappy, bored with life, frustrated, frightened? Does grasping at the tendrils of the phantasy world which the purveyors of mass culture gladly provide (as long as there is a buck or two to be made from it), does it compensate for the traumas which emerge in our real daily lives?

Perhaps mass culture with its incessant advertising does provide a quick narcosis, a surcease from the big problems. But as I see it, day after day, year after year of this plastic view of life, of being the ultimate consumer, the sweet target of the Big Sell, the synthetic tripper to Lotus Land, eventually breaks down the will of millions of Americans to live in any kind of creative self-actualizing manner.

Day after day they turn to mass culture as a magic mirror which will tell them, "Oh, yes, yes indeed, you're the fairest one of all (or you will be if you dash on a few drops of Oil of Olay). You're J. R. Ewing and Farrah Fawcett Major and tomorrow you'll win $1 million in the lottery." And with all sincerity I say that this is a cruel exploitation of the *anomie* that afflicts millions upon millions of Americans.

At a conference I attended at the University of Southern California a few years ago, Richard Wald, former head of NBC News and later senior vice-president at ABC News, put it very honestly. I quote him, "TV harps on a very few themes. Only those eternal verities—lust, violence, sins and virtues—cut across all lines and make broad waves. These themes have always been with us, and in the past we might have confronted them on occasion, such as when we went to the theater. But now we live in a society where this is rained upon us all the time. What is this doing to us? How is TV changing the character of modern man?"

Let me try to draw some of the threads of my argument together now, and then you can formulate your own conclusions. Whether we as a nation have willingly given the vast majority of our leisure hours to the purveyors of our mass culture, or whether the media moguls are so infernally clever that they have seduced us begs the question, or so it seems to me.

The facts are that we are living in an age where the art of exploitation has been cultivated with enormous valence. A few years ago Keven Phillips coined the term mediacracy to express his deep concern over the concentration of persuasive power in increasingly fewer communications conglomerates. To a certain degree, I share Mr. Phillips anxiety about their power, although I feel it is too simplistic to overstate the influence of even such gigantic conglomerates as C.B.S., Gulf and Western, Time, Inc., not to mention a newspaper vulture like Rupert Murdoch, who waits for once viable publications to virtually die so that he can buy them. I doubt that they are the exclusive moulders *per se* of something so complex as our political behavior or moral values. Rather, my brief against the MEDIACRATS is that they are the major collaborators and reinforcers in the demeaning and vulgarization of America! But I suppose I could live with that, since no one *forces* me to partake of any particular mass culture offering. I can choose to read the *New York Times* instead of Mr. Murdoch's scabrous tabloid that bears the name of the once distinguished paper, the *New York Post*. I can turn on my hi-fi receiver on Friday night and listen to a Mozart concerto on the public radio station I help maintain by sending them a few bucks each year, and if 25 million other Americans are glued to the soapy operatics transpiring on "Dallas" or "Dynasty," well, that's their choice.

If I would as soon drink a castor-oil cocktail as sit through an hour of "Dynasty," that's my critical judgement, but those who dote on it are entitled to theirs, for America is a cultural as well as political democracy. "Dynasty" may not have the aesthetic nourishment of a sawdust sandwich, but its effect is essentially innocuous.

However, when it comes to the inordinate amount of violent content that the media moguls apparently feel is necessary to entice a mass public to either the big movie screens or the little TV screens I have the right and the mandate to be concerned. The social environment which this bottom-line violence engenders is one which I *cannot* run away from.

Very few of us go through life without some anxieties, low periods and a variety of inner struggles, but somehow after a while most of us manage to "hang in tough," and we make a rational detente with the problems that are bothering us. But an estimated 15 percent of our population are not so fortunate. Their internal conflicts cause them so overwhelming a sense of turmoil that their behavior becomes quite pathological. The problem is compounded when the source of the difficulty is so complicated and obscure that the symptoms are extremely hard to identify. How can we tell when just one individual out of the 10 to 15 million so-called walking wounded will assassinate a John F. Kennedy, or nearly succeed in doing the same to Ronald Reagan.

Or how do we spot one of the walking wounded who sits quietly at his cubby-hole desk in a gigantic corporation but spends his lunch hour perusing the latest shipment of child-pornography at the ever burgeoning adult book stores? Must we wait until something snaps in him and some child is molested or raped?

The human scum who produce and distribute this particularly noxious form of mass medium are sometimes punished with a slap on the wrist and a misdemeanor fine. So what! In a lawyer-wise society in which smoke screens about the First Amendment are bandied about with solemn protestations, we shouldn't forget that the $100 million spent each year on kiddie-porn contributes to our vaunted gross national product!

Without kiddie-porn a number of people who work in paper mills or on the assembly lines of a factory that makes offset presses might be unemployed. And I say if this is what it takes to raise our gross national product we had better go back and heed what a magnificent religious reformer said in Galilee a couple of thousand years ago, "What is the profit for a man who gains the world but loses his soul?"

It isn't that we haven't been warned of the anti-social effects of mass cultured-violence. Ten years ago the Surgeon General's report on television violence was cushioned with the usual tentative findings that social scientists sometimes use, the kind of academic mugwumpery which they think protects their flanks. Even then they concluded that there was substantial evidence linking television viewing to short-term aggression, but they were unclear whether it had any long-run consequences. Well, in May of this year the National Institute of Health issued a report that is an update of the Surgeon General's findings, and it concludes that there is now "overwhelming scientific evidence" that *excessive* violence on television leads directly to aggression and violent behavior among children and teen-agers. In fact, the report said, and I quote from it: "In magnitude, television violence is as strongly correlated with aggressive behavior as any other behavioral variable that has been measured."

It is becoming more and more clear that violent behavior is acquired from television or theatrical films much the way that cognitive and social skills are learned from siblings, parents, and friends.

What constitutes "excessive violence" one might ask, since what triggers one person may not be the catalyst for thousands, maybe hundreds of thousands, of other people. Precisely. Consider, if you will, some of the most successful motion pictures of the last few years and you will see that they have been violent action pieces or else grotesque horror stories like the current hit "Friday the 13th." The depiction of violence is more graphic than at any time in film history. Some recent high points included Robert De Niro shooting off a man's hand in the gory climax of "Taxi Driver," a film that has gained a sort of grotesque immortality because John Hinckley Jr. viewed it so obsessively. If that wasn't violent enough for your teen-ager, who could have as easily watched it on cable television as at a theater, how about the sharp piece of plate glass slicing David Warner's head off in "The Omen." And those who didn't pay to see Laurence Olivier torture Dustin Hoffman in "Marathon Man" by drilling into the nerve of his front tooth could see it as an ABC Television Movie of the Week in their homes.

Some screen writers seem to specialize in this type of violence. Paul Schrader who gave us "Taxi Driver" also wrote the scenario for "Rolling Thunder." Here we find a Vietnam veteran who has his hand ground off in a garbage disposal, and when he recovers he goes after his attackers wielding his razor-sharp hook as a weapon.

It's a bit of an enigma, a true paradox to me. I suspect that most Americans do not want even to contemplate the almost incredible amount of real-life violence that has occurred during their lifetime. In the six and a half decades I have lived more than 50 million of my fellow human beings have died from the violence of wars, terrorism, genocides, and criminal activities. And it is on the increase. So why do we seek escape from the terrifying reality of these negative aspects of modern life by watching an incredible stream of violence night after night as passive voyeurs sitting in front of the video tube?

I don't know the answer to that question, but I do know that [instances of] violence in movies, both those shown in theaters and those which are shown on television, particularly cable TV, is at an all-time high. If you don't believe me, perhaps you will accept the credibility of the National Coalition on Television Violence, which is chaired by Dr. Thomas Radecki, a psychiatrist at Southern Illinois University. In a recent interview, Radecki said that his Council's monitoring research "has found movie violence at an all-time high, with violence against women and rape scenes common." He added that violence on Cable TV can even be worse than in the movie theaters, and cited the decision by Home Box Office to show a brutal, prolonged depiction of a gang-rape in a film called "Death Wish II." The irony of it was that this scene had been toned down slightly for theater audiences to get an R-Rating, but HBO decided to show it in its original X-rated form.

Throughout this century social critics such as Upton Sinclair and George Seldes have pointed out that the mass media are essentially amoral, but the larger question of WHO is injured has seldom been raised as long as the corporate ledgers showed healthy gains. Well, corporate amorality can and does injure individuals. Sometimes it happens when a motor company like Ford refuses to face up to a serious defect in its Pintos until many people die and only then when enormous lawsuits go against them. But what about corporate greed and amorality among the mediacrats.

Let me give you just one example. On September 10th, 1974, NBC presented a two-hour made-for-television movie called "Born Innocent" staring Linda Blair as a runaway adolescent committed by her parents to a detention center. During the course of the film Ms. Blair is initiated into the center's way of life by a gang-rape in a communal shower. The scene was depicted with extremely graphic realism. Suddenly the water stopped and a look of fear came over Blair's face. Four adolescent girls are standing across the shower room. One is carrying a plumber's helper, you know the sort of plunger that most of us use to unclog stopped-up drains. She is waving the plunger near her hips. The older girls tell Blair to get out of the shower, and she steps out fearfully. Thereupon the fours girls violently attack the younger girl and wrestle her to the floor. She is shown naked from the waist up, struggling, as the older girls force her legs apart. Then the girl with the plunger is shown making intense thrusting motions with the handle until one of them says, "That's enough!"

Four days after this prime-time telecast a violent scuffle occurred on a beach near San Francisco, and before it was over a 9-year-old girl named Olivia Niemi had been sexually assaulted with a beer bottle. This patent imitation of the "Born Innocent" actions induced Olivia's mother to bring a negligence suit against NBC, a suit which obviously raised many difficult sociological as well as constitutional questions.

To me it has come down to one fundamental issue. What was the moral responsibility of the network? Shouldn't it have known that impressionable young viewers might imitate the violent dramatic scene? After legal maneuvering by the highly skillful and expensive lawyers NBC could afford to hire, the case narrowed down to whether this movie actually "incited" that specific real-life attack. So eventually the lawsuit was dismissed when the judge ruled that it was necessary to prove that NBC "intended" viewers to imitate the sexual attack depicted on "Born Innocent."

But I predict that there will be future cases like this, because sooner or later we are going to have to come to grips with the effects of television on human conduct. It was of small solace to Olivia Niemi, who will carry the trauma of what happened to her throughout her life, that some network apologist expressed regret, but glibly added on the witness stand that there were probably hundreds of thousands of young people watching "Born Innocent" that night, and only this small handful of kids in California "acted out" in this pathological manner.

We know that the network recognized that the film might offend or disturb some viewers because it inserted the usual advisory disclaimer at the beginning of the program. "The following program 'Born Innocent' deals in a realistic and forthright manner with the confinement of juvenile offenders and its effect on their lives and personalities. We suggest that you consider whether the program should be viewed by young people or others in your family who might be disturbed by it." What a smug, sanctimonious cop-out that was. Because as a matter of fact such disclaimers generally have the opposite effect, and I suspect that any veteran television network official would acknowledge that this is so, unless he or she were on the witness stand in a future case of this kind. How many parents monitor what their children are watching, and with two or three sets not uncommon in a home, one of them in the children's bedroom or den, it is becoming increasingly difficult to do so.

The question that we in the larger court of public opinion may have to answer sooner than you may surmise is whether such media fare can be justified if indeed only one 1/1000 of *one percent* of those who view it could be influenced in this way. If you think that media violence can trigger such pathological reactions only among impressionable children, consider again one John Hinckley Jr., whose obsessive fantasy about Jodie Foster was initiated by the role she played in the movie "Taxi Driver."

Can America afford the most venal, amoral aspects of its mass culture? I've tried to make it clear that I don't think we can. Although you may think that I am more pessimistic than Jonathan Swift I truly believe that some rational but drastic action must be instituted. And I don't mean anything as simplistic and counterproductive as urging a boycott of certain networks or the sponsors of programs with deleterious content.

We need action that is compatible with the First Amendment but action that will reduce the amount of violence in our mass media, especially now that there is such a proliferation of violence in the movies shown on cable television systems. I agree wholeheartedly with Dr. Radecki of the National Coalition on Television Violence when he urges the United States Congress to meet its responsibility to take legal and constitutional action against proven causes of violence and rape in our society.

Perhaps until now the Congress has been afraid to offend the powerful movie and television entertainment industry and their lobbyists, but I am going to use whatever voice I have to let my Representative know how I feel. I hope some of you will join me.

THE POWER OF THE PRESS: A PROBLEM FOR THE REPUBLIC, A CHALLENGE FOR EDITORS[1]

Michael J. O'Neill[2]

About two weeks after Michael J. O'Neill, editor of the *New York Daily News,* the nation's largest general circulation newspaper, and president of the American Society of Newspaper Editors (ASNE), delivered his presidential address to the Society, Senator Patrick J. Moynihan requested that the speech be inserted in the *Congressional Record.* Senator Moynihan, an outstanding speaker himself and noted for being both candid and perceptive in the Senate and, before that, in the United Nations, praised the speech as an " . . . address of the most extraordinary candor, force, and perception." He added,

---

[1]Delivered on May 5, 1982, during the annual convention of the American Society of Newspaper Editors in a banquet room of the Chicago Marriott Hotel, Chicago, Illinois.
[2] For biographical note, see Appendix.

One recalls that extraordinary series of articles the late A. J. Leibling wrote for *The New Yorker* magazine entitled "Annals of the Press." In those annals there has surely been no (more) important statement by a journalist than Mr. O'Neill's. It is already an event in the history of journalism. As an admiring New Yorker, I can only hope that his analysis and prescription, loving of country and of craft, selfless and patriotic and courageous so far behind the false courage we associate with the herd of independent minds that too often defines public issues will come to be seen as prophetic as well. Ideas have consequences. (*Congressional Record*, My. 27, '82, S6360)

Moynihan inserted the address in the *Record* "so that future generations will know that there lived in our time a man worthy of our past and deserving of the respect and acclaim of our posterity."

O'Neill's talk was the first of three at a luncheon during the ASNE's annual convention at the Chicago Marriott Hotel on May 5, 1982. His audience consisted of approximately 650 members, spouses, and guests. Although the American Society of Newspaper Editors is a small organization with approximately 900 members, it is extremely influential nationally because its members determine editorial and news policy on newspapers throughout the country. The problem O'Neill felt lay in the increasing power of the media.

The mass media, especially television, are not only changing the way government is covered but the way it functions. The crucial relationship between the people and their elected representatives—the very core of our political system—has been altered fundamentally.

O'Neill developed his thesis using a problem-solving method, with the first three-quarters of the speech devoted to the problem and the last fourth to recommended changes or solutions. He enlivened his talk with references to Milton, Samuel Johnson, Wordsworth, Jefferson, Hamilton, and Lincoln Steffens from the past, but also displayed a wide familiarity with current thought on the role of the mass media in society and government from such contemporary observers as Vermont Royster, Daniel Boorstin, Patrick J. Moynihan, Daniel Bell, Steven Spender, George F. Kennan, and Arthur Schlesinger Jr.

Although the address raised difficult professional, ethical, and even moral questions for editors in the mass media, it elicited a highly favorable response. According to the Executive Director of ASNE, O'Neill's speech "was one of the best received luncheon addresses we've ever had" and he noted that many journalism periodicals quoted extensively from it.

Michael O'Neill's speech: Standing on the gallows for the last five months, waiting for the trap door to fall, has been a stimulating experience. As Samuel Johnson once remarked, the prospect of being hanged does powerfully concentrate the mind. In my case, I couldn't help thinking about the mortality of newspapers—the *Daily News,* of course—but also other troubled newspapers and, indeed, newspapers in general because they are probably all quite mortal.

There are in most of us those intimations of immortality that Wordsworth wrote about. We never think of ourselves as ending, just as little children cannot conceive of their parents dying. And so it is with institutions, from large corporations to great cities. We assume they will last forever.

Except if you walk through the ruins of Ephesus in Asia Minor, and realize that a population of 250,000 simply vanished into history, you are reminded of the fragile nature of man and his works. And you get the same feeling, in a more intimate way, when newspapers suddenly disappear. Particularly the ones you have known and loved.

Under these circumstances, it is natural to reflect on our business—to consider what forces are working for its improvement or disparagement, how we are faring generally in the social and economic turmoil now buffeting us all. An editor is inspired to reflect especially on the state of his profession and, in my case, to worry about how well we are fulfilling our obligations to the society we serve. For while there has been an astonishing growth in the power of the media over the last decade or so, I am by no means sure we are using it wisely. The tendency has been to revel in the power and wield it freely rather than to accept any corresponding increase in responsibility.

In fact, the very processes we use to inform the public have been badly distorted by television and, to a lesser degree, by a whole range of other phenomena from investigative excesses to our enthrallment with adversary journalism. So not only have we failed to match new responsibility to new power, we have also yielded to trends that are hurting the cause of a well informed citizenry.

The extraordinary powers of the media, most convincingly displayed by network television and the national press, have been mobilized to influence major public issues and national elections, to help diffuse the authority of Congress, and to disassemble the political parties—even to make presidents or to break them. Indeed, the media now weigh so heavily on the scales of power that some political scientists claim we are upsetting the historic checks and balances invented by our forefathers.

Samuel P. Huntington of Harvard observed that "during the 60s and 70s, the media were the institution whose power expanded most significantly and that posed the most serious challenges to governmental authority." Max M. Kampelman warned that "the relatively unrestrained power of the media may well represent an even greater challenge to democracy than the much publicized abuses of power by the executive and the Congress." And Senator Daniel P. Moynihan, who concedes the press already has the upper hand in Washington, says that if the balance should tip too far in its direction "our capacity for effective democratic government will be seriously and dangerously weakened."

This is flattering, of course, because all newspapermen dream of being movers and shakers and the thought that we may actually be threatening the national government is inspirational. In several respects, it is also true. The Communications Revolution, which is profoundly reshaping all of Western society, has also altered the basic terms of reference between the press and American democracy.

No longer are we just the messengers, observers on the sidelines, witch's mirrors faithfully telling society how it looks. Now we are deeply imbedded in the democratic process itself, as principal actors rather than bit players or mere audience.

No longer do we merely cover the news. Thanks mainly to television, we are often partners now in the creation of news—unwilling and unwitting partners, perhaps, but partners nonetheless in producing what Daniel Boorstin has deplored as pseudo events, pseudo protests, pseudo crises and controversies.

No longer do we look on government only with the healthy skepticism required by professional tradition. Now we have a hard, intensely adversarial attitude. We treat the government as the enemy—and government officials as convenient targets for attack and destroy missions.

No longer do we submit automatically to the rigors of old-fashioned impartiality. Now, not always but too often, we surrender to the impulse of advocacy, in the name of reform but forgetful of balance, fairness and—if it isn't too unfashionable to say to—what is good for the country.

These trends, however, are more symptom than cause. Much deeper processes are at work. The mass media, especially television, are not only changing the way government is covered but the way it functions. The crucial relationship between the people and their elected representatives—the very core of our political system—has been altered fundamentally.

In ways that Jefferson and Hamilton never intended nor could even imagine, Americans now have the whole world delivered to them every day, in pulsating, living color—all of life swept inside their personal horizon. Distant events—Selma, Alabama, the riot-torn Democratic convention in Chicago, the hostages in Iran—are instant experiences, neither insulated by a reporter's translation nor muted by what Theodore H. White has called the consoling "filter of time."

The flashing images mobilize popular emotions on a truly massive scale and with stunning speed, quickly generating and shaping public opinion. The televised battle scenes from Vietnam, as we know, aroused a whole nation against the war, helped reverse our national policy, and ultimately destroyed the presidency of Lyndon Johnson.

"The introduction of modern mass communications," said the sociologist Daniel Bell, "allows us, in many cases forces us, to respond directly and immediately to social issues." Television has thus played a decisive role in the so-called revolution of rising expectations. It has strongly stimulated the consumption culture. It has dramatized the gap between haves and have-nots, helping to create a runaway demand for more and more government services and for equality of result as well as of opportunity.

Time and time again, presidents discover that the public has already made up its mind about issues before they have even had time to consider them. Their hand is forced. The deliberative process that representative government was designed to assure is frustrated.

Television has also indelibly changed the democratic process by establishing a direct communication link between political leaders and their constituents. Now, as never before, these politicians are able to by-pass their parties so that the whole system of party government, built up over nearly two centuries, is now breaking down. This, in turn, is contributing to the crisis of government that Lloyd Cutler and others find so threatening to the American system.

In presidential elections, that most central of democratic functions, media appeal has replaced party screening in the primary selection process. National conventions are no longer relevant. Most of the subtle bonds of political power, whether the ritual dispensing of favors or dependence on party for advancement, have been snapped. From the district clubhouse to Washington, especially Washington, political discipline has almost disappeared.

The president no longer has much leverage over the members of Congress, even those in his own party. Congress itself is in a disheveled state with power so diluted that neither floor leaders nor committee chairmen are able to act with the authority, for example, of a Sam Rayburn.

As a consequence, power has been badly fractured. Our capacity for achieving consensus on national issues has been damaged. George F. Kennan cites fragmented authority as one of the chief causes of the disarray in U.S. foreign policy, and he mainly blames Washington's over-reaction to popular emotions whipped up by the media.

Where power is frayed, as Douglass Cater has pointed out, "public opinion is called on more regularly than elsewhere to act as arbiter among competing policies and politicians." So we have the paradox of the mass media tearing down power on the one hand, and then gaining power themselves at the expense of the institutions they have diminished.

One of the victims of this process is the presidency itself. Although many complex forces have conspired to undermine its authority, television and the national press have played a major role. For one thing, they have focused tremendous attention on the president, as the personal symbol of the nation and its ideals, as the principal instrument of action and the first resort of complaint or redress. They also rely on him for the drama, the glamor and excitement, that television forever craves and must have to survive. Indeed, he happily conspires in the creation of media events and makes all sorts of other concessions in order to present his deeds in a way that TV finds congenial.

A skilled communicator like Ronald Reagan is a master of television. He exploits it with great effect to project himself and his policies directly to millions of people, going over the heads of Congress and, incidentally, making an end run around newspapers.

But television can also be cruel. It raises public expectations far beyond the presidents's reach and then, when he cannot satisfy them, it magnifies the perception of failure. By massive over-exposure, the media also strips away the protective mystery of the Oval Office, inviting the same kind of premature disenchantment that destroys so many TV stars.

A more serious concern is how the media merry-go-round is distorting the news, the information base, if you will, that people need to make sound decisions in a democracy. The capacity to mobilize public opinion is now so great that issues and events are often shaped as much to serve the media's demands as to promote the general welfare.

The result is a blurring of the line between the medium and the message, between substance and shadow, like the shadow on Plato's cave. "In the beginning," as Huntington has commented, "television covered the news; soon, news was produced for television." [Daniel] Boorstin has made the same point, but less politely.

Unfortunately, television is an impressionistic medium that marshals images and emotions rather than words and reason. Its lenses are distorting. They focus on the dramatic and the visible, on action and conflict. News decisions are influenced by what film is available, what events "project" well, what can be explained easily in quickie bursts of audio headlines.

Newsmakers modify their behavior to fit, creating controversy on demand, turning away from debate and petition in favor of protest and demonstration. As the former Tammany Hall chief, Edward N. Costikyan, put it in a manual for political candidates: "Television reporting is not news; it is spectacle. To capture coverage, you must create a spectacle. . . . " Some issues, artificial or real, are churned up to the point that they command national attention and affect national policy. Other issues which may be far more valid and important—lagging investment in basic research, for example—are ignored because they cannot be seen by television's beady red eye.

The raw materials of public deliberation thus become a confusing mixture of the real and unreal, important and irrelevant—a jumble of impressions that confound even the historians. Arthur M. Schlesinger Jr. said that after being involved in the making of history during his White House days, he could never again rely on the testimony of the press.

So we all spin around in a vicious circle. Television first changes the nature of mass communication, including communication between the people and their government. In response, political leaders, single issue groups, and all other players on the public stage change their media, including the national press, react and interact. Masses of people become involved, contributing to the surge of participatory democracy that students of government have decried. Public agendas and priorities are distorted. The thrust of the news, the pace, and even the content of the news, become captive to the process.

Adding to the general turmoil are two other phenomena: the press's harshly adversarial posture toward government and its infatuation with investigative reporting. These attitudes, which have always lurked in the psyche of American journalists, were enormously intensified by Vietnam, Watergate, and the general attack on authority in the 1960s and 1970s. Both news coverage and the conduct of government have been duly affected—but not improved.

It may be foolhardy to say anything uncharitable about investigative reporting; it is in such vogue now. We have all basked in the glory of exposés and gloated while public officials have turned slowly on the spit of newspaper disclosures. I remember the triumph we felt at the *Daily News* when we reported that a congressman had lied about pleading the fifth amendment and then saw him destroyed as a candidate for mayor.

On balance, investigative reporting has probably done more good than harm, although a wise member of the *New York Times* editorial board, Roger Starr, would dispute the point. He once suggested wistfully that journalism schools should ban Lincoln Steffens' famous book, *The Shame of the Cities.* He said that muckraking did so much damage to the cities that he hated to think what havoc modern investigative reporters might commit.

Muckraking has been over-emphasized, tending to crowd out other more significant kinds of reporting. If we had not been so busy chasing corrupt officials, for instance, we might not be guilty of having missed some of the biggest stories of the last half century:

The great migration of blacks from the South to the industrial cities of the North, something we didn't discover until there were riots in the streets of Detroit.

The first mincing steps toward war in Vietnam, which we did not begin reporting seriously until our troops were involved.

The women's liberation movement and the massive migration of women into the job market, a social revolution that we originally dismissed as an outbreak of bra burnings.

In some cases, investigative reporting has also run off the ethical tracks. Individuals and institutions have been needlessly hurt when the lure of sensational headlines has prevailed over fairness, balance, and a valid public purpose. Those uninspiring scenes of reporters and cameramen trampling over Richard Allen's front lawn to hound his wife and children raise questions.

Is our duty to inform so stern that we must exile ourselves from our own humanity? Are we like policemen who have become inured to violence? Have we become too cynical, so hardened by our experiences with sham, that we can no longer feel what an official feels, what his wife and children feel, when he is ripped and torn on TV and in the press? Have we become so arrogant with our power, so competitive, that we cannot decide that the public crime is often not worth the private punishment? That the First Amendment is often abused rather than served by those who would defend it.

" . . . Is it not true," Kampelman asked, "that no man is free if he can be terrorized by his neighbor? And, is it not possible for words as well as swords to terrorize?"

Similar questions need to be asked about our intensely adversarial coverage of government because this, too, is falsely coloring the information flowing to the public.

We are probably the most adversarial people in the world—"the most anti-American," to quote the British poet Stephen Spender—and we are getting worse all the time. The reasons lie deep in the past—in the Enlightenment's victory over authority, in the romantic concept so eloquently expressed by Milton that truth will triumph in any struggle between reason and falsehood, in the industrial age's emphasis on competition to sort out good products from bad, in the checks and balances built into our own Federal system, and in the egalitarian movement that has recently reached such a crescendo in the United States.

In our profession, there are more immediate causes. There are the natural tensions between a President who paints a rosy view of all he does and the messengers who deliver bad news. There is the understandable resentment of officials who feel the media always emphasize the exceptional and negative over the positive, conflict and failure over success. And on the other side, there are the endless official lies and deceits and masquerades that gnaw at the moral intent of reporters.

Within the American context, these tendencies are normal. But they have become much more destructive in the last few years. With Vietnam and Watergate, with new waves of young, committed reporters moving into the profession, with older editors feeling guilty about having been "too soft" in the past, the media's relations with government have taken a sharp turn for the worse. The government has become the enemy.

A regretful [veteran journalist] Vermont Royster has said that the great difference between the Washington press corps of his day and the one now is that then "we did not think of ourselves and the government as enemies."

"We were cynical about much in government, yes," he said. "We were skeptical about many government programs, yes. We thought of ourselves the watchdogs of government, yes. We delighted in exposes of bungling and corruption, yes. But enemies of government, no."

By the time Jimmy Carter was elected, the critic Anthony Smith has observed, the American press had come "to think of itself as an opposition, almost in the European sense, as a counterpower, part of whose *raison d'etre* consisted in the constant search for ways to dethrone the incumbent in office."

Smith may have overstated his point, but the adversarial pendulum has in fact swung too far and this is not good for the press, the government, or society. Contrary to 18th century myth and our own litigious tradition, the adversarial method does not necessarily produce truth. As often as not, it misses the truth and distorts reality. And knee-jerk opposition to government by a free press is only a mirror image of the undeviating governmental support that we criticize in the totalitarian media.

In its more extreme forms, the adversarial attitude creates barriers to the clear observation and analysis necessary for objectivity. It encourages emotional involvement with individual personalities and issues. It invites arrogance. It tempts reports to harrass officials. Ultimately, it undermines credibility because people intuitively sense when the press is being unfair. They are quick to detect a belligerent tone in a story and then discount it in their own mental ledger. And they become deeply skeptical, in Ben J. Wattenberg's view, when all they get from the press is an endless rat-a-tat-tat of failure.

"Is it so absurd to suggest," he asks, "that if all one reads and all one sees is cast under the rubric of crisis and chaos that Americans will either (a) believe the press and think it is on the wrong track or (b) believe their own senses and think the press and the crisis-mongers they headline are elite, arrogant and so far out of touch as to be non-credible and, even worse, irrelevant?"

If the credibility of news coverage has been part, the functioning of government has been damaged even more. Not only are public issues and priorities strongly influenced by the media, every policy initiative, every action, has to run a gauntlet of criticism that is often generated—and always amplified—by the press. In the searing glare of daily coverage, an official's every personal flaw, every act, every mistake, every slip of the tongue, every display of temper, is recorded, magnified, and ground into the public consciousness.

The protests of special interest groups, the charges of publici- ty- hungry congressmen, are rock-and-rolled through the halls of power. Controversy and conflict are sought out wherever they can be found, sapping energies and usually diverting attention from more urgent public business.

In this whirling centrifuge of criticism and controversy, authority is dissipated. Officials are undermined and demoralized. The capacity to govern, already drastically reduced by the fragmentation of power, is weakened still further.

The media have, in short, made a considerable contribution to the disarray in government and therefore have an obligation to help set matters straight. Or at least to improve them. The corollary of increased power is increased responsibility. The press cannot stand apart, as if it were not an interested party, not to say participant, in the democratic process.

We should begin with an editorial philosophy that is more positive, more tolerant of the frailties of human institutions and their leaders, more sensitive to the rights and feelings of individuals—public officials as well as private citizens.

We should be less arrogant, recognizing our own impressive short-comings and accepting Walter Lippmann's lament that we can never claim to be the merchants of truth when we so rarely know what the truth is.

We should make peace with the government; we should not be its enemy. No code of chivalry requires us to challenge every official action, out of Pavlovian distrust of authority or on the false premise that attack is the best way to flush out truth. Our assignment is to report and explain issues, not decide them. We are supposed to be the observers, not the participants—the neutral party, not the permanent political opposition.

We should cure ourselves of our adversarial mindset. The adversarial culture is a disease attacking the nation's vital organs. The lawyers will never escape it, but we must. We should retain a healthy skepticism, yes. Provide socially responsible criticism, yes. But relentless hostility? No.

Reporters and editors are much more attracted to failure than to success. An expression of sympathy, perhaps, because failure is always an orphan while success has many fathers. Yet, if we are truly to provide a balanced view of the world, we must tame our negative nature; we need to celebrate success and progress, not just wallow in mankind's woes.

For if we are always downbeat—if we exaggerate and dramatize only the negatives in our society—we attack the optimism that has always been a wellspring of American progress. We undermine public confidence and, without intending it, become a cause rather than just a reporter of national decline.

We should also develop a more sensitive value system to be sure we do not needlessly hurt public figures while exaggerating the public's right to know. Rights do not have to be exercised, just because they exist or because there is a story to be told. The claim of editorial duty should not be a cover-up for titilation. Legitimate public need should be weighed against personal harm because, among other things, the fear of media harrassment is already seriously affecting recruitment for public service.

Editors also need to be ruthless in ferreting out the subtle biases—cultural, visceral, and ideological—that still slip into copy, into political stories, mostly, but also into the coverage of emotional issues like nuclear power and abortion. Lingering traces of advocacy are less obvious than Janet's Cooke's fiction but, for that reason, are more worrisome. Editors—myself included—have simply not exercised enough control over subeditors and reporters reared in the age of the new journalism.

The problem of television is formidable. Its baleful effect on both government and journalism is beyond repeal. The expanding network news shows and the proliferation of cable promise even more change, confusion, and competition for the attention of busy Americans. And there are no solutions that I can think of, only the possibility of limited damage control.

The key to this is to emphasize the basics, the things newspapers have always been able to do better than television, services that will become even more important as the electronic networks continue swarming over the mass market and, in the process, define a more specialized role for newspapers.

We should be more resistant than ever to media hype—the pseudo event, the phony charges, the staged protest, the packaged candidate, the prime-time announcement and televised interview. Indeed, we should expose these as vigorously as we expose official corruption. For it is our job to cut through the superficial to identify the substantive—to explain and clarify the news, as most newspapers already do, in a reasoned way that television cannot. Although we should be interesting, we should not try to be an entertainment like television because this would be both futile and out of keeping with our special purpose.

Another issue is accountability. A brooding Ray Price, formerly of the *New York Herald Tribune* and the White House, complained that the press had acquired power "out of all proportion" to its ability or inclination to use its responsibility. Walter Wriston, a banker speaking for many in public life, warned that the media should remember that "the effective functioning of a democracy requires the most difficult of all disciplines, self-discipline."

"The freedom of us all," he said, "rides with the freedom of the press. Nevertheless, its continued freedom and ours will ultimately depend upon the media not exploiting to the fullest their unlimited power."

All sorts of remedies have been proposed, from ombudsmen to news councils, even anti-trust legislation. Many critics think it would be wonderful if we were just professionals so there could be the kind of self-policing that doctors and lawyers have—an uninspiring idea, though, when you consider how few doctors or lawyers are ever disciplined.

The fact is that no grievance committees or councils or laws will really work if the general attitude of the profession is not supportive. If the attitude is right, however, all the clanking machinery is probably unnecessary. Our best defense against opponents, our best bet for strengthening reader credibility, is an openness of mind that encourages both self-examination and outside criticism.

With this psychic base, we can expect editors—miracle of miracles—to respond more constructively to complaints, reporters to be more accepting of direction and correction. We can expect a more aggressive pursuit of fairness and a willingness to provide a more effective right of reply than letters to the editor or an occasional op-ed piece.

In the final analysis, what we need most of all in our profession is generous spirit, infused with human warmth, as ready to see good as to suspect wrong, to find hope as well as cynicism, to have a clear but uncrabbed view of the world. We need to seek conciliation, not just conflict—consensus, not just disagreement—so that society has a chance to solve its problems. So that we as a nation can find again the common trust and unity—so that we can rekindle the faith in ourselves and in our democracy—that we so urgently need to overcome the great challenges we face in the 1980s.

ISSUES AND DIRECTIONS IN EDUCATION

THE PLACE OF SCIENCE AND TECHNOLOGY
IN THE LIBERAL ARTS CURRICULUM[1]

David S. Saxon[2]

Concerned with a serious decline in scientific literacy, about sixty leaders in various areas met for three days at the beginning of June, 1982, to formulate a set of actions and strategies that colleges and universities could use to raise the quality of undergraduate education in the sciences, mathematics, and engineering, particularly for students not majoring in these subjects.

The theme of the conference was "Science and Technology Education for Civic and Professional Life—The Undergraduate Years." Sponsored by the Association of American Colleges (AAC) and the American Association for the Advancement of Science, the meeting was the fourth in a series. Earlier AAC conferences on important issues in the undergraduate curriculum were on foreign languages and international studies, the humanities, and the new feminist scholarship.

As keynote speaker, Dr. David S. Saxon, president of the University of California system, titled his address, "The Place of Science and Technology in the Liberal Arts Curriculum." His background as a teacher and scholar in physics, student abroad, university administrator, and author of *Physics for the Liberal Arts Student* qualified him to speak on the subject. He delivered the address at about 7:45 P.M. in the main meeting room at the Wingspread Conference Center in Racine, Wisconsin. His audience of approximately 65 conferees included representatives from higher education, secondary education, business, government, and other professions, and members of the AAC and Johnson Foundation staffs.

At the beginning of the speech, organized around a problem-solution pattern, Saxon posed the problem, one that he had taken seriously for 35 years and about which he had no illusions. He assured his listeners, "you will get no simple prescriptions from me," and stated:

---

[1]Delivered as the keynote address to the conference on "Science and Technology Education for Civic and Professional Life—the Undergraduate Years" held at the Wingspread Conference Center in Racine, Wisconsin, at 7:45 P.M., June 1, 1982, in the Terrace Room. The speech was printed originally in the *American Journal of Physics* (v. 51, p 12). Copyright by the American Association of Physics Teachers.

[2] For biographical note, see Appendix.

The problem is that educated, intelligent, inquisitive people are unable consistently to bring informed judgment to bear on questions connected in almost any way to science and technology, questions often vital to the welfare of each of us and indeed to the future of the world. Instead, the great majority of broadly educated people must rely on, and are at the mercy of, the testimony and assertions of others. Furthermore, the degree of reliance required demands a faith that borders on the credulous.

Developing this contention with specific examples and instances, Saxon turned to the solution: the development of courses that will "educate students for life in a technological society."

Dr. Saxon's address was reprinted in its entirety in the *American Journal of Physics* and was mentioned in an article on the Wingspread Conference in the *Chronicle of Higher Education.*

David Saxon's speech: I am particularly delighted at the opportunity to join you this evening, for I understand the deep importance of your assignment. Also its difficulty. You have been asked to addresss the question of the pervasive lack of knowledge and understanding of science and technology amongst those most educated of Americans, our college graduates. And, at a more fundamental level, to address, at least with respect to science and technology, the question of what constitutes a genuinely liberal education in this technological society and age. But not merely to address these questions; to propose as well a course of action based on your answers.

A significant first step has already been taken; we agree that our technological illiteracy—as it has been called—is a major problem, even a national scandal. Your presence here testifies to the fact that there is a consensus about the seriousness of the problem, so we start out that much ahead.

Teaching science to liberal arts students is something I have always taken seriously, from the moment I began teaching physics more than thirty-five years ago. And I know just how hard it is, having tried to do it myself on many occasions over those three and a half decades, using a variety of approaches, and having been responsible for a failed textbook on the subject. Be assured; I am under no illusions. You will get no simple prescriptions from me. Nor will you get a prescription about just what it is that constitutes a liberal education.

What you will get is, first, an attempt to define exactly what the problem is, to define precisely what I think we mean when we talk about our lack of knowledge and understanding of science and technology. Second, an attempt to understand what the roots of that problem are. Third, a brief attempt to define the proper place of science and technology in the liberal arts curriculum.

I have spoken on—and struggled with—certain aspects of this topic before. I have spoken to my colleagues in the sciences about their share of the responsibility—and perhaps blame—for the extent of our scientific illiteracy and suggested steps they ought to take in their own intelligent self-interest to address that problem. A few years ago, in an address to the Phi Beta Kappa Society, I emphasized the corresponding responsibility of students and faculty in the humanities. I have also talked to a group of broadcasters about the way the news media add to the problem and what they need to do to play a proper and responsible role. As I did on those occasions—and as I've already promised—I will begin by defining the problem.

Simply stated, the problem is that we are quite unable, as a society, to distinguish between sense and nonsense when it comes to science. The problem is that educated, intelligent, inquisitive people are unable consistently to bring informed judgment to bear on questions connected in almost any way to science and technology, questions often vital to the welfare of each of us and indeed to the future of the world. Instead, the great majority of broadly educated people must rely on, and are at the mercy of, the testimony and assertions of others. Furthermore, the degree of reliance required demands a faith that borders on the credulous. One of the distinguishing characteristics of a liberal education is that it should provide just that critical sense which makes it possible to winnow out the meretricious from the meritorious. Yet many liberally educated people are unable to do anything of the sort when it comes to science and technology.

That this is indeed the case is not an original observation, or even a new one. Over fifty years ago George Bernard Shaw summed it up when he said, "We believe (the earth) to be round not because as many as one percent of us could give the physical reasons for so quaint a belief, but because modern science has convinced us that nothing that is obvious is true, and that everything that is magical, improbable, extraordinay, gigantic, microscopic, heartless, or outrageous is scientific."

And this was more than half a century ago—before we had even imagined nuclear energy, neutrons (let alone neutron bombs), quantum field theory, lasers, quasars, black holes, quarks, DNA, or genetic engineering.

"Nothing that is obvious is true. . . . " We are expected and accustomed to accept what we are told without experiencing it or understanding it for ourselves. No wonder we are so often unable to tell the credible from the incredible, science from pseudoscience, sense from nonsense.

That this observation is neither new nor original is a reflection of how old—and how tough—the problem is. Why, then, has a consensus developed at this juncture that something must be done, and done urgently? Because our society is becoming increasingly and irreversibly technological and because scientific investigation is increasingly and irreversibly concerned with almost unimaginable extremes of space and time, which removes it ever further from the realm of our daily experience. Unless we acquire understanding, we will remain where we are right now, at the mercy of experts—or, worse, of charlatans posing as experts.

Let me describe one aspect of what I mean by citing some examples. Here are three statements about microwaves, all from published documents, all items I came across not so long ago:

From a report on the possibility of using microwaves as an energy source:

> The purpose of this report is to call attention to the possible great social benefit that would be derived from the use of microwave radiant energy to provide directly the warmth needed by human beings and other living creatures. A strong motivation for this proposal at this time, in spite of growing concern about possible dangers, is the view that such use could contribute importantly toward alleviating the world energy crisis.

From a book on the impact of microwaves on health:

> Microwave radiation can blind you, alter your behavior, cause genetic damage, even kill you. The risks have been hidden from you by the Pentagon, the State Department, and the electronics industry.

From a story that appeared in the press:

It was proposed that the United States launch space stations that would orbit the earth, collect solar energy, and beam it back to the earth, using microwaves. Such a project, its proponents argued, would largely solve the world's energy problems.

These accounts are similar to dozens of proposals or assertions that we read about daily in newspapers and magazines and hear about on television and radio. You have all heard it said that the world's supply of coal is more than adequate to take care of our energy needs for centuries; but you have also seen reports that use of coal will sooner or later—but irreversibly—cause the sun to heat up the atmosphere and by so doing melt the polar ice caps and inundate the earth. (Incidentally, there are other predictions that it will do just the opposite and cause a new ice age.) And the fierce debate over nuclear power rages more fiercely—and less rationally—than ever. Whom do you believe, and how are you to know?

I bring up these questions to illustrate the problems we have because we live in an increasingly technological society, one in which, to use Shaw's words, we are convinced that "Nothing that is obvious is true, and that everything that is . . . heartless . . . is scientific." Will microwaves kill you or save you from freezing to death some day? What is the feasibility of collecting solar energy in space and beaming it back to earth? Most people don't know. Worse, they don't even know how to go about finding a reasonable answer.

That illustrates the first aspect of the problem. Let me now describe the second, related but different. It has to do with the realm of personal belief and with the largely anecdotal evidence on which people build many of those beliefs. Why do so many educated, intelligent, inquisitive people believe in such things as UFOs, physics, ESP, precognition, psychokinesis, astrology, biorhythms, and pyramid power? On reflection, I suppose the fact that they do isn't all that surprising. After all, many of our own faculty have no difficulty believing in one or more of them. It can be argued, of course, that matters of personal belief—especially when they revolve around such apparently harmless notions as, say, the belief in visits from ancient astronauts—can be dismissed as having significance only to the individual involved. I don't believe that. For one thing, that so many people find it easy to believe in pyramid power, in the supernatural hazards of the Bermuda Triangle, in the reality of precognition reflects a grave misperception of the laws that govern our universe—and a grave failure of our educational system. For another, it is clear that personal beliefs and our state of mind can have a profound and sometimes dramatic effect on individual performance and well-being. There are many instances of this, among them the tendency of beginning medical students to think they have developed the symptoms of each illness they study, one by one.

It is also clear that personal beliefs can influence the decisions we make about our own well-being, decisions that can be disastrously wrong. The Beverly Hills Diet is only the most recent of a long string of fad diets characterized by an amazing ability to inspire faith and an unfortunate tendency to completely ignore nutritional principles. Or take the healing properties of copper bracelets for people who suffer from arthritis. Or the controversy over Laetrile. Some of the many hundreds of popular beliefs about health are harmless, others dangerous. Just about all of them are based on wishful thinking or on undifferentiated and unevaluated anecdotal evidence of one kind or another—sometimes first hand, sometimes second, but evidence that is more often than not negated by anecdotes on the other side of the question, if one only looked.

This brings us to a contradiction. On the one hand I've said that when it comes to science, most people do not have any experience of their own to rely on but must instead rely on the testimony of experts. But I've also asserted that even in the realm of their daily lives, personal experiences is a far from infallible guide. So the question is not just whom do you believe but what do you believe—and on what basis?

This contradiction exists for two reasons. First, modern science deals with the physical world at a level so abstract and so remote from everyday experience that there is no way such experience could act as a guide in distinguishing sense from nonsense. Science expresses itself in the language of abstraction, a language that most people find difficult and forbidding. It is precisely that abstraction, of course, that has enabled science to express relations in the physical world in terms of such great general laws as those of gravity and relativity and quantum mechanics. But it is also the reason why science is an "inaccessible language" for most people, a term the late philosopher Charles Frankel used to describe physics but which is, as far as most people are concerned, applicable to the other sciences as well.

And yet when we turn to the realm of personal experience—to the everyday world in which we must decide whether to plan the day by consulting the horoscope in the morning paper, in which we must choose among the Beverly Hills or the Scarsdale or the Meditation diets—we find that experience often fails, that it doesn't always steer us right. Whether you call it intuition or common sense, that distillation of our experience that we use as a guide in evaluating new information and in making choices about our life is, in its own way, an inaccessible language too. It is inaccessible in the sense that we often don't know how to interpret it or how to translate it into a few solid, reliable, general truths on which to base our decisions and our beliefs. The results of this inability are sometimes amusing and sometimes tragic. It exists because we live in a world in which coincidence and statistical fluctuations are just as likely—or even more likely—to be at the root of much of what happens to us as any causal factor. That makes it extraordinarily difficult to generalize from experience, though the very process of living forces us to do so.

We need to recognize that, in dealing with these kinds of questions, we are dealing with the deep human need to find an explanation for the world and for what happens to us. There is something in all of us that resists the notion that the universe is chaotic and that events are random and beyond our comprehension. The ancient myths, which in virtually every culture explain how the world came to be created and how it works, respond to these universal needs. These myths are attempts to explain not only the manifestly orderly aspects of the cosmos—the regular motion of the sun and the moon and the planets—but also those aspects that are apparently random and chaotic. Earthquakes and volcanos may be no less destructive if you see them as the rumblings of an angry god, but they make a lot more sense. Humankind has always devised stories to explain the inexplicable, to keep at bay the notion that the universe may be not merely hostile but meaningless as well.

If modern science has diminished our capacity to believe these mythic cosmologies in any literal sense, it has in no way diminished our longing for a faith of some kind. This need to find a reason for what happens to us extends to things which may simply have no explanation at all. We all recognize that we can be lucky or unlucky, fortunate or unfortunate. We are less eager to recognize that luck and good fortune are statistical fluctuations. Superstition is the attempt to control events that are really matters of chance, which is why gamblers believe they are more likely to win when they wear their lucky ties or when they bet on their lucky numbers. That we accept anecdotal explanations of chance events, of happenstance, is another manifestation of the stubborn human need to connect events in some meaningful way, even if they aren't connected at all.

In our thinking about liberal education, there has been insufficient recognition of the fact that science and religion and myth attempt to address the same elemental human need, the same unquenchable desire for an organizing principle that can serve as a guide or polestar and help us understand the world and our place in it. The view of science as a destroyer of faith is not merely superficial; it is wrong. Science begins with the assumption—as an act of faith—that the universe is orderly enough to be susceptible to explanation and understanding.

But more than orderliness is required, as the ancient Greek philosophers realized. The universe would be fundamentally incomprehensible were it not fundamentally simple, were it not made up of a few elementary components. And because the Greeks believed that at bottom it must be comprehensible, they postulated the atomic nature of matter. In this century we have finally demonstrated through systematic experiment that the universe is indeed made up of elementary particles, but in a sense which involves modes of description and physical domains entirely outside those accessible to the ancient Greeks. This story, stretching over two millenia, should be understood to mean that more than faith, more than pure reason is involved in science. The tools of science are observation and experiment, but no amount of experiment and observation could produce more than a catalogue were the universe in all its vastness and variety not describable in finite terms. That it has turned out to be so describable, at least thus far, was to Einstein the great miracle, and the most profound of mysteries.

Why then, do we persist in treating science as if it were a separate culture, even as if its values were opposed to those of the humanities, when it is addressing the same universal concerns as those that produced the Bible and the great literature of mankind's ancient myths? Is its language so much more forbidding than Sanskrit or Greek? And how can we provide our liberal arts students with any understanding of science if they, and their mentors, don't first understand and accept the deep connection between science and the humanities?

I've been struggling to identify and spell out what it is we ought to be doing if we are to provide a liberal education in today's technological world. Let me summarize what I've been saying, which reflects the present level of my understanding about this difficult and complicated subject.

What I've suggested is that the problem we need to address is our inability to distinguish between sense and nonsense when it comes to matters connected with science and technology. Liberal education is a failed idea as long as our students are shut out from, or only superficially acquainted with, knowledge of the kinds of questions science can answer and those it cannot. Nor can liberal education be considered a success as long as students are unable to evaluate the evidence of their own experience. Liberal education, in the ideal and in the reality, should establish a common sense or intuitive basis that students can rely on in deciding what—and whom—they will believe.

From this point of view, it seems to me that our goal should not be to teach students the practical side of science—science as a skill. There's nothing wrong with learning the chemistry of cooking or the basics of how an automobile works, but I don't believe that people who have mastered such subjects are any less susceptible to the claims of astrologers or clairvoyants—or scientists, for that matter. Watered-down versions of regular science courses, such as Physics for Poets or Astronomy for Lovers, are as offensive and insulting as would be Poetry for Physicists or Shakespeare for Chemists. And as wide of the mark.

Instead, what I am suggesting is an approach that is at once more modest and more ambitious than that. I don't intend to define a list of courses, but I do believe that any course of study worked out should incorporate the following characteristics.

First, it should be designed to help students understand the nature of physical laws, what they are and what they are not; what they can tell us about the physical world and what they cannot; how they are arrived at; and in what sense they are true.

Second, it should provide some grounding in the laws of probability and chance, and thus some understanding that in a world as complex as ours both statistical fluctuations and the accidental coincidence of unrelated events happen all the time. Many events are unexplainable, are simply happenstance, much as we would like to believe otherwise.

Third, it should convey the important idea that science is not a collection of isolated facts but a highly unified and consistent view of the world. In many ways it can be described as a web—a conceptual, empirical, theoretical, and historical web, nearly but not quite seamless. We need to give our students some sense of why we believe the world and everything in it is made up of small particles; why we believe in our modern grand theories, such as relativity, when past grand theories have been proven wrong. Newton's theory, after all, has been superseded by Einstein's; the chemists' proof that matter is immutable, itself a correction of the earlier views of the alchemists, has been superseded by the discovery through nuclear chemistry that it is indeed possible to transmute base metals into gold. Pasteur's proof that spontaneous generation was impossible has been replaced by the views of modern biologists, who are convinced that life itself most likely began spontaneously.

We also need to make clear, to approach this from a complementary point of view, why it is that scientists can make with reasonable confidence assertions that seem to ignore anecdotal evidence that so many others find persuasive. Our students should be able to understand why physicists accept relativity and not precognition, or why they accept the likelihood of extraterrestrial intelligence and the overwhelming unlikelihood of UFOs, why they regard attempts to describe the first three minutes of the universe as sense and not nonsense.

The reason, of course, is that science has a foundation of large general laws that link together various observations about the physical world and which provide a framework within which various potentialities, facts, and theories can be evaluated. And when a generalization that has long been believed proves no longer true, it is usually because the physical domain in which that generalization was valid has turned out to be a limited one, more limited than actually exists in nature. The discovery of radioactivity demanded radical revisions in our view of nature because it arose entirely beyond the boundaries of what was then known. It should be possible—I have no doubt that it is possible—to convey to students both the power and the limits of general scientific laws and why we can, in the light of both, draw reliable conclusions from those laws.

It should be clear from all of this that what I am talking about does not have to do with the teaching of skills but with education in a broader sense. Not that skills aren't useful and desirable. The more mathematics you know, the more physics you can understand; the more physics, the more chemistry. But I am not so ambitious as to think that it is going to be possible to give all students a thorough grounding in mathematics and the sciences in the course of a liberal education. Obviously, we can't expect liberal arts students to master mathematics and physics and the other sciences to the degree necessary to permit them to understand and use the laws of nature in the same way that physicists and chemists do. For students who don't have those skills, however—that is, for liberal arts students—the sort of scheme I have outlined should nonetheless be an attainable goal. And of course the more science and mathematics they have studied during their school years, the more readily that goal can be reached.

In thinking about the question of how to educate students for life in a technological society, we need to be armed with the recognition that it is no easy task; on the contrary, as our past failures continue to remind us, it is enormously difficult to do. What can be accomplished will depend on the kind and number of people who get involved, on the resources available, and on the kinds of programs that already exist. But I think we are fortunate—and I like to believe that the reason is the general soundness of our educational system rather than happenstance—in having two different sets of institutions within which to address the problem in as serious, thoughtful, and detailed a way as it deserves. Research universities are peopled by faculty who are engaged in enlarging our knowledge and understanding of nature; liberal arts colleges have as faculty members people who are deeply committed to the idea and the ideal of a liberal education. We need to take advantage of both sets of interests, to experiment with and learn from each. We need to take advantage of those two important resources. I hope that you will include in your deliberations some consideration of the best ways to do so.

I have tried to connect science as an intellectual activity to the same wellsprings that motivate us to study the liberal arts. If the ability to distinguish sense from nonsense as an indispensable aspect of a liberal education—and I have emphasized my own belief that it is—then in a technological society science is an indispensable part of the liberal arts curriculum. The study of science and the study of the liberal arts have for too long been considered separate and separable activities. They are not, and at bottom they never were. It is time to bring them together.

SOME EDUCATION REQUIREMENTS FOR THE MANAGER OF THE EIGHTIES[1]

Jacques G. Maisonrouge[2]

Jacques G. Maisonrouge was eminently well qualified to speak on the subject, "Some Education Requirements for the Manager of the Eighties," to the audience in Kauffmann Auditorium at the Institute of International Education (IIE) corporate luncheon on September 16, 1982. His audience included about 60 members of the Institute, business executives, and students. Preceding the speech, other distinguished guests—Guy de Rothschild, Michael Besson, Martin Myerson, and Mrs. Angier Biddle Duke—were introduced.

[1]Delivered shortly after noon, on September 16, 1982, at a luncheon meeting at the Institute of International Education in Kauffmann Auditorium, New York City.

[2] For biographical note, see Appendix.

Maisonrouge had been associated with International Business Machines since 1948 and was now chairman of the board of the IBM World Corporation, which does business in more than 100 foreign countries. Born and educated in France, he worked for IBM in Europe for more than twenty years, and was well acquainted with both education and business in Europe. Later, as a resident of this country for twelve years, a parent of American-educated children, a trustee of Barnard College, and a member of the business task force at Cornell University, Maisonrouge developed ties with a broad understanding of many American institutions.

Noting his close association with the IIE in his speech, Maisonrouge initially referred to his twelve years as a member of its board of trustees. The Institute of International Education, a nonprofit organization, administers fellowships and grants for international education and provides contributor-supported educational services in the academic community.

After indicating what he believed should be the aim of a contemporary education—to give the individual the basic tools to "understand the world, to enjoy the world, and to contribute to the world"—he turned to business careers, observing that "Changes in the structure of society, in the world economy, and in the world's view of our age have changed business so much in the last twenty-five years that demands on the individual are very different from what they once were." Citing these changes, he described four characteristics of business today that should interest the prospective business manager: business has become international; as a result of that internationalization, it has grown extremely competitive; it is subject to very rapid change; and it is affected by a number of social forces.

There were a number of requests for reprints of the speech from academic institutions.

Jacques Maisonrouge's speech: When I say that it's a pleasure to be here, I'm expressing far more than the conventional politeness of a guest speaker. From 1967 to 1974, I worked right next door, at 821 U.N. Plaza, as president of the IBM World Trade Corporation. In that capacity, I was responsible for running IBM's business in more than 100 countries outside the United States.

From the very beginning, IIE (Institute of International Education) and I had much in common, including the conviction that, in a world that was growing smaller every day, the surest road to international understanding and international development was education. I had the privilege of being associated with IIE for a number of years, first as a trustee, then as an honorary trustee, and enjoyed very much Ken Holland's friendship.

My admiration for the Institute's work has never diminished. Wherever I travel, I can see the results of it. The thousands of young people who have come to this country under the auspices of IIE see the real America. The thousands of Americans who have studied abroad thanks to the Institute have increased their understanding and appreciation of foreign cultures. At a time when people are retrenching behind the borders of their countries because of economic problems or for ideological reasons, it is reassuring to know that one vehicle of international exchange is still energetically pursuing the goal of mutual understanding through mutual education. So it is indeed a pleasure for me to be back in this very congenial atmosphere and to have an opportunity to renew old friendships.

Despite the differences in our backgrounds, all of us here today share at least one deep belief—a belief in the enduring importance of education. Since there is no point in preaching to the converted, I'm not going to belabor the point. Instead, I would like to consider the constituent parts of our common passion. What, in other words, makes up a good education? What skills and disciplines must a person master in order to be truly educated today?

Every epoch has had its own answer to that question. In ancient Greece, the answer included physical fitness and politics; in the Middle Ages, the *trivium*—grammar, logic, and rhetoric— and the *quadrivium*—geometry, astronomy, arithmetic, and music; during the Renaissance, Greek and Latin.

Of course, your answer to what constitutes a good education depends largely on what you believe the purpose of an education ought to be. Plato thought it should produce good men who acted nobly. Saint Thomas Aquinas believed its goal was the love of God. And Rousseau thought it should help children realize their unique potential as human beings.

With the rise of science, particularly after Darwin, came a great debate. Did a proper education result from the study of the traditional humanities: language, literature, history, philosophy, and the fine arts? Or, in the light of recent developments, was it time to train young people in such disciplines as geology, paleontology, biology, and chemistry?

The issue was debated in nineteenth-century England by two great educators, who happened also to be eloquent writers, Matthew Arnold and Thomas Henry Huxley.

Arnold maintained that being truly educated meant "knowing the best which has been thought and said in the world." And he believed that this could only be learned through the study of the humanities, particularly literature.

Huxley disagreed, arguing that, above all, a truly educated person ought to understand himself and the world in which he lived and the only reasonable way to acquire such understanding was through mastery of the physical sciences. In a famous metaphor, Huxley compared life to a lengthy game of chess. He explained it in these words:

> The chess board is the world, the pieces are the phenomena of the universe, the rules of the game are what we call the laws of Nature. The player on the other side is hidden from us. We know that his play is always fair, just, and patient. But also we know, to our cost, that he never overlooks a mistake, or makes the smallest allowance for ignorance.

The debate goes on to this day. Which shall it be? The humanities or the sciences? The liberal arts or technology?

I have some ideas of my own on the subject and I'll share them with you shortly, but first I must issue a few disclaimers: I'm not an educator, I'm not even a certified philosopher. However, I do have some credentials.

First, I was a student myself once—and, in many ways, still am. Second, as a father, I have been in close touch with five particular students for a number of years. Third, in my travels I have met and spoken with hundreds—perhaps thousands—of students around the world. And they have not been bashful about expressing themselves. Finally, as a businessman in a high technology industry, I have some knowledge of the skills the world is going to need in the forseeable future.

I said earlier that your definition of a good education depends on what you believe is the purpose of an education. By way of introduction, therefore, let me describe my own feelings on the matter.

When you strip away all the details and get down to essentials, I believe that the purpose of a good contemporary education should be to equip the individual with the basic tools he needs to do three things: to understand the world, to enjoy the world, and to contribute to the world.

To *understand the world,* he needs to know a variety of things, ranging from astronomy to history to psychology.

To *enjoy the world* requires an appreciation of such fields as art, literature, philosophy, and music. I think this is at least partly what Aristotle had in mind when he said, "Education is the best provision for old age."

Finally, to *contribute to the world,* the individual needs certain specialized information, depending on his natural bent and interests, whether they lie in medicine, accounting, law, the computer sciences, or in something else. The young seem to understand this intuitively—a fact they proved during the campus demonstrations of the late sixties and early seventies when, among other things, they demanded curricula that were more relevant to their lives.

Having told you what I think the aim of a good education should be, I'd now like to consider the specific skills and knowledge that young people should acquire, particularly if they are to contribute to the world.

There are certain bedrock skills that all people need simply to get along in the modern world: language skills for one, so that they can give and receive information clearly; and math and science for another, so that they may compete for jobs in a world increasingly dependent on computers, automation, and high technology.

Certain ignorances are unacceptable in our times. An engineer has to know economics—so does a doctor, if he wants to set up a professional corporation. And a business school student must know enough math to understand statistical analysis. The man of action must be a man of culture. And culture today has to include a basic knowledge of math and of the sciences.

Yet, according to *U.S. News and World Report,* 52 million American adults are functionally incompetent at computation, 44 million at solving problems, 34 million at reading, and 26 million at writing. In a world that is growing increasingly complex almost daily, this is unacceptable.

In addition, few young people know what they want to do with their lives. Consequently, the broader their base of general information, the more options they can keep open.

Yet, it is no secret that achievement scores in all these areas have been declining for more than a decade, especially in the U. S. Employers ranging from industry to the military services complain that new recruits cannot function in jobs that require technical understanding. In other words, both the country's economic and military security are being threatened.

And consider these hard facts.

Fact: one-half of all high school graduates in the U.S. took *no* math or science beyond the 10th grade.

Fact: there are today an estimated 1,600 to 2,000 vacant engineering faculty positions—eight to 10 percent of the total—in U.S. universities.

Fact: on a per capita basis, for each engineering graduate produced annually in the United States, the U.K. produces 1.1; West Germany, 1.4; Japan, 2.6; and the Soviet Union, 4.1.

The National Science Board, the U.S. government's top policy-making body for science education, has called the situation critical. Some changes are taking place, I know, and they are to be encouraged because a school curriculum more in tune with society's needs is long overdue.

Now I'd like to confine my remarks to careers in business for two reasons. First, because I believe that speakers should stick to subjects they know something about, for their own sake as well as for that of the audience, and business is what I know best. And second, because most young people are headed for careers in business.

Depending on what qualities of mind and spirit they bring with them, they may find those careers extremely positive, fulfilling, rewarding experiences—or negative and frustrating beyond description. That, of course, has always been true. But changes in the structure of society, in the world economy, and in the world's view of our age have changed business so much in the last twenty-five years, that demands on the individual are very different from what they once were.

Let me cite just four of the new characteristics of business, then I'll discuss what they mean to the employee who wants to get ahead—that is, into management: business has become international; as a result of that internationalization, it has grown extremely competitive; it is subject to very rapid change; and it is affected by a number of social forces.

Take the internationalization of business.

There was a time when a company could anticipate reasonable, even robust, growth within the borders of its home country. If it could also sell its products in one or two other countries, fine. But its primary market was its home country. That time has gone forever—and for several good reasons.

First, because of certain new social, economic, and political facts of life. Common information made instantly available to the peoples of the developed countries, for example, has generated the same economic appetites around the world.

The barriers to international trade have been shrinking rapidly, thanks to such mechanisms as the Common Market, GATT [General Agreement on Tariffs and Trade], and the OECD [Organization for Econimmic Cooperation and Development]. Admittedly, there is a real threat of a revival of protectionism today, but historically speaking, since the end of World War II, the broad trend has been toward freer trade.

Second, there has been a growing need to rely on larger and larger markets. The British aircraft industry, for example, cannot survive if it cannot sell abroad. And for most countries, the same holds true in ship building, in automobile manufacture, and even in the computer industry.

Furthermore, with the complexity of modern technologies, the resources necessary to support R&D demand broader markets.

One major consequence of this internationalization of business has been the increased need for international managers, that is, for managers who, aside from having all the qualities that make good managers of national companies, are also mobile, adaptable, and at ease in cultures other than their own.

In addition, since they will undoubtedly work outside their home countries at some point in their careers, they should have one or two foreign languages, an understanding of the sociopolitical environment in which they will be working, and a world view that inhibits the growth of chauvinistic prejudices.

No matter what a young person's major in school, therefore, he or she can profit in a very real way from the study of such subjects as languages, foreign history, or literature, whatever will add to his or her cultural depth. If young people have the opportunity to live and study for a year or more in another country—as so many do, thanks to IIE—so much the better.

We come next to the internationalization of competition.

Competitiveness on a global scale is quite different from competitiveness in a home country. When you are competing within your own borders, for example, you and the other companies in your industry are all operating within the same environment, according to the same rules. There is a certain equality of opportunity. Once you go global, however, you often find yourself doing business in environments in which some companies—the local ones—are more equal than others.

Their governments see to that through such devices as granting them subsidies and low-interest loans, adopting "buy national" procurement policies, setting standards designed to keep out foreign products, requiring high local content in manufactured goods, and so on.

To be sure, there are ways to compete even under those conditions. But the fierce competition that characterizes the international market-place places a premium on creative thinking and problem solving. Young people who have acquired the ability to analyze problems, gather information, and put the pieces together to form tentative solutions will always be in demand.

I am hard pressed to say what kinds of university-level courses can help in this area. Logic, certainly, which is usually offered by the philosophy faculty, and perhaps any tough courses that require independent research and original thinking on the part of the student.

At a time when there is so much talk about the need for innovation, it's a wonder that there is no formal course of study available in creativity at the university level. At least not to my knowledge. The assumption seems to be that creativity is something you are either born with or doomed to live without. The world has come to rely on the occasional Thomas Edison, Alexander Fleming, or Marie Curie for its breakthrough inventions and discoveries.

Yet, if courses in creativity and problem solving were offered in our schools, I suspect that the world's supply of innovators could be increased significantly. Such courses might offer training in the framing of hypotheses, the search for evidence, critical evaluation, and willingness to accept conclusions based on probabilities rather than certainties. We might not create a race of Sir Isaac Newtons or Albert Einsteins, but we might sensitize a generation of young people to the techniques and joys of solving problems.

Business has also become subject to very rapid change. Consider what we have witnessed in less than a decade: the quadrupling of oil prices, rampant inflation, a prime interest rate in excess of 20 percent, Americans held hostage by a foreign government, global recession, a limits-to-growth movement, an oil glut, war in the south Atlantic, and on and on.

Alvin Toffler, the futurist, has illustrated the staggering rapidity of change by translating the last 50,000 years into 800 lifetimes, then observing that:

of those those 800 lifetimes, only the last 70 could communicate with their descendants—through writing;

only the last eight ever saw a printed word;

only the last four were able to measure time with any precision;

only the last two used an electric motor;

most of the material goods we use in our daily lives were developed within the 800th lifetime;

and more technological progress will be made during the 801st lifetime than during all the lifetimes of the previous 800.

Here is another example. A graduate engineer today has a half-life expectancy of just five years. That means that half of what he's learned by the time he leaves college will become obsolete in the next five years. And what's true of engineers is becoming increasingly true of many other specialists.

Clearly, in a fast changing environment the ability to plan for change becomes a managerial imperative. Consequently, tomorrow's managers will have to demonstrate more awareness of the world around them, more flexibility of mind, more technological literacy than ever before. In a world where new knowledge continues to accumulate rapidly, the most valuable managers of all will be those who have learned *how* to learn.

It's encouraging to see that several American colleges already demand varying degrees of computer literacy as a requirement for graduation. And last fall Harvard began requiring that all undergraduates learn to write a short computer program.

Not everyone welcomes the demand for technological literacy. Some humanists fear that traditional values will be lost in a world that emphasizes quantitative approaches. But I think I can dispel—or at least mitigate—their concerns.

There is today a growing appreciation by business of the fact that society is the larger context in which business operates. Corporate decisions are therefore reached only after many factors have been weighed—for example, the impact on employees, the effects on the environment, the goals of a nation, the law of the land (its spirit as well as its letter), and many other considerations. An important challenge to managers, therefore, becomes to integrate into their business perspective the broader outlook of a responsible world citizen.

This social awareness is a moral necessity. But even for those who still believe in profit as the only motivation, it is an economic necessity. For if industry is unwilling to help make the world a better place in which to live, governments will take measures and that could threaten the existence of free enterprise.

The final disciplines I would urge upon my theoretical college student interested in preparing to meet his or her social responsibilities in a management career, therefore, are some good courses in ethics, sociology, and psychology.

You can see that, unlike Arnold and Huxley, I don't believe that a sound modern education is a matter of *either-or;* rather, it is case of *both-and.* It requires a sound grounding in "the best which has been thought and said" because the human race's accumulated wisdom is what keeps us human and a family. It provides us with a common heritage, a mutual culture. But it also demands that we keep up with the technologies that make it possible to participate in that culture and its system of values and rewards.

Winston Churchill put it more succinctly, perhaps, when he said that there were three acid tests of a truly educated person: "He must be able to entertain himself, to entertain another person, and, above all, to entertain a new idea."

PEOPLE WITH IDEAS, IDEALS, AND THE WILL TO MAKE THEM WORK[1]

LOWELL WEICKER JR.[2]

In a short speech, Senator Lowell Weicker Jr., accepted a certificate of commendation from the Institute of International Education on October 18, 1982, at a luncheon in his honor at the United Nations Plaza Hotel. The citation was presented to Weicker for his support in the United States Senate of the government's educational and cultural exchange programs with other nations.

The Institute, a private, non-profit organization, promotes international understanding and good will through the support of student and teacher exchange programs, the administration of grants and fellowships for international education, cultural programs involving American and foreign artists, and similar events. An important activity has been their sponsorship and coordination for many years of international debate tours involving American college students and students from abroad. These annual tours have recently taken American students to Britain, Japan, and the Soviet Union and brought young people from many countries to the United States to exchange ideas on issues of international concern.

In his speech, Senator Weicker deplored budget cuts by the Reagan administration and suggested that federal support for international education "was on the wane." However, the senator expressed optimism that many of the budget reductions would be restored. Indeed, six months later, a *Christian Science Monitor* editorial noted:

Student exchange programs have been a post-World War II success story of which all the participating nations can be proud. The good news is that the United States is acting to restore the strong role the Reagan administration had once appeared ready to abandon. The need is to ensure that the new initiatives serve the broad purposes

[1]Delivered at a luncheon meeting of the board of trustees of the Institute of International Education in a banquet room of the United Nations Plaza Hotel, New York City, at 2 P.M., on October 18, 1982.

[2] For biographical note, see Appendix.

of individual education and international understanding—rather than any narrow national propaganda purposes. (Ap. 6, '83, p 24)

Weicker's audience consisted of approximately one hundred civic leaders, corporation executives, university presidents, trustees, and friends of the Institute of International Education. (For another address delivered to this body, see Jacques Maisonrouge's speech on p. 123.)

Senator Lowell Weicker's speech: It is a great honor for me to accept this citation from the Institute of International Education today. Just over a year ago, it appeared that internationalism in education was on the wane. For the Fulbright Scholarship Program, we were looking at a proposed 48 percent cut, down to a mere $22 million. The International Visitors Program was to be slashed to less than $10 million. The Hubert H. Humphrey Fellowships were on the verge of extinction. As the *New York Times* warned, the United States was in danger of "declaring unilateral disarmament in the war of ideas."

Today, however, we are seeing the United States rearm for that war by renewing its commitment to the cultural and educational exchange programs in the United States Information Agency (USIA). The Administration grossly underestimated the value that Congress and the education community assign to those programs. It was not prepared for the protests—or for the $43 million the Congress added to their budget.

This year, by way of contrast, it was apparent that the Administration had learned its lesson. Instead of drastic cuts, it recommended a $7 million increase for the exchange programs. In the Senate we saw them raise that $7 million and raised them another $20 million, through an amendment offered by my colleague, Senator Pell. How did this turnabout in public policy come about? For the most part, the programs spoke for themselves. Anyone who has ever come in contact with them knows just how critical they are to the cause of enlightenment and understanding around the world.

Last year, a group of historians associated with the Woodrow Wilson Center in Washington were asked to list the greatest successes of U.S. foreign policy since World War II: Two initiatives topped the collective list. The first, which comes as no surprise, was the Marshall Plan.

The other initiative singled out for highest praise by these eminent historians was the Fulbright-Hays educational exchange program. Launched in 1946, this is the program through which more than 45,000 Americans have studied abroad and over 85,000 foreign scholars have come to the United States.

Last year, in the wake of Administration proposals to slash the funds for these and other exchange programs, a high-level U.S. foreign service officer looked back over the roster of Fulbright-Hays fellows and found 33 men and women who today are national leaders and several hundred more are ministers of government or members of parliament. Thousands of others are prominent in their fields as business people and academics.

When we consider this fact, we realize that the actual course of study of the foreign exchange student is only one of the important facets of the program. Even more crucial, is the opportunity to defuse mistaken assumptions about other parts of the world and the politics they profess. As Senator Fulbright once asked, What could be more important than dispelling the dangerous myth that "different political philosophies cannot survive together in the same world, that sooner or later one must prevail over the other?"

I agree with the Senator that that notion is at the root of most wars and international rancor. If we could only get rid of it, East and West could dispose of their arsenals and live together in peace.

That is why I believe that the educational exchange programs run by USIA are a much better investment than our foreign military aid program. Dollar for dollar, they buy more security than the defense budget. For a small fraction of the cost, they increase immeasurably our stability and the stability of our allies. People armed with ideas, ideals, and the will to make them work won't need guns.

As Chairman of the Appropriations Subcommittee which oversees the USIA's budget, I have fought, tooth and nail, for full funding of these programs, and will continue to do so. And there is something else with regard to these programs that I intend to continue fighting for. While keeping up the flow of students between the United States and Western Europe, I believe we should focus our attention on the Third World.

In the Third World, the Soviet Union offers ten times as many fellowships as we do. That is nothing less than an outrage when you consider the competitive advantage the United States has in education. We have a schooling system in this country to which the Soviet Union's can not hold a candle.

Take, for example, Cuba. When I visited there two years ago, one stop on my itinerary was the Isle of Youth, an island of some 60 senior high school complexes, more than a dozen of which are devoted to students from foreign nations. The one I observed housed 600 students from the African nation of Namibia who are getting their education courtesy of Cuba and the Soviet Union.

These students are going back to Namibia to become the leaders of that nation in every field of endeavor—education, government, business, military and science. And, believe it or not, that fact worries me more than the presence of a few thousand Cuban troops in Angola or elsewhere on the African continent. In the course of time, Africa will, if it has to, swallow up the Cubans just as it has every other foreign nation. But these 600 leaders-to-be will truly determine the fate of this emerging nation.

They worry me because they have been taught to equate America and its capitalist economy with oppression. If they had studied here instead, they would have learned the truth about us, warts and all. They would have been exposed to American authors and ideals. But how many Namibians are studying in the United States? The last time I checked the figures, there were exactly two. What makes this imbalance even more absurd is the fact that the native language of these students in English, not Russian or Spanish, but English.

If you add up all the foreign students studying on fellowships in the United States from Africa, and Near East, South Asia and the American Republics, they do not add up to the number from Western Europe. I'm not saying we don't need to keep up our North Atlantic contacts. But the fact is that your average high school student in Italy or France has no problem going to a library and checking out a volume by Thomas Jefferson or some contemporary American author's writings on democracy or Alexander Solzhenitsyn's critiques of life in the Soviet Union. In the libraries of Cuba's Isle of Youth, these books are nowhere to be found.

The major foreign policy challenges of today lie in the Third World. They lie in the Caribbean, right in our own backyard. And if we are going to meet those challenges we had better increase our understanding of our neighbors and their understanding of us.

These exchange programs are a two-way street. Walter C. Clemens Jr., now a professor of political science at Boston University, wrote recently of his experiences in 1977–1978 as a Fulbright lecturer at the Institute of International Relations in Trinidad.

"What did the United States gain?" he asks. "Future diplomats and educators from a dozen Caribbean islands got to know one American's perspective on world politics, particularly on U.S.-Soviet relations. They learned how seriously many Americans regard the issues of nuclear war and global interdependence. They were guided to books and articles far from their usual fare. They and I learned we could disagree on many points and still be friends. And what did I learn? Perhaps more than my students, I came to understand the outrage that permeates Third World sensibilities and the reasons for it. Living in a fishing village I also saw the joys and anxieties of common folk struggling to improve their lot. I also became colorblind."

Whether or not we believe in the global village, it is clear that we all are citizens of the same world. E. B. White, that great man of letters once said that "it is easier for a man to be loyal to his club than to his planet; the bylaws are shorter, and he is personally acquainted with the other members." But if we are to solve the great challenges facing mankind today, we must demonstrate loyalty to the planet and to the other human beings we share it with.

In this age of austerity, when so many of our own students are finding it hard to scrape together the money for tuition, we will continue to be tempted to discount the importance of these exchange programs. We will be tempted to label them a luxury. They are not. They are nothing short of an absolute necessity.

The only way we will ever be able to live together in peace is through the free and open exchange of ideas. Our principles, our ideals have withstood the test of time. They are the principles, the ideals that offer a better future for people on every continent of the world. And it is clear, at the same time, that we have much to learn from them. With the support of organizations like yours, we will continue to do so.

THE SEPARATION OF ATHLETICS AND ACADEMICS IN OUR UNIVERSITIES[1]

Howard R. Swearer[2]

At a time when the popularity of college sports is at an all-time high, many Americans have been shocked and disillusioned by revelations of altered grade transcripts, false course credits, forgery, violation of recruitment rules, undercover payments to athletes by alumni, hypocrisy in the maintenance of academic standards, and even physical abuse of athletes in intercollegiate athletic competition. Still other revelations of large sums of money earned by schools from televised games, pressures from alumni to produce winning teams, and multi-million dollar salaries offered star collegiate athletes by professional clubs all added to the problem.

Newsweek summarized the situation:

> The shame of the system can be defined in all too many unpleasant contexts. It is fiscal: football and basketball are big business for most schools. It is education: when a kid is cheated out of all chance of learning, the institution is also cheated out of its reason for being. It is social and racial: many victims of the "dumb jock" syndrome, 1980 version, are black. But most of all, it is moral. In the pursuit of victory, the vast majority of fans, alumni, and even coaches and administrators have accepted the notion that a winner may have to cheat. (S. 20, '80, p 54)

University of California sociology professor Harry Edwards said that, "At least 50 percent of the football players at many colleges can't make it academically. Some of them can hardly read and write." (Swift, "Keeping Up with Youth," *Parade,* S. 28, '80.) The president of a university with a reputation as one of the nation's strongest football powers confessed that 330 athletes who could not meet university standards had been admitted in the previous ten years.

Amid charges of academic abuse that put 22 schools on probation, in January, 1983, university presidents joined together at the annual convention of the National Collegiate Athletic Association and passed a proposal to toughen academic requirements for incoming athletes. Far from solving the problem, the new rule only stirred bitter controversy and

---

[1] Delivered to the Corporation of Brown University at its regular midwinter meeting at 2 P.M., on February 12, 1982, in the Corporation Room of University Hall, Brown University, Providence, Rhode Island.

[2] For biographical note, see Appendix.

charges of racial discrimination by black administrators and leaders.

A proposal to resolve some of the problems brought about by the NCAA requirement that college athletes must also be full-time academic students as well was made by President Howard R. Swearer of Brown University to the Brown Corporation on February 12, 1982. Although Brown and the other Ivy League schools, which place less emphasis than most other colleges on intercollegiate athletics, were not caught up in the maelstrom, Swearer pointed out that they were not entirely unaffected because of their interest in the evolving shape of national intercollegiate athletics. His proposal that there be a clear separation between the academic and athletic purposes of a university attracted considerable attention. The *New York Times* (F. 21, '82, p 2S) and the *Christian Science Monitor* (Mr. 17, '82, p 23) reprinted the entire speech and several newspapers, including the *Providence Journal,* carried editorials on the subject.

The speech was made to the board of trustees of Brown University at a regular midwinter meeting at 2 P.M., on February 12, 1982, in the Corporation Room of University Hall on the campus. The audience consisted of approximately 100 trustees and trustees emeriti.

Howard Swearer's speech: The national intercollegiate athletic situation is in considerable flux and, I believe, may have entered a period of rapid transition. Many colleges and universities are facing critical questions which cannot be begged for long.

The driving forces are well known but merit mention anyway, if for no other reason than many of us in the older generations may tend to view collegiate sports through the now misty and romantic filter of our own undergraduate days. However, the tug of nostalgia should not inhibit us from making a clear assessment of the contemporary scene.

At the outset, it is important to note that the playing fields of college sports are populated with many kinds of athletes and there are many types of game plans. It would be a mistake to categorize some as right and good and some as wrong and bad. Institutions and leagues are responding differently to powerful forces at work in the society according to their traditions and perceived self-interests—as they should.

The most significant factors influencing collegiate sports over the last two decades have been the enormous growth in the size and influence of professional sports, and the prominence of television. Professional sports have become big business—for owners and players alike—and TV coverage of sporting events, supported by staggering advertising revenues, has brought big money into the sports world, at both the professional and collegiate level. Large gate receipts have been important sources of revenue to support athletic programs at some universities for many years; but the advent of television revenues has increased the monetary stakes tremendously. Moreover, cable TV is now entering the arena, with the potential of channeling additional millions into the sports world.

These are simply facts, and they are not going to go away unless the public tires of watching these events on television or the corporate world reduces its advertising budgets for their support. The question, then, is how does higher education handle this relatively new world?

There are positive effects of these developments, such as the generation of revenues at some universities sufficient to pay for their entire athletic program. However, I want to dwell on the negative effects of the increased monetary stakes, for both institutions and individual players. They are manifested everywhere:

The scandals of doctored transcripts, academic cheating, violations of NCAA rules on recruiting, and financial support of athletes;

The increased litigation—of universities against the NCAA (which is, after all, an organization composed of the universities and colleges) and of athletes against their universities;

The recent organizational change in the NCAA Division I restricting membership in Division IA to universities with large stadia and high attendance for football which, in effect, sets the level of competition in football solely on a revenue criterion;

Talk of organizing intercollegiate athletes in order to gain compensation in recognition of the revenues produced by sporting events;

The ruling by a federal district judge that the University of Minnesota cannot deny a basketball player the right to play on the team because he has not maintained a sufficient academic record;

The hiring of an athletic director/football coach by Texas A & M at an annual level of compensation of $287,000 and the report a few days later that the University of Nebraska boosters club is seeking to raise $100,000 to supplement the salary of their football coach;

The increasing influence on intercollegiate sports of largely independent booster clubs; and

The internecine conflicts over television contracts.

Obviously, there are powerful market forces at play and the long-established attempts to contain them by regulation may no longer be sufficient. Different strategies need to be devised to cope with them depending on the nature of the institution.

Since the Ivy League, at least this far, has not been caught up in this maelstrom, why should we be concerned? In fact, we have tended to stand apart and to go our own way, sometimes lecturing others from the sidelines. However, I do believe we have—or should have—an interest in the evolving shape of national intercollegiate sports, for we are not unaffected to some degree by what happens elsewhere, as witnessed by the recent redefinition of Division I football.

Practices and attitudes which gain acceptance elsewhere, even if only tacitly, could seep into our institutions. We compete with other institutions for scholar athletes and we compete occasionally with other teams in different leagues. If, in the public mind, the academic integrity of higher education is damaged by scandals in athletics, can we be certain there will be no rub-off on us? Or, on the other side of the coin, what will be the reputation of our teams among the public at large, our alumni, and prospective student athletes if they are totally eclipsed by the media attention to the big football and basketball powers? *Within our own definitions and on our own terms* we do wish to strive for excellence in athletic as well as academic performance.

In effect, the major football and basketball—and to a lesser extent, hockey—powers have become the farm clubs for the professional teams. I find it interesting that in baseball, where the professional farm teams have long existed, the pressures on the intercollegiate sport are dramatically less. May not the time have arrived when it would be desirable to recognize openly this symbiotic relationship between the big athletic powers and professional sports and make the necessary structural changes?

The fictions are wearing thin. I, for one, see no harm in associating a professional or semi-professional team with a university; and I do see a number of benefits. It would clarify what is now a very murky picture. Athletes should, of course, have the opportunity to take courses and pursue a degree, if they wish; but they would be regarded as athletes first and should be paid accordingly.

By so doing, the regulatory and enforcement burden and the temptations for illegal and unethical practices would be dramatically eased. The clear separation between the academic and athletic purposes of the university would be beneficial to both. Who would care if a coach were paid a salary seven times that of the average full professor, so long as the economics of the situation justified it? The ambiguities and stresses which now press on the integrity of the academic programs would be eased.

If the big athletic powers were to choose this course, I think it would benefit all of intercollegiate athletics. High school seniors would be given a more clearly defined choice among different kinds of post-secondary athletic experiences. The general public could recognize more clearly the nature of athletic competition in different leagues. The pressures toward "professionalism" on those institutions which chose a different course might be lessened.

The possibility I have sketched out is not a choice that I believe Ivy League and similar institutions should or would take. However, I hope that the Ivy League will also take a positive and active role in the long-term restructuring of intercollegiate sports. To do so will require that we become more involved in national deliberations and forego our penchant for semi-isolation. We will have to organize ourselves, however, for more sustained involvement.

The philosophy of the Ivy League, as embodied in the Ivy Agreement, has served us well over the last 25 years, and I doubt that we shall wish to make major alterations in its basic principles. Still, we all need to review the Agreement again, making modifications, if required; and reaffirm our allegiance to it. The Agreement should be widely publicized among our alumni, students, and faculty so that the nature of Ivy athletics is broadly understood.

I think it also needs to be said repeatedly that it is not our intention to downgrade the place of athletics or reduce the levels of competition to which our athletes may aspire. We regard athletics as an integral part of our educational programs, and we support superior performance in both academic and athletic programs. However, since we place greater emphasis on the scholar part of the scholar athlete equation than do some other institutions, our search for athletic excellence may take place under somewhat different conditions and environment.

While, as I have said, I believe the Ivy League has become more *isolated* within intercollegiate sports than is desirable, we do need to *insulate* ourselves from trends and developments inimical to the principles we espouse. This suggests to me an expansion of competition with institutions which adhere to similar principles and practices.

There are several ways in which such expansion could be achieved: enlargement of the league itself, joining in looser association with other schools, divisional structures, and yet others. I suspect there are a number of other universities which are now concerned that they are miscast in their exisiting leagues and might welcome an Ivy League initiative. Whether or not this would require a new form of association with the NCAA is too early to say. However, it seems apparent to me that the Ivy League and other similar schools conceptually do not fit well in either Division IAA (where we will be located next fall) or in Division III, where the philosophy is correct but the level of competition may not be sufficient.

Let me make two other points. I do not disparage our athletes who have been able to compete successfully on professional teams; quite the contrary, we are proud of them. And, I would hope that we will continue to provide a level of coaching and competition so that a small number of particularly talented athletes may make it in professional sports. But we are not, nor should we be, regarded by aspiring athletes as an entry port to the world of professional sports.

Nor do I disdain revenues from gate receipts or television to help support our athletic programs. We could use more revenues! Again, however, we are not in, nor should we get into, a position where the need for such revenues drives our athletic programs and decisions about sports.

The Ivy League has its work cut out for itself in the months ahead. I hope we will be up to the task.

PRAYER IN PUBLIC SCHOOLS[1]

LOWELL WEICKER JR.[2]

Curtis J. Sitomer, writing in the *Christian Science Monitor*, observed:

> School prayer—including local and state "moment of silence" laws—is triggering a roar of controversy that could come to a head later this year. The issue has kept civil liberties groups in combat with religious fundamentalists and others for over two decades, since a landmark US Supreme Court ruling in 1962 effectively barred prayers from the public schools. But the tide may be changing. A growing number of communities across the United States are clinging to Bible readings, prayer "moments," and other religious exercises, despite court rulings against them. Congressional interests, particularly those in sympathy with the so-called "religious right," are pushing legislation that would open the classroom doors at least a crack for religious exercises. And they have a powerful advocate: the President of the United States. (Ap. 12, '83, p 1)

Sitomer's newspaper article was prompted by the filing of several bills in the United States Senate to limit or eliminate the jurisdiction of the federal courts over prayer in the schools and in other public places and by President Reagan's proposal that the country enact a constitutional amendment stating, "Nothing in this Constitution shall be construed to prohibit individual or group prayer in public schools or other public institutions. No person shall be required by the United States or by any state to participate in prayer."

Debate on the issue was emotional and divisive. Civil libertarians strongly opposed the legislation submitted to the Senate and the President's proposed constitutional amendment, arguing that nothing under current law regarding school prayer prohibited a student from exercising his/her right to pray voluntarily and that religious freedom and true voluntary prayer for public school children had never been outlawed by the Supreme Court. Religious leaders were divided, with some prominent organizations opposed to prayer in the schools and others supportive of the proposed legislation and amendment.

Among the many articulate and eloquent speeches on the subject in 1982–1983 was Senator Lowell Weicker Jr.'s sermon to the congregation at the United Church on the Green in New Haven, Connecticut, at regu-

---

[1]Delivered at the regular services of the United Church on the Green, New Haven, Connecticut, on the morning of September 19, 1982.

[2] For biographical note, see Appendix.

lar services on the morning of Sunday, September 19, 1982. Coincidentally the prayer issue was on the floor of the Senate at that time. Weicker was invited to deliver the sermon by the regular pastor, the Reverend John Hay, who he said "reminded me that it is an old Congregational tradition for government leaders to speak from the pulpit." Then he apologized for speaking out against another old Congregational practice: "theocracy, the fusion of Church and State into one authority."

Early in the sermon, the Senator stated his topic and theme:

> I want to speak in particular today about prayer in our public schools. The idea is very appealing on its surface. Indeed, it summons up reassuring images of freckle-faced Norman Rockwell children with their heads bowed and hands clasped in prayer. But as inspiring as it sounds, prayer in school has the potential for doing real damage—to children and their families, to the cause of true religion, and to the ideal of separation of church and state our founders embraced.

Senator Weicker made a variety of references from religion, history, the constitution, testimony of authorities, and personal experience in developing his theme.

Senator Lowell Weicker's speech: It is a great honor for me to join you in worship this morning. Reverend Hay has reminded me that it is an old Congregational tradition for government leaders to speak from the pulpit. Forgive me if today I avail myself of this tradition to speak out against what used to be another old Congregational practice: theocracy, the fusion of Church and State into one authority. Until its disestablishment in 1818, nearly two hundred years after the Pilgrims came in search of religious liberty, Congregationalism was Connecticut's official creed.

I don't mean to cast stones but simply to cite facts. On this issue, my ancestors took much the same path. A great-uncle of mine was Archbishop of Canterbury. Nevertheless, I have come to believe with Mark Twain that established religion "means death to human liberty and paralysis to human thought." No greater mischief can be created than to combine the power of religion with the power of government. History has shown us that time and time again. The union of the two is as bad for religion as it is for government. It gives rise to tyrants and inquisitions. It is what drove many of our ancestors to these shores. That is why clergy, lay people, and public officeholders alike must fight radical re-writes of the First Amendment which are masquerading as good old-fashioned morality.

I want to speak in particular today about prayer in our public schools. The idea is very appealing on its surface. Indeed, it summons up reassuring images of freckle-faced Norman Rockwell children with their heads bowed and hands clasped in prayer. But as inspiring as it sounds, prayer in school has the potential for doing real damage—to children and their families, to the cause of true religion, and to the ideal of separation of Church and State our founders embraced.

Today's Gospel lesson goes to the heart of the issue, which is that prayer is—or should be—a personal act of devotion, not an official function. I would like to reread a part of that passage from the Sermon on the Mount, this time from the Phillips translation: "And when you pray don't be like the play actors. They love to stand and pray in the synagogues and street corners so that people may see them at it. Believe me, they have had all the reward they are going to get. But when you pray, go into your room, shut the door and pray to your Father privately. Your Father who sees all private things will reward you."

It seems to me that the kind of prayer Jesus is recommending here is not the sort the school prayer supporters have in mind. He advocates a one-on-one personal dialogue with God, not some kind of officially-sanctioned formula blared through a public address system. Now, to be sure, people are concerned about falling church attendance and the fewer and fewer applicants to seminaries and well they might be. But making prayer a government program won't help matters. Government itself is still in the midst of a crisis of confidence. Look at how few people exercise their right to vote and participate in government. I have never seen a merger between two weak companies that ever worked, and that is what is being attempted here. In this country, government and religion, each must stand on its own two feet. If they cannot, then we must shake them up. We must not yoke them together. When the blind lead the blind, they both fall in the ditch.

If getting the American people closer to God is their goal, why make government the go-between? It reminds me of the Old Testament story of the Tower of Babel. There you had civil leaders commissioning a public works project to bring people closer to God. In the end, of course, the tower not only failed at that but it so insulted God that he made sure such a thing could not happen again by causing the people to speak different languages and scattering them to the winds.

Do I encourage my fellow citizens to pray? Certainly. And I hope that when they do, they will keep those of us in the US Senate in mind. But I do not believe it is up to a Representative or a Senator or even the President to espouse or encourage any one religion or even religion in general. It is not my job to do the convincing, to take up on Monday on the floor of the Senate where the rabbi left off on Saturday or the priest or minister left off on Sunday.

My job is simply this: to make certain that every individual is free to practice the articles of his or her faith, whatever they may be, without fear of reprisal.

Similarly, I believe that our public schools are meant to educate our children, teaching them a healthy respect for people of differing beliefs and disbeliefs. They were never intended to indoctrinate them or inculcate a certain set of beliefs. That is the work of parents and Sunday School teachers and Hebrew School teachers.

There is an old Spanish proverb which says "an ounce of mother is worth a pound of clergy." I would add that both are worth a ton of politicians where prayer is concerned. These days we talk a lot about strengthening families. But we will not do so by imposing some doctrine from without, particularly if that doctrine is alien to the family's own beliefs or traditions.

President Kennedy's comment on the 1962 Supreme Court decision barring prayer in the New York public school system was right on the button. "We have in this case a very easy remedy," he said. "And that is to pray ourselves. And I think it would be a welcome reminder to every American family that we can pray a good deal more at home, we can attend our churches with a good deal more fidelity, and we can make the true meaning of prayer more important in the lives of all our children."

School prayer supporters contend that the prayer they want could be voluntary and vaguely enough worded to embrace all beliefs. But there is nothing voluntary about school attendance; that is compulsory. And what six-year-old is going to stand up and insist on his or her constitutional right to be excused when the prayer is recited? At that age and older, peer pressure is intense. When everybody stands, you stand. When everyone bows their head, you bow your head. When everyone mumbles words, you mumble words. So, in a very real sense, neither is the exercise of the prayer voluntary to a young child.

As E. B. White wrote to Senator Margaret Chase Smith when this issue came up in 1966, "In an atmosphere of 'voluntary' prayer, pupils coming from homes where other faiths prevail will feel an embarrassment by their non-participation; in the eyes of their schoolmates they will be 'queer' or 'different' or 'irreligious.' Such a stigma for a child can be emotionally disturbing, and although we no longer hang and burn our infidels and our witches, a schoolchild who is left out in the cold during a prayer session suffers scars that are very real."

The Reverend Jerry Falwell, founder of the Moral Majority, recently made a very telling remark. He told reporters that because Moral Majority members represented a variety of denominations "if (they) ever opened a Moral Majority meeting with prayer, silent or otherwise, (they) would disintegrate." Well, just what does he expect to happen to our school systems, many of which are equally pluralistic in makeup?

What sort of prayer do they plan to recite: Protestant? Catholic? Jewish? Buddhist? Mormon? Depending on the community in question each of these religions could be in the majority. Is the prayer to be addressed to God, Jehovah, Buddha or the Virgin Mary? Or is it to be a meaningless mishmash of every religion known to man?

M. William Howard, the former president of the National Council of Churches, put it well recently when he said that religious people do not want "a least common denominator prayer addressed to whom it may concern." That is part of the reason why sixty major religious leaders have come out against school prayer.

These leaders are also motivated by a strong sense of our history and our destiny as a free people. In his book, *The Making of the President 1960*, Theodore White wrote: "America as a civilization began with religion. The first and earliest migrants from Europe, who shaped America's culture, law, tradition and ethics, were those who came from England—and they came when English civilization was in torment over the manner in which Englishmen might worship Christ. . . . It was with remembered bitterness they distilled, though not without struggle, that first great landmark in America's unique civilization, that first of the creative American compromises that was to set America apart from the old world: freedom of worship."

If you go to Plymouth, Massachusetts, today, you will find it teeming with tourists. They crowd around the rock with cameras. They clamber on board the Mayflower Two. They patiently file through the first Pilgrim house. How many of them, I wonder, relate what happened at Plymouth to their lives today? On the hill overlooking the sea, there is a monument bearing the names of those 102 English Calvinists who were persecuted because they denied the ecclesiastical authority of the King. There is also this dedication: "to the forefathers in recognition of their labors, sacrifices and sufferings for the cause of civil and religious liberty."

Religious liberty. If you ask me, that was the real rock upon which our country was built.

That was 1620. Unfortunately, not even a century passed before the persecuted became the persecutors. In 1692, for instance, entrenched Puritan hostility to freedom of thought and speech helped cause the deaths of 19 men and women during the Salem witch trials.

In 1802, Thomas Jefferson wrote to the Danbury, Connecticut, Baptist Association: "Believing with you that religion is a matter which lies solely between Man and his God . . . I contemplate with sovereign reverence that act of the whole American people which declared that their legislature should 'make no law respecting an establishment of religion, or prohibiting the free exercise thereof,' thus building a wall of separation between Church and State."

Historians have since discovered that this letter was no casual piece of correspondence. Jefferson had the then Attorney General Levi Lincoln study it before mailing it. Why, twenty years after the adoption of the Constitution and the Bill of Rights, did Jefferson feel compelled to addresss the establishment issue? Because in many parts of the country people weren't taking the First Amendment seriously. As I noted earlier, the Congregationalists had official backing in Connecticut, much to the annoyance of the Danbury Baptists no doubt.

So, the current disregard for the First Amendment and the penchant for religious segregation is nothing new. Even after the last state religion was disestablished, Protestantism was still the unofficial national religion—to the detriment of all other faiths. It was a touchy matter to be a Jew or a Mormon. As recently as 1960 it was widely believed that Roman Catholics should not hold high public office. President Kennedy's election helped tear that barrier down. But prejudices persist.

And I believe that school prayer only serves to reinforce those prejudices. I attended a private school where not only prayer but worship was mandatory, and believe me it was Protestant in form. My Jewish friends either had to attend these services or stand in the park. The same held true for my Catholic friends. And we looked on them as something different just as they must have looked on themselves.

Of my children, and there are eight of them, some go to public schools, some to private. They have not had the same experience. On the other hand, I think they probably have a more profound understanding of the world around them and a greater love and a greater beauty to their lives than I. When I see them working with a group of retarded children, giving of their free time, I can't help suspecting that that really is a form of worship far more exhilarating and far more meaningful than sitting in a pew with hands folded. It is certainly different, far different, from what I did. But according to the matters in which I believe, I think maybe they are closer to Heaven than I am.

The Apostle Paul wrote that "faith without works is dead." And in the Old Testament text read this morning, Isaiah seems to be saying that prayer without actions to match is not heard. It has always struck me how many Biblical passages the Moral Majority chooses to ignore when it sets its legislative priorities. This 58th chapter of Isaiah is one such passage. Isaiah is explaining why the Lord is ignoring Israel's many prayers, fasts, and solemn observances. As I read it, the people's piousness is an abomination to God until they first act on His social agenda. Isaiah writes: "Is not this the fast that I have chosen? to loose the bands of wickedness, to undo the heavy burdens, to let the oppressed go free? Is it not to deal thy bread to the hungry, and that thou bring the poor that are cast out to thy house?"

This, I believe, should be the agenda for each of us as individuals, and indeed for me as a Senator. It pains me to see the Congress diverted onto these moral crusades when there is so much real suffering in our land, when so many people are losing their livelihoods and so many going without the necessities of life. And when there are so many people denied the justice which should be accorded them by law.

Let us rededicate ourselves to taking up this agenda. Let us get involved in our public and private lives to shape a fairer society. Then, and only then, does God promise to hear our prayers. "Then shalt thou call, and the Lord shall answer," writes Isaiah. "Thou shalt cry and He shall say, Here I am."

DETERMINING AND PROMOTING AMERICAN FOREIGN POLICY

FOREIGN POLICY: THE PRESIDENT, CONGRESS, AND PUBLIC OPINION[1]

WALT W. ROSTOW[2]

The Ford Presidential Library in Ann Arbor, Michigan, was chosen as the site for an important symposium, "The Congress, the President, and Foreign Policy," which was held on November 9 and 10, 1982. A group of distinguished public servants and scholars, including three former Secretaries of State and two former national security advisors, gathered to participate in panel discussions. The foreign policy seminar was sponsored by the Gerald R. Ford Foundation; the Association for Former Members of Congress (an 800-member congressional alumni organization); the Atlantic Council; and the University of Michigan, which had initiated a two-year study by former members of Congress and the Atlantic Council to explore in depth the interrelationships between the executive and legislative branches of our government in all matters of foreign policy making.

Dr. Walt W. Rostow addressed the group at a dinner hosted by the University of Michigan on the evening of November 9, 1982. As an historian, experienced public servant, and advisor to Presidents Kennedy and Johnson, Dr. Rostow is regarded as an authority on the role of Congress and the Presidency in the foreign policy arena.

Dr. Rostow delivered his address to an audience of 300 university scholars and administrators, current and former members of Congress, and past Executive Branch officials. He was introduced by former President Gerald R. Ford at approximately 7:30 P.M. His speech was scholarly rather than partisan and he demonstrated a broad historical perspective on conflicts between the executive and legislative branches of government, particularly in this century. Rostow noted that almost two hundred years after Washington's farewell address,

> . . . the major conflicts between the President and Congress in foreign policy are still the consequence of a lack of stable consensus in our society on the national interest. . . . By and large, the behavior

---

[1] Delivered at a banquet on the evening of November 9, 1982, during a two-day symposium sponsored by the Gerald R. Ford Foundation at the University of Michigan, Ann Arbor, Michigan.

[2] For biographical note, see Appendix.

of the U.S. in foreign policy in this century has conformed to Dr. Samuel Johnson's dictum: "Depend upon it, Sir, when a man knows he is to be hanged in a fortnight, it concentrates his mind wonderfully." We have oscillated between isolationism, indifference, wishful thinking, and complacency, on the one hand, and on the other, the panic-stricken retrieval of situations already advanced in dangerous deterioration. We recognized our national interest only when we faced real and present danger—a rather dangerous habit in a nuclear age.

He ended his address with a plea for "a wide bipartisan consensus" and by citing specific examples of presidents from John Adams to the present who had the courage to make what they believed to be the right decisions at the risk of opposing both Congress and public opinion.

Senator William Broomfield, who inserted Dr. Rostow's speech in the *Congressional Record,* said "I commend his cogent remarks to all my colleagues, Republicans and Democrats alike, for we all bear a heavy measure of responsibility to promote bipartisanship in the formulation of foreign policy."

Walt Rostow's speech: A few days ago I suddenly recalled, while in the office of the Dean of the LBJ School of Public Affairs—who happens to be my wife—that I was committed to speak here tonight. I turned to the Dean and asked if she had some books on her shelves on the subject of this symposium. Without a word she began to collect and deliver one armload of books after another until I said: "Thanks; enough." Among others in the pile were Morison, Bemis, Bailey, Spanier and Nogee, Crabb and Holt—even the report of a 1979 joint LBJ School and Library symposium on the Presidency and the Congress. As I refreshed my memory of the accumulated wisdom on this well-worked but still elusive subject, I was struck by the following passage from the lead article in *Foreign Affairs* for the spring of 1979, which was also included in the Dean's pile and underlined in red: " . . . I confess to increasingly serious misgivings about the ability of the Congress to play a constructive role in our foreign relations." The author: J. William Fulbright.

There is a good deal to be said for the distinguished senator's retrospective scepticism. In fact, there were times when I wished he, as an active senator, had accepted this dictum. We all know that the Constitution is written so as to focus the attention of Congress on their districts and states and, therefore, on local public opinion. We all know that Congress is a diffuse and changing body. There are experienced and wise members of Congress, with a knowledge of foreign affairs to match any in the executive branch. Presidents should and often do seek their views; but advice is different from responsibility. Collectively, Congress can, at certain moments act, and evèn act decisively in foreign policy; but there is no continuing locus of responsibility. Moreover, the Congress can change its view on an issue of foreign policy, responding to the swings of public opinion, in a way denied to the President. Above all, Congress can, if it wishes, avoid acting on a problem, leaving the burden of action and political risk to the President.

Wilbur Mills, for example, captured the relationship well at a meeting at the LBJ ranch early in 1968. President Johnson was asking the leadership for prompt legislative action on a controversial balance of payments measure. At the end, Mills delivered his negative response in the following words: "Mr. President, you sure have my sympathy. You've got more troubles than a dog has fleas." On this matter, clearly, the fleas were going to be Lyndon Johnson's, not Wilbur Mills'. And that's a part of what a President is paid for. The Constitution is so written that foreign policy is inescapably the President's problem; whereas the members of Congress, after consultation, can return to the Hill and leave it to the man occupying 1600 Pennsylvania Avenue.

Having been involved in the business of the executive branch, in one way or another, on and off since the summer of 1941, I wish I could, on this occasion, accept the Fulbright doctrine and make a straightforward case for a presidential monopoly in foreign affairs, but neither my knowledge as an historian, nor my experience as a public servant, nor, above all, the dictates of the Constitution permit me to do so. Constructive or not, the Constitution mandates an important role for Congress in foreign affairs; and, in the end, I am sure the Founding Fathers were wise in this as in other matters.

So I am back where, I suspect, you have been since this symposium started this morning: trying to sort out the patterns and lessons to be drawn from 194 years of executive congressional relations in foreign policy: years of quiet, of occasional sturdy partnership, and of stormy contention—never more stormy, incidentally, than in the first quarter century of the nation's constitutional life.

In preparing these brief remarks, I made four lists:

Examples of constructive Congressional initiatives in foreign policy;

Examples of constructive partnership between Congress and the Executive branch;

Examples of costly contention between Congress and the executive branch; and

Examples of essentially unilateral presidential action in which Congress acquiesced without major opposition.

The first is a short but not trivial list. And I am pleased to note, given my initial quotation, that on any such list one would have to place the Fulbright Fellowships. Of greater constitutional interest is the role of certain senators, in the late 1950s, in breaking a kind of schizophrenic deadlock within the Executive Branch on the question of development assistance to Latin America, Africa, the Middle East, and Asia. There was a stand-off within the Administration between supporters and opponents of development aid from 1953 forward which, for whatever reasons, President Eisenhower was not prepared firmly to settle. In the late 1950s a group of senators of both parties took a series of initiatives, of which the Kennedy-Cooper resolutions of 1958–1959 on aid to the Indian subcontinent are a good example. As John Kennedy said on March 25, 1958: "There is no visible political glory for either party in coming to the aid of India. . . . " Nevertheless, his and other enterprises went forward. They not only permitted Eisenhower and Dulles to support the Development Loan Fund but also to respond positively to a series of crises in 1958 in Latin America and elsewhere. The creation of the Inter-American Development Bank and the World Bank's International Development Association were among the fruits of this period.

There are no doubt other examples; but I did not wish to leave Fulbright's somewhat self-flagellating dictum unchallenged.

As for effective partnerships—my second list—there have been a good many and they are worth recalling and studying carefully.

The collaboration of a series of presidents with key senators in the other party to achieve the creation of the United Nations, support for the Truman Doctrine, the Marshall Plan, NATO, SHAPE, and, most recently, the more controversial passage of the Panama Canal treaties.

There was also the collaboration of President Eisenhower with Senator Lyndon Johnson, which, I heard Eisenhower explain to Johnson in the summer of 1968, was a necessary condition for conducting a "civilized foreign policy" in his time of responsibility.

A number of senators, at considerable risk, and President Ford performed that function with respect to the Panama Canal Treaties.

The role of Senators Vandenberg, Dirksen, Johnson, and others who helped unite the Executive Branch, the Congress, and the nation at critical moments is a proud aspect of our Constitutional history.

At this point I would simply note that the key to success in all such ventures in Presidential-Congressional collaboration was the rallying of public opinion—and opinion leaders—by full and effective presentation of the facts. Senator Vandenberg's statement of February 27, 1947, to President Truman of the conditions for supporting the Truman Doctrine is the prototype. He demanded: " . . . a message to Congress and an explanation to the American people, in which the grim facts of the larger situtation should be laid publicly on the line as they had been at their meeting that day." Let me recall that Truman's popularity at the time was low; he was generally regarded as a lame duck; Vandenberg was judged to be a quite likely successor, but Vandenberg was wise enough to understand that only the blunt laying of the facts before the people by the President would permit Vandenberg to carry the Senate and Congress in support of what the nation then required. In short, the successes hinged on making the triangle that links the President and Congress work—the crucial third side being public opinion.

Now my third list: the failures of Presidential-Congressional collaboration. There are more than we would wish, but I will cite only three.

Wilson's failure to carry the Senate on the Versailles Treaty and entrance into the League of Nations.

Franklin Roosevelt's failure to persuade the Congress and the people to abandon isolationism until Hitler controlled the European continent and the Japanese attacked Pearl Harbor.

The division between Presidents Nixon and Ford and the Congress over policy toward Southeast Asia in 1973–1975 leading to the unilateral Congressional destruction of South Vietnamese military capabilities and morale by radical reductions in the military aid promised by President Nixon to the South Vietnamese government as a condition for acquiescence in the terms of the 1973 agreement.

Merely to evoke these painful episodes is to recall how complex the issues in contention can become. There is Wilson's peculiar personality and style and Henry Cabot Lodge's, as well; there is the disabused inter-war interpretation by the Congress and the people of the First World War—an interpretation that played a significant part in the process that led to the Second World War, and, of course, as President Ford's memoir and all other evidence make clear, there is the interweaving of Watergate and the weakening of the Presidency with the destruction by Congress of the peace agreement of 1973, painfully earned, over more than eight years, with the blood of South Vietnamese, Americans, Australians, Koreans, and others who supported the purposes of the Southeast Asia Treaty. (I have stated the nature of the tragedy of 1973–1975 as I feel it; but the tragedy is equally real for those who believed or came to believe we had no business making strategic commitments to Southeast Asia in the first place and that Congress rescued the nation from a costly and misguided policy.)

Before characterizing the nature of these failures, let me give some examples from my list—major unilateral presidential initiatives that occurred with Congressional acclaim or without great or protracted controversy: the Berlin airlift; President Eisenhower's Open Skies proposal of 1955; the Cuban missile crisis; the U.S. intervention in the Dominican Republic in 1965; President Nixon's opening to China; President Carter's negotiation of the Camp David accords.

The reason for the relative success of these initiatives is, of course, that they had substantial majority support in public opinion. They either appeared to move the world in the direction of peace, or they dealt with a potential source of military conflict without significant bloodshed and promptly.

Here, I believe, is the clue to the cases of tragic failure—my third category—and to the essential nature of the relations of President and Congress in foreign policy. The failures are all cases where public opinion was a key variable. The Presidents either failed to sustain public support or could not do so because there was no lucid, deeply-rooted concept of the nation's abiding interests on the world scene to see the nation through a protracted crisis.

Wilson did not explain our declaration of war in 1917 as necessary to protect the nation's abiding interest in avoiding hostile control of the Atlantic and in maintaining a favorable balance of power on the European continent. He held up a transcendent vision of a world made safe for democracy—an admirable vision but beyond the capacity of the United States to achieve. By the time the battle over the Versailles Treaty occurred, it was clear to the American people that, League of Nations or not, it was going to be, still, a pretty ugly world; and a revulsion began that persisted and even gathered strength in the 1930s. Democratic liberals like Harry Hopkins converged with Republican conservatives like former President Hoover to argue, with overwhelming majority support in public opinion, that we could and should keep out of the conflict of the 1930s raging in Asia and obviously about to break out in Europe. The eloquence of one of our most popular and persuasive presidents could neither evoke U.S. action to try to prevent the coming war nor even prepare the nation to defend itself.

With respect to Southeast Asia in 1975—despite overwhelming support for the Manila Treaty two decades earlier—there was no solid understanding in the Congress or public opinion of why seven successive presidents, from Franklin Roosevelt to Gerald Ford, had made or reaffirmed serious strategic commitments to Southeast Asia. (With President Carter's and President Reagan's reaffirmation of the application of the Southeast Asia Treaty to Thailand, the number is now nine.) The opening to China and apparent détente with the Soviet Union converged with Watergate and other forces to lead Congress and a popular majority to believe that, without significant cost to the national interest, we could turn South Vietnam over to the Communists.

I conclude much in the vein of President Washington's Farewell Address, after eight years when he tried to protect the interests of a young country with no lucid or stable sense of its national interest. Almost two centuries later, the major conflicts between the President and the Congress in foreign policy are still the consequence of a lack of stable consensus in our society on the national interest. With respect to Europe and the European balance of power, perhaps something of a consensus has been achieved and institutionalized; although the consensus is periodically challenged and cannot be taken for granted. And we have three times reacted strongly to reestablish, after going slack, what we hoped was an adequate military balance with the Soviet Union—after the invasion of South Korea in June 1950; after the Soviet launching of Sputnik in October 1957; and in the wake of the Soviet invasion of Afghanistan. But, by and large, the behavior of the U.S. in foreign policy in this century has conformed to Dr. Samuel Johnson's dictum: "Depend upon it, Sir, when a man knows he is to be hanged in a fortnight, it concentrates his mind wonderfully." We have oscillated between isolationism, indifference, wishful thinking, and complacency, on the one hand, and on the other, the panic-stricken retrieval of situations already advanced in dangerous deterioration. We recognized our national interest only when we faced real and present danger—a rather dangerous habit in a nuclear age.

That is roughly what Alexis de Tocqueville, writing a century and a half ago, said we would do. And that oscillation explains, I believe, a high proportion—not all—of the tensions between the President and the Congress in foreign policy. By and large—without higher intellect or virtue and with some exceptions—Presidents have perceived the national interest in a steadier way than public opinion or a Congress mandated by the Constitution to be attentive and sensitive to public opinion.

The remedy for this dangerous cyclical behavior, to the extent there is a remedy, clearly lies in a sustained effort by our political leaders to develop a wide bipartisan consensus on the nature of the nation's abiding interests on the world scene—an effort not rendered easier because there is an ideological strand embedded within us which would deny that we, like other nations, have abiding interests.

That is about all I have time for tonight except for a final reflection. We can hope that our society evolves a more mature and stable notion of its relation to the rest of the world; and we can all try to contribute to the emergence of a more stable, forehanded consensus. But, we shall still need from time to time, I suspect, the exercise by our Presidents of a little noted extra-constitutional dimension of our political life.

The White House is, in a good sense, a haunted house. The family quarters are cheerful and, indeed, modest by standards of other homes of heads of state. All the presidents since John Adams lived there—Adams for only a few months. Lincoln slept and ran the war from what is now known as the Lincoln Bedroom. It is hard for a President in that house to escape a living sense of his predecessors and successors. He knows that his predecessors often left office defeated—and, if not defeated, with the mob howling at their heels, as President Washington. Often this was because they did what they deeply believed was the right but unpopular thing for the country. Presidents are and should be politicians, and they don't like to be unpopular, but they also wish to be worthy of the best in their predecessors and to be respected by their successors.

From, say, John Adams' determination to avoid war with France at the cost of the possibility of his re-election, down through Harry Truman's firing of Douglas MacArthur and Lyndon Johnson's stoic pursuit of a cautious and unpopular strategy in Southeast Asia to Gerald Ford's response to the *Mayaguez* incident in the midst of a political mood that simply wanted Southeast Asia to disappear from the face of the earth, we have needed that kind of lonely, unilateral courage by our Presidents. We shall continue to need it.

PROMOTING FREE ELECTIONS[1]

Jeane J. Kirkpatrick[2]

The invasions of Afghanistan and the Falkland Islands by totalitarian countries, suppression of the Solidarity movement in Poland, the struggles for power in Lebanon and Central America all focused attention on the conflict between people desiring freedom and those determined to impose their will on others. Responding to these events, in a speech to the members of the British Parliament in London on June 8, 1982, President Ronald Reagan proposed that freedom-loving nations join together

> . . . to foster the infrastructure of democracy—the system of a free press, unions, political parties, universities—which allows a people to choose their own way to develop their own culture, to reconcile their own differences through peaceful means.

On November 4-6, 1982, the Conference on Free Elections, sponsored jointly by the Department of State and the American Enterprise Institute for Public Policy Research, was held in Washington in response to President Reagan's project for the promotion of democracy outlined in his speech to the British Parliament. In the interest of "assisting democratic development," the conference was designed to provide a forum for the exchange of ideas on elections, the democratic process, and basic political institutions in many countries of the world and to explore practical options for encouraging free elections and constitutional governments. The 24 individuals from 15 countries attending included political party leaders, diplomats, election administrators, government officials, scholars, and legislators from both developed and developing countries where democracy was imperiled.

Secretary of State George Schultz opened the conference and was followed by addresses from the Prime Minister of Italy and the President of Costa Rica. The President of Nigeria sent a message which was read to the delegates. President Reagan hosted a luncheon for the participants.

On the first day of the conference, Ambassador Jeane J. Kirkpatrick, United States Representative to the United Nations, addressed 150 participants and observers in the Loy Henderson Room of the State Department. As a delegate to the United Nations and a former professor of political science at Georgetown University, Ambassador Kirkpatrick is well respected in spite of some controversial opinions she has expounded in her speeches. Disagreement with her views by students, faculty mem-

---

[1]Delivered to the Conference on Free Elections at 3 P.M., November 4, 1982, in the Loy Henderson Room of the State Department, Washington, D.C.

[2] For biographical note, see Appendix.

bers, and others had led to interruptions of her speeches on some campuses, cancellation of lecture invitations at other schools, and a consequent refusal by Ambassador Kirkpatrick to accept honorary degrees at those institutions. As a result, some major universities are reexamining the freedom of speech on their campuses.

How successful was the "Conference on Free Elections?" The conference moderator in his report observed,

> . . . the participants invariably asked their questions and made their arguments in a manner that was polite, orderly, and in every way conducive to a thoughtful exchange of ideas. I personally acquired a great deal of new information, many new ideas, and a better understanding of the problems and possibilities of free elections in the many different kinds of polities in the modern world. From their comments to me, I know that many conferees had the same reactions.

Following the conference, David D. Newsom, former Undersecretary of State and currently director of the Institute for Study of Diplomacy at Georgetown University, wrote in the *Christian Science Monitor:*

> As one who had expressed some skepticism about the feasibility of government-sponsored efforts to promote democracy abroad, I attended the conference with questions in mind. Would such a conference see the problems of creating democratic regimes only as United States competition with the Soviet Union? Would such a conference be prepared to face up to the challenges to democracy from both left and right? Would the spectrum of opinion be sufficient to generate discussion on some of the basic issues involved?
>
> My questions were largely answered—and answered positively. ("Can Democracy Be Promoted Around the World?," N. 24, '82, p 23)

Jeane Kirkpatrick's speech: Democratic elections and democratic government are a core concern, of course, for all of us concerned with human freedom in our times. As everybody knows, everybody claims the title but very few people in very few countries today, as in much of the past, desire to incur the associated risks of democracy and so we have the proliferation of a lot of labels like people's democracies, guided democracies, one-party democracies, and so forth.

In fact, it is not difficult to distinguish between systems which do possess the distinctive characteristics of democracy and those which do not, because as the distinguished commentator on this panel, Giovanni Sartori, has written, "Democracy is a term which carries a historical experience whose meaning is stabilized." That is, it has a specific meaning, a determinant meaning.

The historical content of democracy is inextricably bound up with the long struggle against arbitrary power. Modern democratic institutions have their origins in the persistent efforts of Englishmen to limit the power and jurisdiction of their kings. Those efforts began before a reluctant King John was persuaded to sign the Magna Carta early in the 13th century. And, although progress was made, it was not until the 18th century that the outlines of modern democracy began to emerge in new doctrines of legitimacy that made just government dependent on the consent of the governed; in doctrines of contract that not only attributed natural rights to people but asserted that the protection of those rights was the very purpose of government; and in doctrines of representation that insisted that each person was entitled to speak for himself about how the laws affected him.

The actual history of democratic government then definitively established that the expansion of individual liberty, the rise of popular rule, and the institutionalization of limits on government's power have developed together alongside one another.

In this sense, all democracy is liberal democracy. All democracy is liberal democracy in the precise sense that it provides for public participation in basic decisions about who should rule; to what broad ends under conditions that provide choice among would-be rulers; freedom to discuss; freedom to criticize, organize, and proselytize; and protection against reprisals by government for the exercise of those freedoms.

Elections, as everyone here knows, are the central institution of democracy. All the essential elements of democratic government are present in democratic elections. Of course, there are elections and elections and I'm speaking only about democratic elections; not the kind of elections that provide no choice or the kind in which all the candidates are chosen by the same governing power. Those are not democratic elections.

Democratic elections are competitive, periodic, inclusive, and definitive. Each of these characteristics has important consequences for the character of the process. Periodic elections, as everyone understands, limit the tenure of those elected and guarantee that before they or their group can continue in office, they will be required to submit themselves again to the voters in order to insure that they still have the voters' approval.

Competitive elections are elections in which opposition and criticisms are permitted and alternative leaders compete for office under conditions of free speech, press, and assembly. Inclusive elections are those in which large portions of the adults in a population are authorized to participate. Definitive elections are those whose outcomes largely determine the partisan composition of government.

Democratic elections operationalize and institutionalize some distinctive and determinant views of legitimacy, representation, and participation—some distinctive views of personal freedom and public power and of the relation between private ends and public goals.

First is the distinctive conception of legitimacy. It is very clear that legitimate government in this view is government whose chief decision makers are chosen through democratic elections. Only those governments are legitimate, and, not only that, but the persons chosen in this fashion through democratic elections must respect the limitations of their power necessary to preserve this system of selection. In other words, legitimate power flows from the people and respects constitutional limits on its exercise.

Democratic elections produce governments that are not only legitimate in this democratic sense but representative as well, because it is assumed, of course, that the people having chosen their governors through competitive, periodic, and inclusive determinant processes will choose people who, broadly speaking, represent their own views and values.

Democratic elections produce representatives that are chosen by their people whom they are to represent. Democratic elections guarantee that laws will not be made simply in the name of a community but with the consent of the community.

No substitutes are acceptable. Democratic representation postulates that each citizen is the best judge of his own interests and insists that no elite, hereditary or self-made; no vanguard, however enlightened; no group, however virtuous, is capable of representing the people unless chosen by them under appropriate circumstances.

Their participation, therefore, is sharply distinguished from the participation in systems in which people do not make the decisions but only ratify decisions made elsewhere. Choices made in democratic elections have real consequences.

Democratic elections, then, institutionalize the processes of meaningful participation and representation. They constrain as well as empower, limit as well as authorize. They not only implement the belief that legitimate power flows only from the people, but also that institutionalized continuing restraints are required to protect people from those who govern them.

Democratic elections insure that the goals of government are consistent with those of a majority of citizens. Democratic elections never leave people who govern free to pursue very far goals or visions which violate those of the majority of the public. The next elections bring them sharply back to the realities of their dependence on the public.

It's generally recognized, of course, that, as compared to autocracies, democratic governments are difficult to establish and to maintain. They have some quite specific legal requisites which include a constitutional system that features a rule of law and respect for basic democratic rights and electoral laws that permit broad participation, active competition, and an honest count.

They also have some sociopolitical requisites in the form of informal institutions. The most important of these are political parties, which in fact, of course, have developed wherever democratic elections exist. The parties, as we all know, recruit candidates, conduct campaigns, structure the electorate, articulate and aggregate the views of individuals and groups, and basically link government to society in such a way that the subordination of the rulers to the ruled is guaranteed.

Let me just mention that democratic institutions require that persons who would desire to exercise power run the risk of defeat. It's a very real risk that some of the people who went down to defeat day before yesterday in the American elections well understood. Leaders must have sufficiently strong egos to risk defeat. They must not be too proud to ask for the support of others, including many lowly, ordinary persons. They must renounce violence and the threat of violence in the pursuit of political power.

This all requires a very high degree of restraint and of initiative. The demand for participation and restraint that democratic elections impose is much more complex than either the demand for passive obedience or undisciplined participation of some other system.

Because democratic elections submit those who rule to demanding disciplines of government by consent, they constitute the best protection ever for persons against tyrants imposing themselves on people. That is why democratic elections are the best protection possible for this human legal right of individuals.

That is also the reason that those who value power above freedom avoid the test of democratic elections. For let us be clear, democratic elections pose real, substantial risks to those who seek or hold power. Ask Jimmy Carter, Giscard d'Estaing, Napoleon Duarte, Jerry Brown, Helmut Schmidt. To compete in a democratic election is to endure criticism, risk defeat for one's party and one's administration and one's self. Why bother?

Why not instead embrace a different doctrine of legitimacy— one that justifies the indefinite possession of power on grounds, for example, that one has a divine mandate to rule or on grounds like the late Italian dictator, one is always right; or, because like contemporary Communist leaders, one knows that one is the chosen instrument of history.

There are a lot of associated views of representation at hand to complement these doctrines of legitimacy. One can always claim that one doesn't really need to be chosen by the people because the people, in fact, do not know their own interests.

There are always available convenient doctrines of false consciousness to explain why a given people have been too confused and misled to know their own will and are, therefore, unable to make valid decisions. And, of course, one can always turn out participation and claim for a nondemocratic regime that one's regime also boasts participation; it just won't be the participation associated with democratic systems.

The nondemocratic doctrines of legitimacy, representation, and participation have the great advantage from the autocrat's point of view that they do not limit either the scope or the duration of his power. Democratic leaders come and go with the regularity of elections, but nondemocratic leaders, while they may be brought down by a sudden coup, may also stay on for decades. Furthermore, while they're there, they suffer no unwelcome constraints on how they may define "public" goals.

The autocrat is free to use the coercive power of the state to translate his private dreams into public goods. The autocrat is free to pursue with all the power at his disposal the dream of a new man, a new society, without much concern about the impact of his efforts on actual men in actual societies. Elections are a good instrument, then, for protecting people against the abuse of power; they are no help at all to the autocrat interested in maximizing or extending his power.

Why, then, do rulers anywhere submit themselves to the test of democratic elections? Only, I think, because they believe that government should rest on consent. Only because they believe people should have the right to choose their rulers and have, moreover, the capacity to do so. Only because they value public above private good.

Two governments in this hemisphere illustrate the alternative attitudes toward democratic elections. One was the government of Napoleon Duarte, the former president of El Salvador, who last March sponsored elections which, as it turned out, he and his party lost. The other approach is illustrated by Nicaragua's government which steadfastly refuses to permit elections or otherwise submit its policies to tests of consent.

El Salvador's election, with its enormous turnout of voters, was a tribute to the Salvadoran people and also to the vitality of the democratic idea. What extraordinarily courageous and unflinching people the Salvadorans proved themselves. In spite of massive violence at the polling places and threats of retaliation by guerrilla forces against voters, they voted in unprecedented, huge numbers. And when it became obvious that the government had failed to persuade a majority of the correctness of their leadership, El Salvador's leaders resigned. Why did the people behave that way? Why did the government behave that way? The people behaved that way because they desired profoundly to shape their own destiny.

The *Wall Street Journal* reported an interview with one woman who was the mother of two children. She got to her polling place around 5 o'clock in the morning. By 9 o'clock, she was still two blocks from the gate to the entrance. She said to the *Wall Street Journal* reporter, "I'll wait here all day if I have to. The rest of the world seems to have made decisions about El Salvador. Now, it's my turn."

Some people had said that free and fair elections could not be held in El Salvador, perhaps because of the reasons suggested by President Monge at lunch today, that "democracy doesn't thrive in the tropics" or that they are too poor to enjoy democracy. The Salvadoran people proved those judgements wrong.

Some opposed the elections in principle, regarding them as a tool of the bourgeoisie and a misrepresentation of the popular will which could best be expressed through armed struggle. In El Salvador, the view of preferring the bullet to the ballot is held by the various guerrilla factions whose coordinating front is appropriately named after one Farabundo Marti, the Salvadoran Communist. One of those guerrillas, Commandante Ana Guadalupe Martinez, was quoted in an issue of the *Economist* of London as saying that "Elections are there to ratify a popular government. . . . If laws exist which represent the people, elections are not very important."

The idea that the will of the people can be better expressed through a revolutionary elite than free elections is, of course, a fundamental tenet of Leninism. It is incompatible with democratic elections and democratic government, and of course, fundamentally at variance with Article 21 of the U.N. Universal Declaration of Human Rights.

El Salvador's Farabundo Marti National Liberation Front is not the only element in Central American politics that opposes free elections. Nicaragua's Sandinista leadership also opposes such elections and called the Salvadoran election "an absolute denial of democracy and civilization." They did not always speak that way. One month before achieving power, the Sandinistas promised—here in Washington and elsewhere—the Organization of American States that they would hold free elections when they assumed power. Once in power, however, they quickly reneged on that promise.

In the spring of 1980, the Sandinistas consolidated their control over the Council of State, enlarging it and packing it with their own supporters to insure a permanent majority. In July 1980, Sandinista Defense Minister Humberto Ortega announced that there would be no need for elections since the people had already "voted" during the revolution. "Elections," he said "could not be held until the people had been 're-educated.'"

The following month, in August 1980, Humberto Ortega announced that elections would be put off until 1985. Even then, it was said, these would not be "bourgeois" elections—the kind of elections called for in the Universal Declaration of Human Rights—but "people's" elections, which, in the words of Interior Minister Tomas Borge, power "will not be raffled off." In the interim, no "proselytizing activities" on behalf of any candidate would be permitted, neither would any discussion of candidacy be permitted, before candidates were offically designated by an electoral agency, which would not be created until 1984. Violations would be punished by terms of 3 months to 3 years in jail.

Meanwhile, vigilante mobs have been encouraged to intimidate the opposition. The Nicaraguan Democratic Movement and the Social Democrats, two of Nicaragua's principal opposition parties, have repeatedly been the victims of semiofficial mob violence. In a speech delivered last fall, Humberto Ortega stated that the Sandinista regime is "guided by scientific doctrine, by Marxism-Leninism" and threatened to hang dissenters against the regime's policies "along the streets and highways of the country." Shortly thereafter, four Nicaraguan business leaders who signed a letter protesting against this speech were arrested and sentenced to 7 months in prison. They have since been released, let me say.

Partisans of nondemocratic politics have no trouble finding reasons why the people of El Salvador—or any other country—should not be permitted to choose their rulers and hold them accountable through competitive elections. "The people have been brainwashed," say the brainwashers, "and do not know their own minds." "The people are intimidated," say the intimidators, "and will not dare express their own views."

We have heard these claims many times before: in Rome, as Mussolini deprived Italians of the right to choose their government; in Moscow, when Lenin decided elections were not a proper instrument of revolution; in Berlin, as Hitler decided German "voting cattle," as he called them, were too corrupt to choose their rulers; in Venezuela, when violent insurgents sought to keep the people from the polls; and so forth. Always those who seek power without the consent of the people find reasons why their rule should not be subjected to the discipline of popular elections.

In conclusion, let me say that it would be vastly preferable if all elections could be held where there is mutual trust and civic peace. But governments come into being even where these conditions do not exist. Everywhere, someone decides who shall rule. Can any democrat seriously argue that the decision is better made by a small minority operating under unstable conditions than by a larger majority operating under those same conditions?

Certainly, some social and economic conditions, some political traditions, some cultures make holding democratic elections and functioning within a democratic government easier. But the experience of recent decades suggests that all that is finally required is a government willing to submit itself to opposition and competition because it is willing to risk power for the sake of freedom.

IN MEMORIAM

A MEMORIAL TO AMERICAN VIETNAM WAR VETERANS[1]

ALBERT KELLER JR.[2]

On a cold, rainy Saturday, November 13, 1982, more than two hundred thousand people gathered on the Mall in Washington, D.C. for the dedication of a memorial honoring the veterans of the Vietnam War. The monument, according to Charles McDowell of the Richmond *Times-Dispatch,* is much more than a memorial:

> It seems to me it's a symbol of all our needs to come to terms with that war and to come to terms with ourselves. So on the Mall, with Lincoln and Washington and the great museums of our heritage, we have a new monument for a war we didn't win, a war that wore away at most of the things that hold us together, a war that divided the generations—young and old—and a war that divided the young generation against itself. . . . The bitterness of the division of that generation left its mark on all of us to this day. ("Washington Week in Review," PBS, N. 12, '82)

Veteran journalist Richard L. Strout described the monument:

> It is one of the most moving things in América I think—it is just names. Acres of them. When it was proposed it caused controversy— it is not like most monuments built around some splendid temple like the Jefferson Memorial or a thrilling sculpture like the Lincoln Memorial. This is just lines and lines of names, 58,000 of them, carved in slabs of polished black granite, the names of those killed in Vietnam. They went out to far-off jungles at the order of the state and gave their lives. I defy you to see it without being moved. (*Christian Science Monitor,* Ap. 4, '83, p 22)

The dedication ceremonies at the memorial site on November 13 began with a prelude by the United States Marine Corps Band, a welcome, the presentation of colors, an invocation, and the introduction of speakers by the founder and president of the Vietnam Veterans Memorial Fund.

---

[1]Delivered at outdoor dedication of the Vietnam Veterans Memorial in the Mall in Washington, D.C. at approximately 2 P.M. on November 13, 1982.

[2] For biographical note, see Appendix.

Of the several persons who spoke briefly, it was fitting that Al Keller Jr.,
national commander of the American Legion, was called upon to speak
first. Not only was Mr. Keller a veteran and former prisoner of war in
World War II, but his organization had raised and donated $1.17 million
for the memorial, more than any other group. He began his short address
at approximately 2 P.M.

Vietnam veteran Art McGovern, who was present, said that the men
who spoke at the ceremony "deserve recognition for real moral courage.
They delivered messages of love, pride, and humility when other words
and feelings might have pleased some of the crowd even more."

Albert Keller's speech: Thank you, Jan. Today we dedicate a memorial to a generation of Americans who fought a lonely battle.
We dedicate the Vietnam Veterans Memorial to those who died
in that war, yes. But, more than that, we dedicate it to those count-
less thousands who survived that war, only to face a battle that
honor bound them to.

In the jungles and the dusty deltas of Vietnam, our young soldiers stood together and cared for their wounded and dead. If no
other characteristic distinguished the Vietnam veteran, it was his
unfaltering devotion to his comrades. They let no wound go un-
tended. They left no dead behind. And they came home expecting
the nation to care about their comrades as they did.

But instead, they encountered indifference and a deep desire
to have Vietnam, and those who fought there, left behind.

But this generation of veterans would not have it so. For years
the wounded spirit festered. And for years the Vietnam veteran
tended to himself and did what he would alone. And for years the
wounded memory of his comrades cried out to be healed, waiting,
hoping, crying out in a hundred tortured ways.

The Vietnam veterans yearned for a way to tend to this last
wound of the war. And, finally, they decided, as they had learned
in the war itself, that they would have to tend to one another alone.

But today, we know they were wrong. The American people,
inspired by the undaunted determination of those men and wom-
en, responded in a historic conversion of compassion, caring and
generosity. Standing at last before them was the opportunity to express the gratitude and the honor that they longed to give, but
knew not how to grant.

There are those who say that the war in Vietnam brought shame on America. There are those who say this memorial would bring shame on those who fought the war. But there are those, like the men and women that I represent, who say, "Not so." There is no shame in answering the nation's call. There is no shame in serving with honor and courage in difficult times. And there is no shame in enshrining the names of fallen comrades in immutable stone for generations to recall.

There is a legacy left for us from the Vietnam experience, and it was left to the young who fought there to show it to us. And that is the rediscovery of our capacity to care, to give, and to honor. That is no small legacy for a nation to receive.

This memorial symbolizes, not only the supreme gift of nearly 58,000 young Americans, but also the priceless gift of renewed awareness in our capacity as a people.

With this dedication, we come not to the end of America's commitment to Vietnam veterans, but the beginning of a new awareness of their unparalleled contribution to the nation.

Generations to come will walk before these gleaming walls and, like them, will reflect. They will consider the memories of those who died. They will consider the legacy of the living veterans left. And they will take from this Memorial a promise to be ever true to their American heritage.

My fellow veterans, families and friends, we are here today to honor, to remember and to consecrate forever this piece of America, to insure that coming generations understand how dearly we hold those who served our nation in Vietnam. How painfully we recognize that the debt we owe those listed here can never be paid. And how hopefully we stand together as a nation of peace.

There are some very special people here with us today. They symbolize America's future. They are the children of our nation's Vietnam veterans.

Let us salute this nation's Vietnam this afternoon by joining hands in a silent pledge that together we will care for their children, as we pray that Vietnam was America's war to end all wars.

A MAN OF STEEL AND VELVET AND PEACE: DWIGHT D. EISENHOWER[1]

WILLIAM BRAGG EWALD JR.[2]

Eulogies, speeches honoring the deceased—leaders, heroes, scholars, distinguished personages and others—are an important element in the fabric of any society because they serve as reminders of the contributions of their predecessors, provide continuity, and serve as a source of inspiration for succeeding generations. A eulogy has two distinctive characteristics that sets it apart from most other forms of public address: (1) it is meant to be delivered at a ceremonial occasion to honor the subject; and (2) it is designed to be heard by an audience that already shares the speaker's respect, affection, or admiration for the person being honored. The speaker's task, then, is to heighten the auditors' feelings of regard, love, or appreciation, which can constitute a formidable challenge.

On October 14, 1982, a reunion of the "old guard" of the President Dwight D. Eisenhower Administration was held at the L'Enfant Plaza Hotel in Washington, D.C. Over 1,000 persons who served in the Eisenhower administration attended the banquet which was held on the General's birthday and marked the 30th anniversary of his 1952 presidential campaign and inauguration. Those present included White House staff, cabinet and sub-cabinet members, and other administrators of the Eisenhower era.

The principal speaker was Dr. William Bragg Ewald Jr., who not only had served as a member of the Eisenhower White House staff but had also assisted the President with his memoirs and written a biography, *Eisenhower the President: Crucial Days, 1951–60.* As a newly graduated Ph. D. and a Harvard instructor, Ewald was closely associated with Eisenhower as a political campaigner, staff member, aide, and biographer.

Senator Ted Stevens, who served in the Department of the Interior under Eisenhower, was deeply moved by Dr. Ewald's eulogy. The senator said the address: "brought back memories of the dedication we all shared toward the goal of American peace, prosperity, and independence." (*Congressional Record,* D. 9, '82)

William Ewald's speech: It is an unutterable pleasure and an unutterable honor to speak to this audience, which includes so many beloved friends of so many years.

[1]Delivered at a banquet honoring Dwight D. Eisenhower on the evening of October 14, 1982, in L'Enfant Plaza Hotel, Washington, D.C.

[2] For biographical note, see Appendix.

As Governor Adams said when I walked into his office up at Loon Mountain after many years in which I hadn't seen him: "OK, let's get to work."

No shooting war.

No lives lost.

No territory surrendered to aggression.

The consumer price index going up at an annual average rate of 1.4 percent.

Real GNP increasing 47 percent over an 8-year span.

I don't have to tell you, of all people, what years I'm talking about. Because in loyalty and devotion and service, you helped shape them. As Arthur Burns said the last time we met here, "Those were good years." Years, in his wonderful metaphor, of "Eisenhower weather."

He never forgot the first time he saw Dwight Eisenhower, as he joined his fellow faculty members for Ike's inauguration as president of Columbia. The day had been threatening. The procession approached the place where Burns was waiting. The clouds parted, the sun burst out. And Eisenhower turned to Arthur with that great grin and quipped: "Eisenhower weather." The Supreme Commander had it on D-Day in 1944, when the blinding storms over the English channel subsided for 36 hours to permit the invasion.

He had it at his second inaugural as President in 1956, on that bleak January afternoon when, once again, the clouds divided and the sun came out, and he spoke of the winds of change sweeping the earth.

And he had it at the funeral. It was not a gloomy funeral, as many of us remember on what was our first reunion after his death. No sad songs for him: just that magnificent Scottish setting of the 23rd psalm, "Onward Christian Soldiers," and that heroic Bach chorale prelude, "Wir Glauben All'." It was a happy day. Like St. Paul, he might have said at the end of a long life: "I have fought a good fight. I have finished my course. I have kept the faith."

Sure, he had made some mistakes: the removal of the Marshall paragraphs in 1952; the decision in 1956 not to speed up the launching of an earth satellite and thus beat out the Russians'

Sputnik; the scheduling of the U-2 flight on the eve of the Paris summit conference in 1960. He wasn't perfect. Who is?

The plain fact is that in the past half century, since October 24, 1929, when the stock market crashed and since September 18, 1931, when the Japanese invaded Manchuria, we've had few years indeed without one of three things: a shooting war; a deep depression; or murderous inflation. Except the Eisenhower years. Not bad.

Now, all these things being true, why? Why have the myths—the myriad myths—persisted? Including that unspeakable myth concocted by the Select Committee on Intelligence chaired by Senator Frank Church that Ike ordered the assassination of Patrice Lumumba in the Congo.

He didn't order Lumumba's assassination. He didn't order anybody's assassination. He hated the very thought of assassination. I've laid out the facts on all this—facts that start where the Church committee left off—and I wish to God people would stop parroting the myth and pay those facts some attention.

The biggest myth—the myth of the golfing president, the do-nothing president, the know-nothing president—that myth is silly on the face of it as every one in this room knows. But the myth persisted.

Then two things happened: Vietnam and inflation.

In 1963, as we were going to press with "Mandate for Change," Eisenhower did what he usually did with long chapters—chopped and chopped and chopped. He chopped and chopped away at the chapter on the 1954 Indochina war. It was ancient history. Who would want to read about it? So he cut page after page of commentary on the folly of sending unilaterally, without allies, American forces into the jungles of Southeast Asia.

A few years later, when we were unilaterally engaged in the folly of sending American ground forces by the hundreds of thousands into the jungles of Southeast Asia, the wisdom of the 1954 Ike decision struck like lightning and started people thinking.

Next, inflation. Ike worried when it edged up past two percent. He gave us three balanced budgets. And nobody cared. Until inflation skyrocketed into double digits. And we realized that those three Eisenhower balanced budgets were three of the five we've had in more than thirty years.

Another thing happened: the record started unfolding.

First, the Ann Whitman files, which the President took with him to Gettysburg, and drew on heavily for "Mandate for Change" and "Waging Peace," and which are now being opened for research.

Then the diaries of Bern Shanley, C. D. Jackson, and Jim Hagerty.

And I can tell you that when the voluminous minutes of the meetings of the National Security Council are opened, they will fill out with overwhelming evidence a portrait of Eisenhower at work, quick of intellect, decisive, wrestling with the most intractable problems in the world.

So here we stand, with this historical legacy. Is this what brings us together tonight? Great as it is, I believe the answer is no. Because every President has two legacies: a historical legacy—what he did; and a biographical legacy—what he himself was. And the biography determines the history.

Lyndon Johnson wanted history to remember him for the Great Society. He will be remembered for Vietnam. Richard Nixon wanted history to remember him for reshaping the geopolitical structure of this planet. He will be remembered for Watergate. And the fault in both instances was not in the stars, but in the men themselves—something down there inside, in the flesh, the bone, the nervous system.

The conduct of the presidency is not a science. The conduct of the presidency is an art—an art that turns on what lies in the mind and heart and soul of the man in the Oval Office.

On February 12, 1959, Carl Sandburg addressed a joint session of Congress on the 150th anniversary of the birth of Abraham Lincoln. And with his first sentence a rare hush fell over the hall. This is what he said: "Not often in the story of mankind does a man arrive on earth who is both steel and velvet, who holds in his heart and mind the paradox of terrible storm and peace unspeakable and perfect." Nothing about Lincoln's legislation, nothing about the Civil War. Only words about steel and velvet, rock and fog, storm and pure peace; the interior landscape of the soul of the man—an incredible man.

At the center of the wheel there is a point—a theoretical point—that does not turn—what T. S. Eliot called the "still center of the turning world": a point infinitely small, perpetually still.

This image leaped alive one afternoon several years back when I went to interview Ed McCabe. I'd gone to see Ed about Ike's labor legislation. But then he began to reminisce, to wander into other fields of memory. And he recalled that July afternoon in 1958 in the cabinet room when Eisenhower told the congressional leaders he was sending U.S. Marines into Lebanon. The congressmen drew in their breath with audible apprehension.

And then Ed, who was sitting behind the President, looked at him, and what he saw was this: one big hand draped over the arm of a chair, a hand relaxed, with no sweating palm, no agitation, no nervousness. Eisenhower had outsized hands—hands good for kneading pie dough or firing a gun—hands with knuckles broken years earlier in football and boxing (the only hands I've ever seen comparable were those of Gene Tunney), yet hands which could, incredibly, make swift, tiny, impeccably accurate editings in the margins of a typed text.

I never forgot that image. And as I thought about it, a pattern—a pattern of parallels—began to form, from many sources:

Bill Robinson's diary account of his first meeting with Eisenhower during the Battle of the Bulge—a meeting in which everyone at SHAEF headquarters was going crazy, and only Ike was calm;

The picture of Ike out on the White House lawn during the 1956 Suez crisis, with the looming possibility of World War III; banging one golf ball after another, grinding his teeth and cussing to himself about the perfidy of his old friends the British and the French;

The memory of that Gettysburg day in 1962 during the Kennedy Cuban missile crisis when Eisenhower suddenly left our editing session, took a briefing call from the White House and returned with the buoyant exclamation: "Boy, that was good news," reflecting, "You know, most of the worst things you expect to happen never do happen;"

And that almost unbearable moment in the midst of his final illness at Walter Reed, several months before the end, when, as nationwide TV news reported the physicians' fear that he probably wouldn't live through the night, I spoke with John over the phone and he confirmed that stark prognosis and then added: "The only person who is not gloomy around here is Dad. He's kidding with the nurses and still having a great time."

The pattern formed—formed around the central image of that Lebanon afternoon: the image of wheeling power: of the planet-shaking movement of ships and troops and planes—a thousand SAC aircraft bombed and ready—the greatest emergency deployment of military force in our peacetime history—a supreme demonstration of the Eisenhower principle that he would enunciate again and again, eyes flashing, riveting the listener: "Look, when you appeal to force, there's just one thing you must never do—that's lose. There's no such thing as a little force. When you use it, you use it overwhelmingly."

And at the center of all that wheeling motion—at the still center of this turning world—that single hand: no sweating palm, calm, relaxed: the symbol of a man four-square in heart and hand and mind: A man of command and objectivity and courage and control.

Not often in the story of mankind does a man arrive on earth of steel and velvet and peace unspeakable and perfect. Something like that resided in the mind and heart and soul of Dwight Eisenhower. In the midst of many threatening clouds it brought us a beautiful golden season of Eisenhower weather. For what he did, and above all for what he was, we thank God from the bottom of our hearts tonight.

BEGINNINGS

NOW FOR THE HARD PART[1]

Thomas J. Stevenin[2]

Although speeches by prominent figures delivered in the nation's capital and major cities, or at large universities are usually accorded attention by the press and television, interesting and influential public address is not restricted to centers of power or academic prestige. Many addresses that deserve recognition are presented to audiences on occasions that are largely unobserved by the national media. One such speech was Thomas J. Stevenin's address at the ninetieth commencement exercises of Sterling College on Saturday, May 22, 1982, at 3 P.M.

Sterling College is a school of approximately 500 students located in the small central Kansas town of Sterling. The school seeks to provide a "Christian higher education with excellence in the liberal arts and with career orientations. The college is committed to an evangelical Christian emphasis in all aspects of its program."

The main speaker at the commencement exercises was Thomas J. Stevenin, vice-president for human resources and administrative services for Farmland Industries. He was known as an outstanding and inspiring speaker, and his services were widely sought as a speaker, seminar conductor, and corporate trainer.

The commencement exercise took place outdoors at Smisor Stadium on the Sterling campus. A musical prelude, the procession of graduates, faculty, and administrators, the invocation, and reflections by two graduating seniors preceded Dr. Stevenin's address. The audience of approximately 900 (in addition to the graduating seniors, faculty, and staff) included parents and friends of the graduates, supporters and alumni of the college, other undergraduates and local community members. The speech was favorably received as evidenced by audience comments such as "It was the best I've heard" and "the best in many years." Much of the success of the speech probably can be attributed to Stevenin's surprising and unusual theme, his candor and humor, and his reliance on personal experiences with which most listeners could identify.

[1]Delivered at the commencement exercises of Sterling Colege at 3 P.M., May 22, 1982, in Smisor Stadium, Sterling, Kansas.

[2] For biographical note, see Appendix.

Thomas Stevenin's speech: In preparing for my assignment today, I read a number of recent commencement addresses. I found that the speakers in one way or another usually made three points: 1) As graduates, you deserve to be congratulated for your hard work. 2) The college has prepared you well for a future life of success. 3) Because of numbers 1 and 2, today marks the start of a great and wonderful new period in your life.

Now there is, of course, some truth to each of these points, and I have no wish to give you a cynical perspective on this truly wonderful day in your life. At the risk of offending you, however, I would like to take issue with each of these three traditional points, and stress the opposite truth. 1) Truth number one: Now you've finished the easy part: the hard part is about to begin. 2) Truth number two: Sterling College did not prepare you for the future (no college can). 3) Truth number three: Many people never do much of anything after college, and whether you do or not is entirely up to you.

When I say that today you have finished the easy part, I'm certainly not saying that college was easy. I'm sure for most of you it was hard. I know this school has a reputation for high standards. By attending a private college of the liberal arts and sciences, you have given yourselves a commendable foundation for a career.

In my work, I have the privilege of being associated with many colleges and universities all over the Midwest. I can tell you that colleges are not like industries—they do not get better as they get bigger. In the small private college, there is an ability to put various disciplines and subjects together in such a way as to enable the student to see life steadily and whole that may not be possible in any other type of educational format.

Nevertheless, I still insist that today you have finished the easy part for reasons you may fully understand today. For example, in college you are guaranteed attention, supervision, caring, especially in a college like Sterling. For four years, someone has read your papers when they were worth reading and when they weren't worth reading; answered your questions when they were good questions and when they were not good questions; given you attention and respect both when you had something to say and when you just had to say something! You have been the center of a loving, caring community of parents, relatives, friends, administrators, and teachers, all of whom cared about you and wanted you to succeed. Do you have any idea of the extent to which this environment, this extraordinary environment that so few human beings on earth ever have the privilege of being part of, has contributed to the success you enjoy today? I hope you do and that you will express it to those who have provided it for you before this day is over.

There are a couple of other things that make college just a little bit easier than the world of work. For one thing, there is a certain freedom in college that you will no longer enjoy. From now on, Thanksgiving is Thursday; Christmas is the 25th of December; and summer is just like the rest of the year! There is also a certain freedom of choice in college, freedom of choice in instructors, courses, majors. From this point on, freedom is always sacrificed to the will of the corporation, or to the demands of your job.

Another thing that makes college a little easier than you may have realized is that to some extent college is always like a game. You can always do it over again. If you fail a course, you can repeat it. If you do poorly on one test, you can do better on the next one. If you oversleep and cut a class, you can make up the material. There were standards, but if you failed to meet them, it was no big deal, you could meet them the next time around. From this point on, there will be no new starts. Everything tends to be cumulative in a career. Mistakes tend to stay on your record; every job you lose has to be explained later, and if you lose too many of them, no explanations are acceptable.

If you haven't had enough bad news already, let me mention one more thing. In some ways, college is more fun than the world of work. College is more fun because it's more varied. From now on, you may not be able to deal with four or five different subjects in one day. Particularly in the beginning days of your careers, you may deal with only one subject. Instead of intricate puzzles to solve or profound questions to wrestle with, you may find a seemingly endless series of routine tasks (many of which would not have required a college education).

I always become uncomfortable listening to college graduates tell me they want to get into "meaningful work." The problem with this is that it seems to place the entire burden on the employer. The truth is that our economic system, the free enterprise system, allows us to make work meaningful through our own goals and our own determination to succeed. Not all work can be creative and interesting, and exciting and rewarding. Every job, including those at the very senior management level of an organization, has routine, daily chores that have to be completed with a high standard of excellence.

People are always saying to me, "I want a job with a future. I have to tell you today that jobs don't have futures; only people have futures. It is not the job itself that gives meaning to your life, it is your life that allows you to put meaning into your job.

One of the amusing things that job applicants frequently say is "I want a job working with people." Do you know what? We don't have a single opening for a hermit anywhere in Farmland Industries. All of our jobs involve working with people. No matter what technical skills you have mastered at Sterling College, well over 50 percent of your future success will depend on your ability to work with people; your understanding of yourself and others; your willingness to be a member of the team, and part of your task in being a member of the team may be to spend thousands of hours doing work that is dull, uninteresting, boring, and terribly important.

I like what Norman Vincent Peale once wrote. He said, "Think enthusiastically about everything, but especially about your job. If you do; you'll put a touch of glory in your life. If you love your job with enthusiasm, you'll shake it to pieces. You'll love it into greatness, you'll upgrade it, you'll fill it with prestige and power."

One of your toughest jobs in the next few months will be to find a job at all. Nothing is more discouraging to a college graduate, who has spent four plus years preparing for an exciting and rewarding future, than to suddenly find out that the world has not been waiting with baited breath for you to finish your degree. The world has gone on, and the U.S. is in the midst of a serious economic recession. Don't think for one minute that because it may take you six or eight months, or more, to find a job, however, that you've wasted your time in college. Part of the test of what you have become here will be your willingness to discipline yourself to stay at what may be the toughest challenge you have ever faced—the challenge of simply getting a job.

Let me give you one more job tip. Don't be so concerned about the job you get, as the organization that provides it. Find an organization, if you can, that cares about people, that develops people, holds people accountable for their performance; an organization that has a reputation for ethical and moral conduct of its business affairs, an organization you can be proud of, and then take any job they will offer you including a job that in no way ever required you to attend college. Remember that Sterling College was not attempting to get you ready for a job—it was attempting to get you ready for a career, and more importantly it was attempting to get you ready for a significant life.

My first job after returning to Kansas City was a job for which I still have the job description in my scrapbook. It carried the official title of "clerk/typist." My job was to check the training schedule at our corporate Training Center, find out when films, filmstrips or slides were being shown by the various instructors, move the necessary equipment into the classroom, and offer to either show the film or leave it for the instructor to show. When the presentation was finished, I took the equipment out of the classroom, rewound the film, put away the slides, and checked the equipment to see that it was in good working order. When the class was on coffee break, I erased the blackboards, sharpened the pencils, and emptied the ashtrays. I could have performed any aspect of my job at the end of elementary school.

But by pure dumb luck, I had the good fortune of choosing an organization that met all the criteria I outlined above. Everything that I have achieved in my own business career, I attribute to the fact that it was such an organization. Don't be so concerned about the job; be more concerned about the company. If you can't find an organization to work for that you respect and admire, don't forget the great freedom you have in this country to be an entrepreneur yourself. I know an individual in Kansas City who lost his job several years ago with a large organization. After months of searching for a job, he began to do the humiliating and degrading work of mowing lawns for other people. Today, he owns one of the largest lawn services in the Midwest. He took his disappointment and made it into a success. He didn't sit around waiting for meaningful work, he brought meaning to his work. I know another individual who lost his job with a major corporation, finally had to take a job as a busboy in a restaurant. He began to become interested in the service industry, became a waiter, a maitre d', and today a successful restauranteur. "If you love your job," said Norman Vincent Peale, "you'll fill it with greatness, you'll upgrade it, you'll fill it with prestige and with power."

The most fortunate ones among you today are those who have had to work your way through college. Personally, I never did believe that it was a good idea to get people ready to work by having them spend four years not working. I've had the privilege of completing three higher education degrees, but I always worked at least forty hours per week while pursuing those degrees. I never completed a degree and then went out to get a job—I had the job and I completed the degree in order to improve my standing in that job. (By the way, that is probably the future of higher education in the United States, but that's another subject.) When I was having this experience, of course, I was very envious of other students. I remember my college roommate whose parents were wealthy. Every week he would open up an envelope that had more money in it, and he would exclaim, "Now, there they've sent me more money. What am I going to do with it!" Over the years, however, I've traced his career and I found that he was never able to make the very transition that I'm talking about today, because the truth of the matter is that he never really learned how to work.

One of the problems in the United States today is that we have a very large group of people who have simply never learned how to work. If you want to see what is wrong with the economy of the United States, I invite you to watch your television set on any given evening and notice the image of the successful person. The successful person is calm, cool, collected, and, of course, is never supposed to lift anything heavier than a cocktail glass. And one thing more, of course, you're not allowed to sweat. Sweating is forbidden. If you are ever found to be sweating, you must immediately spray it with something. The only time it is socially acceptable in the United States today to sweat is if you are jogging! The truth

is that we have spawned not one generation, but several generations, in the United States who simply do not know how to work.
And the further truth is that it is beginning to catch up with us
in overwhelming economic ways.

So I say again that those of you who have had the great privilege of having to work like a dog so you could get your college education are the most blessed of all today. You may not have
graduated at the top of this class, or even with honors, and the
yearbook may list few, if any, extracurricular activities by your
name, but you may have also learned something else along the way
that will stand you in good stead in the years ahead. You have
learned how to work!

Getting out of school when you have never done much of anything except go to school is much tougher. I am not saying that
those of you who are in that position today cannot succeed, but I
want to warn you that many graduates do stumble right at this
point. You will have to summon all the strength and inner resolve
that you have to make sure that you now take the great privileges
which you have had and translate them into hard work and success in a completely different realm.

I might have surprised you a few moments ago when I said
that neither Sterling College nor any other college can prepare
you for the future. I must tell you in all honesty that ten years from
today you will have to say, as I have to say, that 95 percent of the
knowledge you use in your work is knowledge you learned on the
job. If you join a large corporation, you will find that a large cor-
portion today is in itself a school. It might surprise you, in fact,
to know that last year more money was spent by business corporations on the training and development of their workforce than was
spent on all of higher education in the United States. Corporate
training is the major form of adult education in the Western hemisphere. But not only through participation in formalized corporate training programs, but also through your own immense desire
to learn, to develop, to pick the brains of your colleagues and associates and learn from them, this is the avenue which leads to success. I believe that a large, well managed business corporation is
truly the most creative entity on earth today. But those who succeed will not be those who sit back and wait for the corporation

to make them a success—it will be those who bring meaning to their work in terms of their own goals, their own value system, and their own dedication to the importance of work. Above everything else that I hope you carry away from Sterling College today, I hope you carry away a love of learning, a desire to learn, and an appreciation for how important it is to learn.

My last irreverent point was that you may or may not be on the verge of an exciting future. I might as well be honest today and tell you that many people never make the transition from college into the world of work. Some people simply can never adjust to going from an environment in which most people want you to succeed to an environment in which most people really don't care whether you succeed or not, and there's no small number around who would just as soon you would fail because it would then help them succeed.

When I was in college, I read a book that was a bestseller at that time called *Games People Play* by Dr. Eric Berne. In this book, Dr. Berne says that immature people spend most of their lives playing silly games. One of these games he identifies as the game "If Only." If only my parents had been different. If only my parents had been rich. If only I were married. If only I were not married. If only I lived in a different part of the world. If only, if only, if only. If only somehow I could get all the circumstantial furniture of my life arranged in the right way, then I'd be a success.

One of our favorite games in this country today is, if only the government—if only the government would do this or that, then I'd be a success. So often, I hear my fellow citizens say, what we need to do to solve this problem is to get what they always euphemistically call "federal money" into this project. Somehow I always want to tap them on the shoulder and remind them that what we call federal money is money we used to have before we gave it to the government to give back to us to help us with the problem of not having enough money. Someone I think wisely observed that this makes about as much sense as giving yourself a blood transfusion in the right arm by taking blood out of the left arm (and spilling half of it somewhere in between).

Certainly the message of our day which the current administration is trying to get across to all of us, is that government is not the solution to our problems. In many ways, it has become our problem. But I think it is only symptomatic of this whole national feeling that has spread abroad in America, that somehow "they" are supposed to get busy and solve all of our problems for us. We don't know who "they" are or when they're coming, but we're convinced that it's somehow their responsibility. We speak of "Reaganomics" as though the economic future of our society were his responsibility.

Here is my central message to you: You are the person who is fully accountable for your own success, for your own future. Many people have contributed to your life up to this point. They have made their contribution very imperfectly because they are all very imperfect people. But they have done their best. From now on, it's up to you. While some of the things in your future may be difficult beyond belief, you have a tremendous number of things going for you—your health, your strength, your families, your backgrounds, the tremendous education you have received here in one of America's finest colleges, this great and good land, and above and beyond all else the opportunity to have been exposed for four years to teachers whose professional dedication to you have been their expressions of the love of God.

I leave you with a verse from the Old Testament taken from the 40th chapter of Isaiah. These will be encouraging words as you enter the hard part: "They that wait upon the Lord shall renew their strength; they shall mount up with wings like eagles, they shall run and not be weary, they shall walk and not faint."

THE FUTURE IS NOW: A ZEST FOR LIVING[1]

WALTER F. STROMER[2]

Handicapped children face special problems in getting an education that will prepare them for useful, productive lives. Parents of these children often are understandably apprehensive when it comes time to send them to school, so to alleviate such fear, many schools attempt to provide parents with information and guidance. A preschool conference for parents was held at the Indiana School for the Blind on April 23, 1982. The program was conducted by teachers, counselors, administrators, and other personnel at the school. It was the special challenge of the guest speaker to inspire hope and inspiration with his keynote address.

Dr. Walter F. Stromer of Cornell College was invited to be guest speaker because it was felt that a blind person who had competed successfully in a sighted world might provide a good example of how people can be successful despite a handicap. Several persons on the staff knew Dr. Stromer and had heard him speak at similar conferences at the Iowa Braille and Sightsaving School.

The speech was made at 10:30 A.M. on the first day of the three-day conference. The audience of about 150 people included parents of preschool blind children, visiting guests, and the staff of the school.

Dr. Stromer began with a bit of humor at his own expense and a brief history of how handicapped persons had been treated through the centuries. He used examples from various cultures to show that serious hurdles remain despite progress.

Finally, addressing the future, Dr. Stromer offered suggestions to parents who have the awesome responsibility of raising a blind child. Not minimizing the problems, he remained optimistic that human beings, despite blindness, can still lead a useful and happy life.

Walter Stromer's speech: When a man has to travel four hundred miles to find an audience to listen to him you have to wonder how things are going for him back home. But my excuse for being here is that some wonderful people who heard me speak years ago have been kind enough to invite me back and that kind of flattery is hard to resist.

When I was told that the title of this talk was to be "The Future Is Now," I was puzzled. When I was also told that it had been

[1]Keynote address delivered at 10:30 A.M., April 23, 1982, at a preschool conference for parents, in the main auditorium of the Indiana School for the Blind, Indianapolis, Indiana.

[2] For biographical note, see Appendix.

suggested by a psychiatrist, my first impulse was to turn the tables and to analyze the analyst. On second thought, I decided that this was a topic I could live with and that it expresses something which I truly believe. I feel strongly that we should learn from the past and that we have a responsibility to those who come after us, but that the most important task for us is to live this day and this moment to the best of our ability.

Since many of you here are parents of blind children, I want to talk first about what has been done in the past for the blind and other handicapped. Then I want to make some tentative suggestions that may be of help to you in the future, which begins now.

Those wonderful Greeks of twenty-five hundred years ago, to whom we owe so much, used to put defective babies in clay jars beside the road and let them die. In Rome such children were put into wicker baskets and put out on the Tiber river, to be swept away and drowned somewhere downstream. In many countries defective babies were staked out on the mountains to die of exposure or to be eaten by animals.

These earlier ancestors of ours were not entirely lacking in compassion; but, they were often in real danger of being exterminated by famine or flood or marauding enemies, and survival of the group had to be put ahead of the weakest members who could not help themselves. Caring for the handicapped, as we know it, could not really take place until societies became somewhat stable and had some surplus food and some leisure time for some members.

Lack of resources was not the only factor that kept society from humane treatment of its disabled members. Attitudes were also involved. Epilepsy was once thought to be caused by the moon. To be moonstruck was to be deranged or insane. What we call mental illness was once attributed to possession by demons, who in one case in the Bible were driven out of the man into a herd of swine. Blindness and other conditions were connected with sin, as when the disciples asked Christ, about the blind man, "who sinned, this man or his parents?" As long as the causes of disability are thought to be supernatural, either godly or satanic, the only cure will have to be supernatural, such as prayers, incantations or exorcisms; but, not much will get done at the local human level.

Slowly attitudes began to change. In the 4th century A.D., a Christian bishop urged compassion for the retarded. In the 9th century in Baghdad, the Caliph orderd that those getting out of hospitals should be given a sum of money to tide them over until they could go to work. Yet, at this same time, in other parts of Europe people were being blinded for committing such crimes as poaching, that is hunting on land which they did not own. Ironically the church fathers of that day approved of blinding instead of putting the person to death because they felt that blinding would give the victim more time to repent of his sins.

Centuries later the defectives—the stutterers, those with pointed heads, the grossly deformed—were exhibited in cages, in carnivals and sideshows for the amusement and amazement of the public. After that, came the asylums and the institutions where the defectives were locked away. Others were locked away in attics or back bedrooms until their tortured bodies became torturing skeletons in the family closet.

As late as World War II, the federal government did not include blind people in this country as eligible for rehabilitation funds. It was thought that they could not be rehabilitated but would simply have to exist on welfare. Consider how far we have come. Last year was the International Year of the Disabled Person. This year has been declared the National Year of the Disabled Person in this country. We know that there are between 30 and 40 million disabled persons in this country and about 450 million in the world. Just the fact that we can count them, even approximately, is a mark of our progress. In the Middle Ages young children were not even counted in the census because it was assumed that most of them would die by the age of twelve. Why bother counting?

Another indication of concern and our openness to the subject is the fact that there are 120 organizations for disabled. There are more than 130 wheelchair basketball teams. A totally deaf woman holds the world speed record for driving a vehicle on land. The president of Hofstra University is a man with cerebral palsy. Recently a young blind woman was involved in a down-hill skiing competition in Switzerland, while two other blind skiiers and four sighted companions set out to ski across Lapland.

In the area of entertainment, we have had the play "Butterflies are Free," about a blind young man, and "Whose Life Is It, Anyway?" about a quadraplegic veteran. The movie "Inside Moves" deals with disabilities. The television movie, "Elephant Man," dealt with one who was grossly deformed. A retarded boy was permitted to play himself in a movie about the retarded instead of having the role played by a professional actor. From Seattle, you can rent a film about a boy who lost both legs and went on to become a football coach. In Dallas, a televison station devotes several minutes each day to advertising available children. These children are not for sale for immoral purposes but they are handicapped children available for adoption.

Yet with all this progress we must admit that there are still problems. Many of them are in the area of employment. Of those who are paralyzed, almost 90 percent are unemployed. Of the blind, Job Opportunities for the Blind estimates that 70 percent of the blind are unemployed or underemployed. Harold Krents, graduate of Harvard Law School, and inspiration for the movie and play, "Butterflies are Free," applied to forty law firms before he got a job.

Taking it all together, the good and the bad, I think it is not unreasonable to say that if one must live as a handicapped person, this time and this place is one of the best that history has known.

Next, I would like to talk especially to those of you who are parents of blind children about some tentative suggestions as to how you can help your child and yourself. I do this with some hesitation because I knew so much more about child rearing before we had children than I do now.

One of the first things you can do is to believe sincerely that raw fish tastes good. I use this example because we have a Japanese student who has stayed with us often who assures me that raw fish is delicious. My mind says it's true. My stomach says, don't touch it. It is hard for us really to believe that people can enjoy food which we consider repulsive. In the same way, it is hard for us to believe that others can be happy without all the things that make us happy. For example, people will look at one who is blind and say, "How terrible, how tragic, how miserable it must be without sight." Yet, I can assure you from my personal experience and from contact with many blind people, that blindness need not result in constant unhappiness. Keep in mind that we have no reliable external measures of happiness, no brain scan, no blood test. About the best we can do is to ask people if they are happy. While I may be better informed on the happiness of blind people than you, still when it comes to deaf-blindness, my own reaction is very similar to yours. I find myself thinking, "How tragic, how difficult." I read recently about a man and wife, both deaf-blind, taking training at the Helen Keller Center on Long Island. When they want to communicate, one goes to the kitchen table and pounds on it to make the floor vibrate. Then they meet at the table and if they are angry they spell words into each others hands rapidly. My reaction was, "How tragic, how inadequate, how frustrating. How much better it would be if they could shout at each other, or better still if they could see each other and make faces." Or would it be better? Who are we to say that their way of communicating feelings or frustration is better or worse than ours? This same deaf-blind man laid tile for his basement floor; he hung paper on the walls of his kitchen, and he travels around the city by subway. Is he less happy than we are? I doubt it. Yes, he does miss out on things you and I take for granted. Is he aware of what he is missing? Yes, to some extent I am sure the deaf-blind are aware that life could be simpler and less frustrating if they could see or hear, or both. But I doubt that they spent much time fretting about it. In general, it seems to be the nature of living organisms to adapt as best they can to the circumstances that exist. Does the worm wish it could fly like the robin? Does the robin regret not having the wings of an eagle? But you will say people are different from the lower animals. Yes, they are. Yes, humans can worry and envy and regret. Still, it is amazing how people with stable personalities can have their bodies broken and pick up the few remaining pieces and make a life of them.

You and I can help handicapped people by letting them define happiness for themselves. We can make life more miserable for them if we constantly remind them of how terrible we feel because of what they are missing. When we do that we are really saying to them, "Please get rid of your handicap because it makes me so uncomfortable."

Let me illustrate how disabled people can be happy in their ignorance. Sometimes during a long Iowa winter I walk to class in the morning and decide it's a nice day because I can feel the sun warming my back. Then some sighted person comes along and says, "It's such a dull, depressing day." To him it is dull because the sun is under the clouds. That doesn't really destroy my happiness, and I do need to be aware that other people perceive the world in ways other than I do. I need to recognize that, just as I need to turn on lights in a room for the benefit of others even though I don't need them. So I will continue to be happy about the warm sun while my friend is depressed by the gray clouds. And, on other days, I will be depressed by the cold while he enjoys the bright, but cold, sunshine. We can each find happiness in our own way.

Is this so different from what happens to any of you? You are all missing out on some success or happiness. You fathers are all disabled in some ways. Some of you are too short to be successful basketball players, and others of you are too scrawny to be professional football players. Do you cry yourselves to sleep every night because of what you are missing? I doubt it. And, you mothers who are lacking the face or the figure to appear on a movie screen, do you beat your fists on the kitchen counter all day and moan about the things you can't do? I'm sure you go on with the business of living and do the best you can. Allow handicapped persons to do the same. If they like raw fish, let them eat it.

My next suggestion for you as parents is that you be like the character in magazine ads for Hastings piston rings years ago. They showed a picture of a big muscle man with a scroungy beard with a friendly smile, and the caption was, "Tough, but oh so gentle." That is a good motto for parents—to be tough, but gentle. It is especially apt for the parents of handicapped children. Just being a parent, of any child, means that you have to be gentle and protective or the child will not survive the first few years of life. Yet, somewhere along the way, you have to be as tough as the mother bear who cuffs the cubs on the snout to let them know that now is the time to leave home and get out on their own. It will be especially hard for you as parents of a blind child to watch your child bump into things or get cut and bruised and still to sit back calmly and say, "live and learn." But handicapped children, more than others, need to have such toughening experiences if they are to grow up as sturdy oaks instead of delicate African violets. All through life, society will tend to overprotect and shelter those who are disabled. They will need a little extra measure of toughness, of assertiveness, of independence if they are to get their fair share of rights and freedoms. It may help you in learning to be tough if you will remember that most of the accidents that happen to blind people are not serious, and almost never fatal. The greatest damage is always to the loved ones who watch things happen, and to the pride of the blind or disabled person.

Last winter I was hurrying to the chapel for a convocation program. I took a short cut along a narrow sidewalk, got too far off to the left side, and got clipped just above my left eye by a tree branch stump where it had been cut off. The branch drew blood, and I knew it. I had no more than sat down in the chapel than one of my students came along and said, "Oh, you're hurt; are you all right?" I said, "Yes," and I wanted to tell him to go away and let me suffer in silence. After chapel, I did not want to go back to the office because I knew the secretary would notice and make a fuss. I didn't even want to go home for lunch because I thought my wife would wrap me in bandages and keep me in the house for a month. What was hurt was my pride. I had demonstrated to others that I was careless, or worse, that blind people can't walk across the campus without bumping into things.

You can help most if you will encourage your child to be independent, to move out, to take risks. If there is a cut or a bruise, be cheerful about cleaning it up and applying a Bandaid and then go about your business. If you can do that, you will be saying most eloquently to your child, "I have confidence in you; keep trying."

My last suggestion to you is to believe in yourself. You are here at this conference to get help and reassurance from various experts. I am sure they have much to offer and I hope you will learn from them. Never forget that in one way you are more expert than any teacher, counselor or psychiatrist you will ever meet. You are expert in knowing how it feels to have your life and your life blood wrapped up in a handicapped child, and to live with that investment twenty-four hours a day, every day of the year. That

is very different from being a professional helper who deals with
the problem for an hour a week, or an hour a day, or even six
hours a day. We need professionals who can be detached and objective and sometimes we, as parents, need to learn some of that
detachment of perspective. If ever the professional helpers get so
detached that they forgot the depth of our feelings, please feel free
to remind them that you, too, have some expertise. Some years
ago, I came across a book by a French psychoanalyst, Alfred Ad-
ler. In the first chapter of his book he wrote, "When parents come
to me with a problem about their child and they tell me what they
have been doing, my first response is to say, 'I think you're on the
right track,' because parents carry a heavy burden and they need
all the support they can get." I wish I could meet that psychoanalyst and hug him and say, "Thank you for understanding."

I want you to learn all you can from the professionals here or
wherever you are. I might even agree with them that you need to
change your behavior in some ways. I do not want you to feel that
you are stupid and worthless and that you are not doing anything
right. If you do that, you won't be a good role model for your child.
I want your child to be happy, but part of that will come about
if your child sees you as parents who find life enjoyable and challenging. So—listen to the experts, but also trust yourself.

If I may summarize briefly, let me remind you how far we
have come in a mere two thousand years, such a little time in the
long history of the world. Next, believe in raw fish; that is, give
handicapped people much freedom in deciding what they enjoy.
Try to be both tough and gentle; and, finally, listen to others but
also trust yourself. I think the greatest gift you can give your child
is a zest for living, a spirit of wonder and adventure, and a confidence that the problems of life can be solved or endured.

In the words of a Chancellor who was both a tyrant and a romantic, Otto von Bismarck, "With confidence in God, put on the
spurs and let the wild horse of life fly with you over stones and
hedges, prepared to break your neck, but always, always, without
fear."

If that is a bit too romantic, let me suggest two lines from a
Kipling poem. A Russian who spent seven years in Siberia said
that these lines helped sustain him. And, if you will update the

sexist language to make it "man or woman," perhaps these lines will help you begin the future now: "If you can fill the unforgiving minute with sixty seconds worth of distance run, yours is the world and all that's in it, and which is more, you'll be a man, my son."

TO CREATE A BETTER SOCIETY FOR ALL

WOMEN IN LEADERSHIP CAN MAKE
A DIFFERENCE[1]

GERALDINE A. FERRARO[2]

When the National Association of Women Judges was created in 1979, its founders expressed the hope that one day there would be no need for such a group. The objectives of the Association are to promote the administration of justice; to discuss and formulate solutions to legal, education, social, and ethical problems encountered by women judges; to increase the number of women judges to reflect more appropriately the role of women in a democratic society; and to address other issues particularly affecting women judges.

When the members of the Association gathered in New York City for their 1982 convention, they presented U.S. Supreme Court Justice Sandra Day O'Connor with their first "Judge of the Year" award. Pride in her 1982 appointment to the nation's highest court was tempered, however, by disappointment that women held only five percent of the nation's judgeships and that only four of the 84 Federal District and Appeals Court judges named by the Reagan administration had been women. In addition, in places where women had formerly been totally excluded from judgeships, only token appointments were made, even though women were graduating from law schools in record numbers. Political scientist Beverly B. Cook found in her investigations that twenty states had never named a woman to the appellate bench and two states never appointed a woman to a state court at any level.

The keynote speaker at the fourth annual conference of the Women Judges Association was United States Representative Geraldine A. Ferraro of New York's ninth district, who is also a lawyer. Following a dinner at the St. Regis Hotel, Congresswomen Ferraro delivered her address at 7 P.M. on October 9, 1982, to about 300 women judges and lawyers from across the country.

In a note to the editor of this volume, Representative Ferraro explained why she chose to deliver an address on the subject of women's rights to an audience of women judges and lawyers:

---

[1]Keynote address at the fourth annual conference of the National Association of Women Judges. It was delivered at 7 P.M. October 9, 1982, in a banquet room in the St. Regis Hotel, New York, New York.

[2] For biographical note, see Appendix.

Women judges have traditionally refrained from involvement in the women's movement; they have tried to remain slightly detached from it. This speech was an attempt to gently raise women judges' and lawyers' consciousness about the women's rights issues—to tell them what's happening, why they should be concerned about them, and why they should become more involved.

Geraldine Ferraro's speech: When I was an assistant district attorney in Queens it used to make me terribly nervous to get up and argue a motion in front of one judge. So you can imagine how I feel standing up here in front of hundreds of judges.

Of course, I am not here today to argue. But I am here to plead a case. My case is that women in leadership positions make a real difference in the way our society works. And I believe that women like us must continue to make that difference.

All of our futures, and our daughters' futures, are at stake. I am talking about the future of every woman, from the migrant farm worker or ghetto mother to United States Supreme Court Justice Sandra Day O'Connor, a founder of this organization and your honoree earlier today.

I speak to you as a Member of Congress who has not forgotten that she is a lawyer who never forgets she is a woman. How could I?

I was one of just two women in my law class at Fordham in the late 50s. In 1960, five job interviews at one of our prestigious New York law firms culminated with a "you're terrific, but we're not hiring any women this year." As a bureau chief in the DA's office many years later, I learned that I was being paid less than men with similar responsibilities. When I asked why, I was told "you don't really need the money, Gerry, you've got a husband."

Getting to Congress wasn't easy either. The biggest problem in running as a woman, if by some quirk you get the organization endorsement, is raising money. I remember going from bank to bank in 1978 for a campaign loan and being told that my husband had to cosign. Forget that I was a lawyer with a good deal of trial experience. Just remember that even if I wanted my husband to sign, I couldn't because I would be in violation of the FEC laws. Once elected, I applied to Eastern Airlines for a Wings card to make billing for the shuttle flights to Washington a bit easier. Despite the fact I was a member of the Aviation Subcommittee of the House Public Works and Transportation Committee, I was turned down. It was only after I mentioned it, to everyone's embarrassment, at an ERA luncheon with an Eastern Airlines lobbyist present, that I received my card. I know what the law is, and so do you. But that doesn't mean it is observed.

Four months ago, I applied to Citibank for a VISA card, listing my salary, American Express, and Eastern Airlines as credit references, my savings banks, and my employer. Again, I was turned down. It was only after I commented to a friend of mine who is a vice president of Citibank that I was going to write to inquire the basis on which my credit had been disapproved that I received a note from the credit department, along with my card, welcoming me into the fold. There was no reason to turn me down other than I am a woman. Fortunately for me, I am a woman with clout. But what about the woman who is not a member of Congress?

As recently as two weeks ago, Capitol Hill police stopped me at four different locations, the last when I entered the House for a roll call vote, and demanded identification. Four years I've been walking in and out of those hallowed halls. Clearly, they found it more difficult to recognize me—one of just 20 women in the House—then any of the 415 men.

Yes, the "old boy network" is alive and well and living in our courthouses and our legislatures and our boardrooms. As women, we still have to be better than men at most of the things we do, we have to work harder, and we have to prove our worth over and over and over again.

It is not just those of us who have reached the top who are fighting this daily battle. It is a fight in which all of us—rich and poor, career and home-oriented, young and old—participate, simply because we are women.

Look at the facts. More women than men are poor and it is harder for them to escape poverty. Indeed, more and more women are struggling to support children alone, earning 59 cents for each dollar a man earns and lower pay translates into smaller pensions or checks from social security in old age. As a result, more and more women are sinking deeper and deeper into poverty. In our wealthy society, poverty is becoming a women's issue. Cuts in domestic programs, seemingly gender-neutral, actually hit women and children twice as hard as they do men because women are the greatest number of recipients. Ninety-two percent of the participants in Aid for Dependent Children are women and children. Sixty-six percent of the recipients of subsidized housing are women. Sixty-nine percent of food stamp recipients are women. Sixty-one percent of Medicaid recipients are women. And why are women dependent on federal help? It is not because they are lazier than men or less moral than men. Or less intelligent.

Women are in greater need because they often have less education. They are the ones who must care for the children. They must work part-time or in menial jobs and they get paid less for the work that they do. After a lifetime of work, in or outside their homes, they often enter old age dependent solely on Social Security benefits.

There are nine million families in the United States where a woman, not a man, is the breadwinner. Fully a third of these families are welfare cases. Still more of them require other federal aid—food stamps, Medicaid, public housing. Woman and children are 75 percent of all Americans living in poverty. And by the year 2000 that figure will rise to 100 percent.

What can women do when their government and, I admit, that includes Congress, takes a meat ax to the programs they depend on so heavily? They can, and do, turn to the Legal Services Corporation when the welfare office stops the food stamps, the landlord shuts off the water, the ex-husband forgets the child support check, or the Social Security Administration cuts their benefits. Yet this Administration has persistently tried to abolish this source of legal hope and help by eliminating funding. So far Congress has refused to go along.

Cuts to Legal Services becomes a double-edged sword for women. Not only are women 67 percent of the Legal Services clients, but this public benefit agency has served as an important training ground for women attorneys. It has provided jobs for well-qualified lawyers who still find the doors of many rich corporate law firms open to "old boys" but closed to young women. At a time when 29 percent of law school graduates are women—an amazing development in itself—almost 36 percent of Legal Services 5,678 lawyers are women.

And what about the working women? Is it any better for them? Our society has changed over the past thirty-five years—but our attitudes have not.

More and more women are working outside the home. Many work for personal satisfaction and achievement like many of us here. But most—two-thirds—work to support themselves and their children and husbands who cannot earn enough alone to keep the family above the poverty line. There are now 43 million women in the workforce, triple the number just prior to World War II. Sixty percent of all women between the ages of eighteen and sixty-four are workers, with eighty percent of all women who work concentrated in so-called "pink collar" jobs, jobs dominated by females and dominated by low salaries.

A woman with a college education can expect lifetime earnings equal to those paid to a man who never finished eighth grade. Grounds-keepers are paid more than nurses. Parking lot attendants are often paid more than experienced secretaries. We entrust our children, our most precious resource, to teachers who frequently earn less than truck drivers.

Who will fight for the worth of women's work? A series of hearings I conducted recently in Washington with two other Congresswomen provided some interesting answers. We found that the fight for equity in the workforce is in full swing. But it is not happening in the marble halls of Washington. It is happening in the statehouses, the union offices, and the courts.

More than twenty-five states and local governments have launched studies of the comparative value of the work their male and female employees do. Spurred on by public employee unions, they are beginning to question the assumption that a tree trimmer should be paid more than an intensive care nurse.

In 1981, Minnesota became the first state to pass a law establishing a state commitment to comparable worth and earmarked budget funds for pay adjustments that might result.

Unions in the private sector have also brought successful pressure to bear on companies like AT&T. Non-union groups like 9 to 5—The National Association of Working Women—have embarrassed companies like John Hancock Insurance into granting raises for clerical workers.

In the courts, 1981 was the crucial decision of Gunther vs. Washington which explicitly links the Civil Rights Act to the issue of wage discrimination against women whose jobs are similar, but not identical, to those performed by men. At a time when the federal government seems to lack the funds, or the staff, or the will to vigorously enforce laws which promote fairness in the workplace, it is only before judges such as yourselves that these vital issues can, literally, have their day in court.

So what does this all mean to us? I did a little research the other day. I wanted to find out how many women in America earn more than $60,000 a year. I picked that number, frankly, because that is what I, as a member of Congress, earn. I learned that there are only 18,000 women in the entire United States, working full-time who earn more than $60,000. We represent just one-tenth of one percent of all the women who work full-time in America. By contrast, 885,000 men, 2.1 percent of full-time male workers, are in the $60,000-plus bracket.

It would be easy to say "gee, it's great to be part of such a tiny minority." It would be easy to say, "I'm all right, Jack—or Jill" and leave it at that. But that would be denying the real role we can, and must, play as female legislators and judges.

I said earlier that I believe women in leadership make a real difference in our society. Now, there are really two reasons why there needs to be more women in leadership—more than the bare five percent of Congress, more than the eight percent of the federal judiciary. More than the six hundred women in state court systems.

The first reason could be called the "Me-First" reason. We are smart, we worked hard, we deserve this job, we are entitled to it and we will do anything necessary to get and keep it. Women of merit do indeed deserve their fair share of society's rewards, a share previously denied to us only because we were women.

The second reason, though, is more important. Women leaders are different. Despite our frequent political and philosophical differences, there are certain generalizations that can be made about women judges and women legislators. We care more about other women. We show more concern for children. We try to resolve controversies by cooperation, rather than conflict.

Harvard University Professor Carol Gilligan has written a book entitled *In a Different Voice* in which she discusses how men and women make decisions. Women, she suggests, are more likely to think about human relationships when they make decisions. They think about what the impact of their decision will be on the people it will affect. Men, on the other hand, are more likely to follow a set of rules and procedures to a conclusion. Women worry more about the effect of their decisions. Men worry more about making the decisions the right way. In short, men often worry more about rules and processes. Women often worry more about outcomes.

We have an obligation to use our unique perspective when we make the laws, as I do, and interpret the laws, as you do.

Your distinguished honoree, Justice O'Connor, has made this kind of difference on the Supreme Court even though I am sure we would all agree that she is neither a professional feminist nor, certainly, a liberal Democrat. In fact, if I may be so bold as to characterize Justice O'Connor's first year, she has shown herself a staunch supporter of states' rights and a reduced court presence in legislative affairs.

Yet, in at least one opinion, setting a male nurse against a Mississippi nursing college for women only, Justice O'Connor focused the argument against sex discrimination in a way which may not have occurred had our highest court still been an all-male enclave. Let me quote her opinion: "Rather than compensate for discriminatory barriers faced by women, Mississippi University for Women's policy of excluding males tends to perpetuate the stereotyped view of nursing as an exclusively women's job." Justice O'Connor went further. She added a footnote citing evidence that the small number of men in nursing keeps wages down. So, the Justice argued, keeping men out of an all-women's nursing school actually punishes women, rather than helps them.

I am not here to give you a campaign speech. You know that I am a Democrat and you know that, with the exception of the appointment of Sandra Day O'Connor, I have not had very many good things to say about President Reagan.

But I do not think that you have to look at the world through Democratic spectacles to see that women judges made greater strides under President Carter than in any other period of our history. Sixteen percent of Carter's appointments to the federal bench were women. Forty-one women out of 260. More than all of his predecessors combined. Not enough, after years of exclusion, but a good start compared to Reagan's percentage of four percent. Four percent. At a time when our federal judiciary is eight percent female, the Reagan Administration is not even keeping up.

The President's record of female appointment to other top jobs is also poor. U.N. Ambassador Jeane Kirkpatrick is the only woman of Cabinet rank, but she is not a member of the Cabinet. Given a chance to name the highly qualified Republican Betty Southard Murphy as Secretary of Labor, Reagan instead chose Raymond Donovan. Need I say more?

What the President does, especially in the area of minority and women's rights, creates a national climate. That climate can be a climate of fairness for women in our society. Or it can be a climate of regression. It can be a return to an era when women were not vital participants in public policy-making.

I have long supported the Equal Rights Amendment—and have sponsored its reintroduction—because I see how government can lose the will to protect the rights of all citizens without the Constitutional imperative.

When women are named to federal courts, there is pressure to name them to state and municipal benches as well. Significantly, it was not until 1979, during the Carter Administration, that every one of our states could finally say it had a woman in its judiciary system. When women become judges, when more and more women graduate from law school, not only government, but private enterprise, has to realize that women are a force to be dealt with and treated with respect.

On the other hand, the sight of top Administration officials capering at Bohemian Grove, that sexist California summer camp for overgrown boys, probably made it easier this past summer for the American Bar Association to undo a progressive new policy. That policy would have put the ABA on record against private clubs which refuse to admit women.

It is not my place, as a maker of laws, to tell you how to do your job of interpreting that law. I am a firm believer in the system of checks and balances established by our Constitution. I am strongly opposed to the efforts that are being made by some members of Congress to strip our courts of their proper jurisdiction.

Yet I do not think it is presumptuous of me to remind you that the courts in this country are in every sense courts of last resort for the poor and the powerless. Increasingly, those poor and powerless are women and children. If we, as women, don't look out for other women, who will? If we as women don't care what happens to women it will not just be the waitress or the welfare mother who loses. It will be every one of us. Every one of us who thought when we made it, all women had it made. Or who thought "if I make it, it doesn't matter who else makes it."

It is too easy to divide the world into "us" and "them." And it is far too easy for us—secure, successful, well-off—to become them. A simple thing—an illness, a divorce, widowhood, alcoholism, economic depression—could turn any of our hard-won gains into a struggle for mere existence.

I didn't go to Washington to represent the women of this nation. But if I don't, who will? I ran, and was elected, not as a feminist, but as a lawyer. And as a lawyer I can argue more effectively for equity and fairness for all Americans.

As I was preparing for this speech tonight I was reminded by one of your publicity aides that "judges are people too." Women judges are women, too. Congresswomen are women in Congress. As each of us devotes energy, talent, and time to the "man's" work we are doing, we owe it to our nation to remember that we are in the same boat with more than half of all Americans. As women, as judges, as lawyers—we must make a difference.

As women we are a majority, but as judges and legislators we are still an all-too-small minority in America. As a minority, our responsibilities—to our sex, our professions, and our nation—are heavy ones. A majority may have the luxury of being a "silent majority." A minority in defense of its rights must speak up.

As members of a minority we have a responsibility to be role-models for all women. As a minority, we bear the burden of expressing the minority viewpoint and keeping it ever before the

American public. Our responsibilities are heavy but they are not oppressive. We have an opportunity as well as an obligation—an opportunity to help create a better society for all Americans, men and women.

Madam Justices, I rest my case. The verdict is yours.

VIOLENCE AND PUBLIC HEALTH[1]

C. Everett Koop[2]

On October 26, 1982, the nation's top health officer, the Surgeon General, addressed the American Academy of Pediatrics (AAP), an organization he helped to found 35 years earlier. The 23,000-member academy is a professional society of medical doctors engaged in the health care and medical treatment of children. Dr. C. Everett Koop chose as his topic, violence as a public health concern. It is an uncomfortable subject, Dr. Koop said, because "we are admitting that mankind still has quite a distance to travel in its long march toward civilized living." Nevertheless, he stressed that the issue must be discussed, studied, and investigated because "violence has grown to become one of the major public health problems in American society today."

In his speech, Koop urged physicians generally, but pediatricians especially, to consider violence as a treatable public-health family problem. Statistics show there are periods of striking changes in the incidence of violence. Koop argued that the country had entered just such a period, in the late 1960s and speculated that it is unlikely that mortality rates from violent acts will return to the levels of the early 1960s. He expressed his belief that violence is "treatable," in the sense that pediatricians know enough about the symptoms of violent personality in children and parents to make diagnostic, predictive, and preventative decisions.

Dr. Koop was the featured speaker at the AAP annual convention. He delivered his speech at 9:30 A.M. in the Grand Ballroom of the Hilton Hotel in New York City to an estimated audience of 2,000, most of whom were members of the academy. Toward the end of his speech, the Surgeon General stated that the effects of video games on certain children "are not constructive. Whether they show soldiers or space-craft or men from Mars or just from the 'other side,' we zap them—and that means

---

[1]Delivered at the American Academy of Pediatrics annual convention in the Grand Ballroom of the Hilton Hotel in New York City at 9:30 A.M. on October 26, 1982.

[2] For biographical note, see Appendix.

annihilation." He repeated this theme in a speech two weeks later in Pittsburgh, rekindling the debate over whether the games are good or bad for children and whether they do produce "aberrations in childhood behavior." His remarks met with objections from teachers, child psychologists, and, of course, manufacturers of the games. (Miranker, Baton Rouge *State-Times,* N. 10, '82, p 2A)

Syndicated columnist George Will described the speaker in his newspaper article on the speech in the *Birmingham Post Herald* ("Violence; Treatable Health Problem?" N. 15, '82):

> With his beard and armor-piercing gaze, Dr. C. Everett Koop resembled an Old Testament prophet who has discovered his neighbor is making graven images. Actually he is not fierce, but is determined to be heard, which is good because that is his job. He is Surgeon General of the United States.

C. Everett Koop's speech: The Academy has had 35 annual meetings since the day I sat with seven other surgeons in Atlantic City and founded the surgical section. Of the meetings since then, I've attended two-thirds. Of the seven surgeons, five have died.

I'm still here, and it is always a comfortable occasion coming back to be with you. In a sense, it's like a homecoming. It provides another opportunity for me to say "thank you" once again to the Academy for giving the pediatric surgeons a haven, a pulpit, and a future.

I appreciate this opportunity to speak to you this morning on a subject that is uncomfortable to raise: violence as a public health concern. It is uncomfortable because, when we do raise that issue, we are really admitting that mankind still has a quite a distance to travel in its long march toward civilized living.

I'm not limiting my remarks just to child abuse this morning. Rather, this is a call to action on your part, individually and collectively, to address this issue of violence by discussion, study, and research.

We've got to do this because violence has grown to become one of the major public health problems in American society today. It is not new, of course. Violence of some kind—murder, suicide, assault, armed confrontation of neighbor against neighbor—these have appeared in our national history since the 17th century. In the past 80 years or so, as we improved our ability to collect vital statistics, we have been able to identify periods when there were changes in the incidence of morbidity and mortality caused by violence. We are coming through just such a period now.

Violence in this country surged in the late 1960s and into the 1970s. All the indicators went up, but the toll upon young people—pre-schoolers, early adolescents, and young adults—has been particularly high. The mortality rates have risen during this period and there seems to be little likelihood that they will return to the levels of the 1950s and early 1960s.

Let me isolate the recent mortality history just for 15- to 24-year-olds in three different areas of trauma and violence:

In motor vehicle fatalities, the death rate per 100,000 of this age group in 1960 was 38. In 1970, it hit its peak of 47.2. By 1978, it had abated only slightly to 46.4. That is the history for all men and women ages 15 through 24. Among white males the numbers are far worse: from a 1960 rate of 62.7 to a 1978 high of 75.4 deaths per 100,000, nearly *twice* the rate for the entire age cohort. One-half of the fatalities are caused by the combination of driving and drinking. We can do something about that.

The story in homicide is the same. From a 1960 low of 5.9 murders per 100,000 men and women age 15 to 24, to a rate of 11.7 by 1970, and to a high of 13.2 in 1978. The carnage among black males, however, is particularly alarming: From a rate of 46.4 deaths by murder in 1960 to a high of 102.5 a decade later, and then down to a homicide mortality rate of 72.5 in 1978.

In suicide, my third and last example, the mortality rate for men and women ages 15 through 24 rose from 5.2 in 1960 to a peak of 13.6 in 1977 and then dropped slightly to 12.4 in 1978. The story among white males bears some study: their rate had been 8.6 back in 1960. It then rose in virtually a straight line to a level of 20.8 in the latest year we have, 1978.

Motor vehicle accidents, homicide, suicide—these violent death categories now have new and higher death rates per 100,000 population in almost *any* grouping of persons between 1 year and 24 years of age. I picked the 15- to 24-year-olds not only because their mortality trends are so clear or because they are about to cross the threshold to adulthood and become the workers and voters and leaders of this country. They are also the products of the pediatricians' efforts in the preceding decade and a half. If, of course, they have survived.

Something happened in this country about a decade or so ago. Or, maybe we should say some things, since no single cause or event could be responsible for results so widespread, so pervasive, and so destructive. And, it may be too soon for us to know with any certainty what those things were. We may not yet have the historic distance, the detachment, to come to any reasonably sound conclusions. But, we still must try to understand, even with our contemporary myopia, just what has been happening and why— and what the effects seem to be upon the American people. I am, by speciality and training, *not* a social historian. But, it *is* my job to monitor the health status of the American people. If I sense something wrong, I am obliged to bring it out into the open and talk about it.

And that's precisely what I'm doing right now.

Rather than resurrect much of the literature of violence, with which many of you may be familiar anyway, I want to take a few careful steps forward to see what the role of the physician might be in understanding and possibly preventing the loss of life— through these violent premature deaths.

I have chosen this particular occasion because, of all physicians, I believe the pediatrician has a unique relationship with children and with parents. You gain certain insights about individuals and families that other physicians may not have the chance to see.

I base that opinion, by the way, on the reflections of my own career of 35 years in pediatric surgery. Dealing with the young children who were my patients I saw firsthand the stresses of childhood and was aware of both the strengths and weaknesses of children trying to cope. I also had to understand the families of those children. I had to gain their confidence and win them as allies in the battle to help their children.

In the process, I think I began to understand a great deal about the contemporary American family.

I tried to absorb that information and then focus it upon the problem to be solved by surgery. Sometimes, when it was clear to me that I was gaining insights into a serious family problem not directly related to the surgery, I would be open and available to that family, just in case they wanted to talk it through. But, I knew that I lacked a clear understanding of the need for me to become involved and to what extent I should become involved and what I might hope to accomplish.

Now, after looking at the data from my new vantage-point as surgeon general, and appreciating the special access to and relationship with the Ameri:an family that pediatricians do enjoy, I think my message to you today on violence in our society and its effects on children and families is appropriate and necessary.

Let me propose as a starting-point the proposition that physicians need to become more familiar with the symptoms of violent personality in child and parent alike. Unfortunately, we don't have available some stock, off-the-shelf profiles of persons who are disposed toward violence. But the research literature does provide us with some clues that seem sturdy enough to follow.

For example, according to the work done by Dr. Dorothy Otnow Lewis of the N. Y. U. School of Medicine, homicidally violent children also tend to have a history of attempted suicide. Many of them have a history of psychomotor seizures. Their fathers are usually characterized as "very violent," particularly to the mothers. These children also tended to have mothers who at some time had to have inpatient psychiatric care. Other studies indicate that violent adolescents had seen severe physical abuse occur at home or were themselves the victims of family violence.

High-risk families also tend to be socially isolated from their neighbors. This is the case across all social, racial, and economic lines. Such families lack strong friendships. They can't seem to get close to other families, particularly families that do *not* show evidence of stress or violent behavior. High-risk families have difficulty coping with pressures outside their own home—pressures on the job or pressures while looking for a job, or the internal pressures that may build up while trying to negotiate such social transactions as shopping or using public transportation. Such families also have difficulty coping with stress inside their own homes: children making noise—loud radios, television sets, or stereos—and a whole range of marital upsets, including those produced by alcohol and drugs.

We know that violence within the family, particularly parental violence toward children, tends to escalate during periods of economical stress. Indebtedness, lack of work, eviction, lay-offs, repossessions, these are the stuff of trauma for many families. They can overwhelm parents and open them to the terrible impulses of violence against each other and against their children. In some areas of the country we are experiencing very difficult economic conditions and, if the research and the anecdotal material we have is any guide, those areas are also experiencing a rise in family violence.

These may show up in marks on battered spouses and abused children. They are never well explained. The victims are often embarrassed, evasive, or simply tight-lipped. The physician needs to understand how to "read" those intensely personal and human signals of the victim of family violence.

I have spent some time on the family because of its overwhelming influence in the shaping of individual behavior. Educational research has demonstrated again and again that a family environment that supports study and learning, that rewards the child that is successful in school, will produce children who do well in school and in life later on, all other things being equal. And the reverse is true, also. A family environment that is cruel and uncaring will send cruel and uncaring children into the world as aggressive, violent adults. These are not hard-and-fast rules. Human beings are not pigeons and don't fit into neat, consistent pigeon-holes. But the weight of experience and evidence does indicate that some signals, such as the ones I mentioned, ought to be noted and respected by the physician.

The physician, suspecting that a patient may be predisposed to violent behavior, should provide the same kind of counseling or referral service as if the patient showed a predisposition to cardiovascular disease, obesity, or diabetes. With the patient's consent, it may be possible to involve a spouse or a child in the discussion of this health problem. This is a sensitive area and we need to give it our professional study and attention in order to provide guidance to pediatricians and other primary care physicians. The objective, let me repeat, is not to intervene into a patient's private family life for intervention's sake but to prevent violent behavior from occurring and endangering the health or the life of another.

I recognize that not all physicians would agree with that assessment of their role. They would object to it as being yet another example of the "medicalization of social problems." And I fully appreciate the uneasiness felt by many physicians and other health professionals with society's habit of casually turning to medicine to solve what may simply not be a health or medical problem. But with violence, I think there is a difference.

This point was also made at a workshop last summer by the Institute of Medicine. The subject was the prevention of violence. On this matter of the "Medicalization of Violence," the participants made several good points, which I will summarize:

First, there seems to be no other institutional focus for research into the causes of violence that takes into account the multiple biological, psychological, social, and societal dimensions of crime, its victims, and its prevention. The institutions closest to being able to provide a multidisciplinary approach to research in the prevention of family violence, for example, would be the National Institute of Mental Health and the National Institute of Child Health and Human Development.

Second, the National Institute of Law Enforcement and Criminal Justice, the research arm of the Justice Department, sees "prevention" as a way of stopping a *recurrence* of a criminal act. In effect, the Justice Department does not have what would be in our discipline of medicine a "primary prevention" strategy, and, on reflection, one would have to admit that such a strategy under the criminal justice system could very well come in conflict with traditional civil liberties.

And, third, the workshop participants agreed that the morbidity and morality from violence are extremely costly to society not only in productive years lost but in the hard dollar terms of the impact upon the health care system. This is particularly true in the cases of abused children, who frequently have chronic disabilities even after treatment. Young women who have been sexually abused by family members frequently develop chronic illnesses requiring repeated inpatient psychiatric care. They also make increased use of gynecological health services, as their total personal health status declines.

We might not want this very complicated issue to gravitate toward medicine for answers, but I believe we need to accept the fact that we may have a contribution to make. I believe that we do and we are obligated to make that contribution.

In addition to learning more about the issue of violence and how it manifests itself in patient behavior, I believe physicians need to see themselves as capable of prescribing some rudimentary, preventive behavior for such patients. This may be more easily proposed than done, but I think it's time we looked at this as a serious aspect of pediatric and family practice for contemporary American society.

I spoke before of seeing patients with predispositions toward violence as needing our help, as if they were patients predisposed to hypertension. As physicians, we do not hesitate to counsel patients to avoid salt and salted foods or to avoid simple sugars. And, I think we all would agree that there is a profound difference between advising a patient to avoid sugar and advocating that the government remove all sugared products from the market-place. The former is good medical practice, the latter is bad government.

Similarly, if we have a patient with a predisposition for violent behavior, especially against family members, I think we need to advise that patient to get some professional counseling and also suggest that he or she monitor their entertainment "menu" and avoid the kinds of television or motion picture fare that stimulates and contributes to the violence in their personalities. I don't like the violence in so-called "entertainment" shows today, but I do not believe the answer is government censorship. That does not leave me powerless as a physician, however. I believe it would be completely within the canons of my profession to advise patients predisposed to violence to self-censor their entertainment diet.

I don't know how many times the government has to come out with yet another study of television violence to make the point that it is harmful to children. There has been an interminable amount of bean-counting to quantify the obvious:

Children spend a least 2 hours and a half in front of a T.V. set each day;

Many of today's high school graduates will have spent more of their lives in front of a T.V. set than in the classroom;

By the age of 18, a young person could have witnessed over 18,000 murders on television. This does not count the documentation of violence that seems to be in every T.V. news report;

Adults spend about 40 percent of their leisure time watching television, which ranks third—behind sleep and work—as an occupier of an adult's average day.

Last year the California Commission on Crime Control and Violence Prevention considered these and other facts and concluded that there *is* a relationship between the violence that is televised and the violence that takes place in the "real world." Not only are the specific details of a fictional crime re-enacted by viewers—often young children or adolescents—but there is a strong suspicion that the aggressive behaviors by the "heavies" on television are mimicked by viewers also, whether consciously or unconsciously, in a variety of relationships and settings.

This is directly related to another potential result from extensive viewing of television or motion picture violence: We begin to believe that violence is a socially acceptable and credible way of responding to frustration or insult or some other direct, personal hurt. And, frequently, violent behavior that stops just short of murder seems to go unpunished. Children especially become "desensitized" to violent interpersonal conflict and, when seeing another child being hurt, will tend *not* to do the thing that civilization requires be done—step in and protect the victim. Instead, they will watch, as if this too were dramatized entertainment.

I have not mentioned video games because I don't want to duplicate what another speaker on your program may present. Also, we are just beginning to assess the data. But I do know these games are not constructive. Whether they show soldiers or spacecraft or men from Mars or just from "the other side," we *zap* them—and that means annihilation.

It seems to me that the weight of evidence—whether it has a solid research base or is purely anecdotal—the weight of evidence strongly suggests that physicians ought to recognize that a diet of violent entertainment for the violence-prone individual is as unhealthy as a diet of sugar and starch is for the obesity-prone individual.

I have indicated the need for physicians to recognize the signals of the violent personality and the violent home and I have suggested that there are some things we can "prescribe." Such as a lower intake of violent entertainment. These are ways of responding to the phenomenon of violence as we see it develop or deal with its aftermath. But there are things we ought to do, as physicians, that are *pro*-active, as well as *re*active.

One task we have is to put the full weight of our profession on the side of strengthening positive, healthy family life in this society. In this matter of violence, as in other matters, we tend to look all about for other palliatives—magic potions of one sort or another, real or figurative, exotic therapies, all sorts of diverting possibilities keep cropping up.

But, that's what they are: diverting. We need to return to the business of holding the family together, the fundamental, irreducible social unit.

I believe that it is primarily and substantially within the limited physical and emotional space occupied by the family—its "home"—that one human being can get used to the work of loving and truly caring about the welfare of another human being. Of course, we know that the reverse is true, also. But the family violence we talk about is the *exception* to the human rule. We need to deal with those exceptions, but, in doing so, we must not cut adrift the healthy families from our constant support and attention.

The family relationship is rich, but it is also fragile. Physicians providing family care and concerned about the maintenance of peace as well as of health in a family, need to understand the influence of work—or the influence of the lack of work—upon family members; also understand the symbolism of material goods, which are supposed to convey a sense of well-being for the family but rarely do all by themselves; and also understand the healthy ways in which people grow up and grow old, and the possibility that some families face their own aging with anger and fear.

This is a very difficult request to make of any physician. Most have not been trained in these areas, which tend to be more the province of the sociologist, the psychiatrist, the psychologist, or the social services worker. The work of sociologists Murray Straus of the University of New Hampshire and Richard Gelles of the University of Rhode Island tends to be unknown among physicians, yet Straus and Gelles are among the leading researchers in the field of family violence.

Physicians tend to be unclear about the roles of these and other professionals. Communication between the practitioners of physical medicine and those who practice other disciplines tends to be limited and unclear. Physicians are also generally unfamiliar with the education and training of personnel engaged in the delivery of social services. Nor are they always aware of the similarity of ethical imperatives shared by both medicine and the social services.

Because of this, physicians, especially those in private practice, tend not to refer patients as often as they should nor do they seek the counsel of social services professionals when a possible incident of family violence comes to their attention.

This may be a problem now, but I believe it will be less of a problem in the future as physicians become more familiar with the total constellation of research and service becoming available for the protection of victims of family violence. Let me note just one example where we are making some progress. This is the work of Dr. Eli Newberger at Boston Children's Hospital.

Dr. Newberger is a pediatrician and editor of a new book on *Child Abuse* for the Little, Brown series on clinical pediatrics. With the support of the National Institute of Mental Health, he has been carrying out a program of interdisciplinary training and research in the detection and treatment of victims of family violence. In this program, Dr. Newberger brings together a group of professionals on the staff of Boston Children's Hospital. They include pediatricians, social workers, researchers, psychologists and psychiatrists, sociologists, and computer analysts.

Working as a team, they provide hands-on clinical care for children who have been abused. They also seek to understand the causes of the violence within the family, to prevent it from recurring. The result is a program that draws upon a variety of skills right at the time they are needed most. The program generates new information regarding family violence and this new information, plus other research data, are translated into direct patient care.

These are the kinds of projects that benefit not only the immediate persons under care, but can also benefit the practice of medicine itself. These projects are dedicated to the protection of innocent victims of violence, especially family violence. I hope to see more of these kinds of efforts begun, whether supported by government research funding or not. Eventually, the medical profession should be engaged, as a routine matter and without the benefit of research dollars, in such interdisciplinary practices as the treatment of victims of violence and the protection of potential victims as they come to our attention. When that time arrives, then we may indeed be close to understanding and controlling violence, which is one of the most extensive and chronic epidemics in the public health of this country.

I have talked of violence on the highways, and of the influence of alcohol and drugs on our escalating violence. I have given you some statistics on homicide and suicide, and I've once again underlined the destructive impact of T.V. on our children and I've added video games to the list. I know I have laid a great burden on you. I share it.

Can we handle it? When that question is asked, I am reminded of that point in the book called *The Little Prince,* by Antoine deSaint Exupéry, in which the Little Prince talks with the fox. The fox says, rather plaintively, "one only understands the things that one tames. Men have no more time to understand anything. They buy things already made at the shops. But there is no shop anywhere where one can buy friendship, and so men have no friends any more. If you want a friend, tame me."

The fox can be tamed and it can become a friend. Violence can also be tamed and people who are disposed to violence can also learn how to live in peace with the rest of us—and all of us should feel secure. It's not a task that can be done easily or in a short space of time. But it has to be done.

CALDICOTT, HELEN MARY (1938–   ). Born, Melbourne, Australia; M.B.B.S., University of South Australia, Adelaide, 1962; intern, Royal Adelaide Hospital, 1962–63; intern, Adelaide Children's Hospital, 1972–73, resident 1973–75, staff member 1975–76; fellow in nutrition, Children's Hospital Medical Center, Boston, 1967–68; fellow in cystic fibrosis, 1975–76, associate in cystic fibrosis, 1977–   ; member, American Thoracic Society, Royal Australian College of Physicians, Physicians for Social Responsibility, president, 1981–
(See also *Current Biography*, October 1983.)

CISNEROS, HENRY G. (1947–   ). Born, San Antonio, Texas; B.A., Texas A. & M. University, 1968, M.A. in Urban and Regional Planning, 1970; M.P.A. in Public Administration, John F. Kennedy School of Government, Harvard University, 1973; Ph. D. in Public Administration, George Washington University, 1975; administrative assistant, Office of the City Manager, San Antonio, Texas, May, 1968; administrative assistant to the city manager, Bryan, Texas, September, 1968; assistant director, Department of Model Cities, San Antonio, 1969; assistant to the executive vice president, National League of Cities, Washington, D. C., 1970; White House fellow, assistant to the Secretary of Health, Education, and Welfare, 1971; Ford Foundation research grantee; Harvard University, teaching assistant, Department of Urban Studies and Planning, Massachusetts Institute of Technology, 1972; faculty member, division of Environmental Studies, University of Texas at San Antonio, 1974–   ; assistant professor, 1974–   ; member, San Antonio city council, 1975–81; mayor of San Antonio, 1981–   ; trustee, City Water Board, City Public Service Board, 1981–   ; selected "Outstanding Young Man of San Antonio," Jaycees, 1976, one of "Five Outstanding Young Texans," Texas Jaycees, 1976, one of "Ten Outstanding Young Men of America," U.S. Jaycees, 1982; awards, Torch of Liberty Award, Anti-Defamation League of B'nai B'rith, 1982, Jefferson Award, American Institute for Public Service, 1982; member, President's Federalism Council, United San Antonio, National Council for Urban Economic Development, Governor's Council of Mayors, Council on Foreign Relations of New York, Police Foundation of Washington, D.C., Texas Municipal League, Philosophical Society of Texas.

Cox, ARCHIBALD (1912–   ). Born, Plainfield, New Jersey; A.B., Harvard University, 1934, LL. B., 1937; LL. D. (honorary), Harvard University, 1975, Loyola University, 1964, University of Cincinnati, 1967, University of Denver, 1974, Amherst College, 1974, Rutgers University, 1974, University of Michigan, 1976, Wheaton College, 1977, Northeastern University, 1978; admitted to Massachusetts bar, 1937; in general practice, 1938–41; attorney, Office of Solicitor General, U.S. Department of Justice, 1941–43, Solicitor General, 1961–65; associate solicitor, Department of Labor, 1943–45; lecturer law, Harvard University, 1945–46, professor 1946–61, Williston professor of law, 1965–76, Carl M. Loeb University professor, 1976–   ; Solicitor General of the U.S., 1966; special investigator for Massachusetts Legislature, 1972; director, Office of Watergate Special Prosecution Force, 1973; co-chairman, Construction Industry Stabilization Commission, 1951–52; chairman, Wage Stabilization Board, 1952; member, board of overseers, Harvard University, 1962–65; American Bar Association, American Academy of Arts and Sciences, Common Cause; co-author (with Derek C. Bok), *Cases on Labor Law* (1948 to eighth edition, 1976); (with Mark DeWolfe Howe and J.R. Wiggins), *Civil Rights, the Constitution and the Courts* (1967); author, *Law and the National Labor Policy* (1960), *The Warren Court* (1968), *The Role of the Supreme Court in American Government* (1976). (See also *Current Biography*, July 1961.)

EWALD, WILLIAM BRAGG JR. (1925–   ). Born, Chicago, Illinois; A. B., Washington University, 1946; M.A., Harvard University, 1947, Ph. D., 1951; instructor, English and Humanities, Harvard University, 1951–54; special assistant to the White House staff; assistant, US Secretary of the Interior, President Dwight D. Eisenhower, in preparation of memoirs, *White House Years, Mandate for Change,* and *Waging Peace,* 1954–64; public affairs advisor, Directory of National Studies; executive secretary and member, Committee on Corporate Responsibility; program director, communication studies, International Business Machines Corporation, 1964–   ; president, Bruce Museum Association; author, *The Masks of Johnathan Swift,* 1954, *Rogues, Royalty, and Reporters: The Age of Queen Anne Through Its Newspapers,* 1956, *Eisenhower the President: Crucial Days, 1951–60,* 1981.

FERRARO, GERALDINE ANNE (1935–   ). Born, Newburgh, New York; B.A. Marymount College, 1956, J.D., Fordham University, 1960, postgraduate study, New York University Law School, 1978; admitted to the New York State bar, 1961, United States Court of Appeals bar for the Second Circuit, 1975, United States District Court bar for the Eastern District of New York, 1975, United States Supreme Court bar, 1978; practice of law, New York City, 1961–74; assistant district attorney, Queens County, New York, 1974–78; member, 96th-97th United States

Congresses from 9th New York district, 1978–   , advisory council on housing, Civil Court, New York City, 1978–   ; Queens County Bar Association; past president, Queens County Women's Bar Association.

HART, GARY (1937–   ). Born, Ottawa, Kansas; B.A., Bethany College (Oklahoma); LL.B., Yale University, 1964; admitted to the bar, 1964; attorney, U. S. Department of Justice; then special assistant, Secretary of the U.S. Department of the Interior; practiced law in Denver, Colorado, 1967–70, 1972–74; national campaign director for George McGovern in Democratic presidential campaign, 1970–72; U.S. senator from Colorado, 1975–   ; past member, board of commissioners, Denver Urban Renewal Authority, Park Hill Action Committee; student volunteer organizer Robert F. Kennedy presidential campaign, 1968; author, *Right From the Start.*

KELLER, ALBERT JR. (1915–   ). Born, Peoria, Illinois; attended the University of Illinois; served with the 15th United States Army Air Force to rank of sergeant; 1943–45; cost accountant, David Bradley Mfg. Company, 1945–50; office manager and accountant, Azzarelli Construction Company, 1955–59; Chief Deputy County Clerk, Kankakee, Illinois, 1959–64; Administrative Assistant, Kankakee County, Illinois, 1964–82; alderman, City of Kankakee, Illinois, 1969–   ; accountant, American Red Cross, 1973–   ; senior vice commander, American Legion Post 83, Kankakee, Illinois, 1951–52, commander, 1952–53; 18th district commander, Illinois Department of the American Legion, 1954–55, department senior vice commander, 1953–54, department commander, 1958–59; member, Americanism Commission, the American Legion, 1960–66; vice-chairman of select committee on Special Problems of the Veterans Affairs and Rehabilitation Program, 1977–80; chairman, National Economics Commission, 1974–80, national commander, 1982–   ; member, Elks, Disabled American Veterans, Veterans of Foreign Wars, Non-Commissioned Officers Association, American Ex-Prisoners of War Association.

KIRKPATRICK, JEANE DUANE JORDAN (1926–   ). Born, Duncan, Oklahoma; A.B., Barnard College, 1948; M.A., Columbia University, 1950, Ph.D., 1967; fellow, University of Paris Institute de Science Politique, 1952–53; L.H.D. (honorary), Mount Vernon College, 1978; research analyst, Department of State, 1951–53; research associate, George Washington University, 1954–56; Fund for the Republic, 1956–58; assistant professor of political science, Trinity College, 1962–67; associate professor of political science, Georgetown University, 1967–73, professor, 1973–   ; Leavey professor in Foundation of American Freedom,

1978-   ; resident scholar, American Enterprise Institute for Public Policy Research, 1977-   ; co-chairman, task force for presidential election process, 20th Century Fund; consultant to American Council of Learned Societies, Departments of State, Health, Education, and Welfare, and Defense intermittently, 1955-72; member, credentials committee, Democratic National Convention, 1976; Permanent United States Representative to the United Nations, 1981-   ; author, *Foreign Students in the United States: A National Survey*, 1966, *Mass Behavior in Battle and Captivity*, 1968, *Leader and Vanguard in Mass Society: The Peronist Movement in Argentina*, 1971, *Political Woman*, 1973, *The Presidential Elite*, 1976, *Dismantling the Parties: Reflections on Party Reform and Party Decomposition*, 1978; editor and contributor, *Elections U.S.A.*, 1956, *Strategy of Deception*, 1963, *The New Class*, 1978, *The New American Political System*, 1978; Stephens College alumna award, 1978, Earhart fellow 1956-57. (See also *Current Biography*, July 1981.)

KOOP, CHARLES EVERETT (1916-   ). Born, Brooklyn, New York; A. B., Dartmouth College, 1937; M.D., Cornell University, 1941; Sc.D., University of Pennsylvania, 1947; LL.D., Eastern Baptist College, 1960, M.D. (honorary), University of Liverpool, 1968, L.H.D., Wheaton College, 1973, D.Sc., Gynedd Mercy College, 1978; intern, Pennsylvania Hospital, 1941-42; surgeon-in-chief, Children's Hospital of Philadelphia, 1948-   ; with University of Pennsylvania School of Medicine, 1942-   , professor, 1959-   ; fellow in surgery, Boston Children's Hospital, 1946; consultant, U.S. Navy, 1964-   ; member, board of directors, Medical Assistance Programs, Inc., Daystar Communications, Inc., Eastern Baptist Seminary and College; fellow, American Academy of Pediatrics; member, American Surgeons Association, Society of University Surgeons, British Association of Pediatric Surgeons, International Society of Surgery, Societé Francaise de Chirurgie Infantile, American Medical Association, Deutschen Gesselschaft für Kinderchirurgi, Societé Suisse de Chirurgie Infantile, Order Duarte, Sanchez y Mella, Dominican Republic; contributor to surgical, physiological, biomedical, ethical, and pediatric journals.

MAISONROUGE, JACQUES GASTON (1924-   ). Born, Cachan Seine, France; diplomed engineer, Ecole Centrale de Paris, 1948-   ; assistant to sales manager, France, 1954-56, manager, marketing planning and research, IBM Europe, 1956-58, regional manager, Europe, 1958-59, assistant general manager, 1959-62, vice-president, World Trade Corporation, 1962-64, president, IBM Europe, 1964-73, president and chief executive officer, IBM World Trade/Europe/ Middle East/Africa Corporation, 1974-   , chairman of the board, 1976-   ; director, Philip Morris, Inc., L'Air Liquide; board of directors, European Institute of

Business Administration; chairman, board of trustees, Ecole Centrale des Arts et Manufacturers; member, Institute of International Education (honorary).

O'NEILL, MICHAEL JAMES (1922-   ). Born, Detroit, Michigan; B. A., University of Detroit, 1946; graduate student at Fordham University, 1946–47; L.H.D. (honorary), University of Detroit, 1977; public relations consultant, 1945–46; radio commentator at station WJBK in Detroit, 1946; writer, Standard News Association, 1946–47; United Press International, 1947–56; Washington overnight editor, 1954–56; Washington correspondent, *New York Daily News*, 1956–66, assistant managing editor, 1966–68, managing editor, 1968–74, executive editor, 1974–75, editor, 1975–   , vice-president, director, 1971–   ; served with the United States Army, 1943–45, decorated with bronze star; member, State Department Correspondents Association, president, 1964–65; president of Overseas Writers, 1965; member of New York Academy of Sciences, Council on Foreign Relations, China Council; recipient of National Affairs Reporting Award, National Headliners, 1956; author, (with L. Tanzer) *The Kennedy Circle*, 1961, *China Today*, 1976.

REAGAN, RONALD WILSON (1911-   ). Born, Tampico, Illinois, B.A., Eureka College (Illinois), 1932; sports announcer, radio station WHO, Des Moines, Iowa, 1932–37, motion picture and television actor, 1937–1966; program supervisor, General Electric Theater; president, Screen Actors Guild, 1947–52, 1959; captain, US Air Force, 1942–45; governor, California, 1967–74; unsuccessful candidate for Republican presidential nomination, 1976; US President, 1980–   (See also *Current Biography*, February 1967.)

ROSTOW, WALT WHITMAN (1916-   ). Born, New York; B.A., Yale University, 1936, Ph.D., 1940; Rhodes scholar, Balliol College, Oxford University, 1936–38; instructor, economics, Columbia University, 1940–41; assistant chief, German-Austrian economic division, U.S. Department of State, 1945–46; Harmsworth professor, Oxford University, 1946–47; assistant to executive secretary, Economic Commission for Europe, 1947–49; professor, American history, Cambridge University, 1949–50, economic history, Massachusetts Institute of Technology, 1950–60; staff member, Center for International Studies, 1951–60; special assistant to President for national security affairs, 1961; counselor, chairman, policy planning council of the U.S. Department of State, 1961–66; special assistant, President, 1966–69; United States representative and ambassador, Inter-American committee of the Alliance for Progress, 1964–66; currently professor of economics and history, University of Texas, Austin; served as major, O.S.S., United States Army, 1942–45;

awards, Legion of Merit, Honorary Order of the British Empire, Presidential Medal of Freedom with distinction; author, *The American Diplomatic Revolution* (1947), *Essays on the British Economy of the Nineteenth Century* (1948), *The Process of Economic Growth* (1952), *The United States in the World Arena* (1960), *View from the Seventh Floor* (1964), *A Design for Asian Development* (1965); *Politics and the Stages of Growth* (1971), *The Diffusion of Power* (1972), *How It All Began* (1975), *The World Economy: History and Prospect* (1978), *Getting From Here to There,* (1978); co-author, (with A.D. Gayer and A.J. Schwartz) *The Growth and Fluctuation of the British Economy, 1790-1850* (1953); (with A. Levin and others), *The Dynamics of Soviet Society* (1953); (with others) *The Prospects for Communist China* (1954); (with R. W. Hatch) *An American Policy in Asia* (1955); (with M.F. Millikan) *A Proposal: Key to an Effective Foreign Policy* (1957), (with William E. Griffith) *East-West Relations: Is Détente Possible?* (1969); editor, *The Economics of Take-Off Into Sustained Growth* (1963). (See also *Current Biography,* May 1961.)

SAXON, DAVID STEPHEN (1920–   ). Born, St. Paul, Minnesota; B.S., Massachusetts Institute of Technology, 1941, Ph.D., 1944; L.H.D. (honorary), Hebrew Union College, 1976, University of Judaism, 1977; LL. D., University of South Carolina, 1978; research physicist, Radiation Laboratory, Massachusetts Institute of Technology, 1943–46, Philips Laboratories, 1946–47; member, faculty, University of California at Los Angeles, 1947–75, professor, physics, 1958–75, chairman, department of physics, 1963–66, dean of physical sciences, 1966–69, executive vice chancellor, 1968–74, university provost, 1974–75; president, University of California at Berkeley, 1975–   ; visiting scientist, Centre d'Etudes Nucleaires, Saclay, France, 1968–69; visiting professor, faculty of sciences, University of Paris, Orsay, France, 1961–62; awards, Guggenheim fellow, 1956–57, 1961–62; Fulbright grantee, 1961–62; member, American Physics Society, American Association of Physics Teachers, American Institute of Physics; author, *Elementary Quantum Mechanics,* 1968, (with A.E.S. Green and T. Sawada) *The Nuclear Independent Particle Model,* 1968, (with Julian Swinger) *Discontinuities in Wave Guides,* 1968, (with William B. Fretter) *Physics for the Liberal Arts Student,* 1971.

STEVENIN, THOMAS J. (1939–   ). Born, Kansas City, Missouri; B.A., Wheaton College, 1962; M.A., Midwestern Theological Seminary, 1965; Ed.D., Nova University, 1982; training assistant, Farmland Industries, Inc., home study supervisor, director of sales training, executive director, Farmland training center; vice-president, Human Resources and Administrative Services, 1965–82; president, Stevenin and Associates,

1982–   ; member, Association of Cooperative Educators, American Society of Training and Development; awards, Distinguished Service Award, Future Farmers of America, 1976, Outstanding Contribution to Education award, Association of Cooperative Educators, 1980, Graduate Research Award, Cooperative League of the U.S.A.

STROMER, WALTER F. (1920–   ). Born, Iowa City, Iowa; attended Nebraska College of Commerce, Hastings; worked two years as a clerk-stenographer; B.A., Hastings College, Nebraska, 1949; M.A., University of Denver, 1950, Ph.D., 1953; United States Army, 1943–1945; professor, speech communication, Cornell College, Iowa, 1954–   ; member, Speech Communication Association, American Association of University Professors, American Civil Liberties Union; author, more than 30 articles in *English Journal, Quarterly Journal of Speech, The Speaker, Education, Today's Speech, Social Work, Journal of Creative Behavior,* etc.

SWEARER, HOWARD ROBERT (1932–   ). Born, Hutchinson, Kansas; A.B., Princeton University, 1954; M.A., Harvard University, 1956, Ph. D., 1960; professor, political science, University of California at Los Angeles, 1960–67; program officer-in-charge, office of European and international affairs, Ford Foundation, 1967–70; president, Carleton College, 1970–77, Brown University, 1977–   ; first lieutenant, United States Army, 1958–59; director, Textron Inc; board of directors, A Better Chance, Inc., German Marshall Fund U.S., American Council on Education; member, Council on Foreign Relations, Phi Beta Kappa.

THOMAS, FRANKLIN AUGUSTINE (1934–   ). Born, Brooklyn, New York; B.A., Columbia College, 1956, LL. B., Columbia University, 1963; LL.D. (honorary), Yale University, 1970, Fordham University, 1972, Pratt Institute, 1974, Columbia University, 1979; member, United States Air Force, 1956–60; admitted to New York State bar, 1964; attorney, Federal Housing and Home Finance Agency, New York City, 1963–64; assistant United States attorney for South District, New York, 1964–65; deputy policy commissioner for legal matters, New York City, 1965–67; president, chief executive officer, Bedford Stuyvesant Restoration Corporation, Brooklyn, 1967–77; president, Ford Foundation, 1979–   ; director, Citicorp/Citibank, CBS Incorporated, Aluminum Company of America, Allied Stores Corporation, Cummins Engine Company; trustee, J.H. Whitney Foundation, Columbia University, 1969–75; awards, L.B. J. Foundation award for contribution to betterment of urban life, 1974, Medal of Excellence, Columbia University, 1976. (See also *Current Biography,* October 1981.)

WEICKER, LOWELL PALMER JR. (1931–   ). Born, Paris, France; graduate, Lawrenceville School, 1949; B.A., Yale University, 1953; L.L.B., University of Virginia, 1958; admitted to Connecticut bar, 1960; United States Army, 1953–55; Connecticut General Assembly, 1963–69; first selectman, Greenwich, Connecticut, 1964–68; 91st U.S. Congress, fourth district of Connecticut, 1969–71; United States senator, Connecticut, 1971–   ; member, senate committees, Energy and Natural Resources, Appropriations, Small Business.

WHITE, DAVID MANNING (1917–   ). Born, Milwaukee, Wisconsin; A.B., Cornell College, 1938, M.S., Columbia University, 1939, Ph.D., University of Iowa, 1942; L.H.D., Columbia University, 1964; teaching fellow, University of Iowa, 1940–42; instructor, English, College of William and Mary, 1945–46; member of faculty, Bradley University, 1946–49; research professor, Boston University, 1949–75, chairman, division of journalism, 1964–72; professor, mass communication, Virginia Commonwealth University, 1975–   ; visiting professor, Centro International de Estudios Superiores de Periodismo American Latina, Quito, Ecuador, 1970–71; news commentator, station WBZ-TV, Boston, 1949–50; project director, Center for International Studies, Massachusetts Institute of Technology, 1951; research director, New York office of International Press Institute, 1952–53; research adviser, Sarpay Beikman Institute, Rangoon, Burma, 1957–58; correspondent, NBC News, Rangoon, 1957–58; supervisor, Gallup Poll in Boston area, 1952–56; special elections editor, AP, Boston, 1954–62; member, UNESCO relations committee, State Department, 1954–56; consultant, department of mass communications, UNESCO, Paris, 1954–62; lecturer, Burma School of Journalism, 1957–58, Centre International d'Enseignement Superieur de Journalism, Strasbourg, France, 1957, '60, '61, '62. Inst. for Publizistik, Free University, Berlin, 1962, '66; general editor, Beacon Press, 1966–   ; chairman, Governor's Committee on Communications, 1965–70; served to ensign, U. S. Navy Reserve, 1943–44; awards, Chevalier d'Honneur et de Merite, Ordre Souverain de Saint-Jean de Jerusalem, Chevaliers de Malte, Order of Polonia Restituta; Yankee Quill award, 1970; member, Illinois Academy of Science, Boston Author's Club, Historical Society of Iowa, Association for Educational Journalism, Council on Communications Research chairman, 1954–57, New England Academy of Journalists (honorary), Phi Beta Kappa; co-author, *Elementary Statistics for Journalists* (1954); author, *Mass Culture: The Popular Arts in America* (1957), (with Al Capp) *From Dogpatch to Slobbovia* (1964), (with Richard Averson) *Journalism in the Mass Media* (1970), (with Richard Averson) *The Celluloid Weapon: Social Comment in the American Film* (1972); editor, *Pop Culture in America* (1970), *TV Quarterly* (1969–71); co-editor, *Introduction to Mass Communications Research* (1958), *Publishing for the New Reading Audience* (1959), *Identity and Anxiety: Survival of the Individual in Mass Society* (1960),

The Funnies, An American Idiom (1963), *People, Society, and Mass Communications* (1964), *Sight, Sound and Society* (1968), *Electronic Drama: Television Plays of the 1960s* (1971), *Mass Culture, Revisited* (1971), *Popular Culture: Mirror of American Life* (1977).

CUMULATIVE SPEAKER INDEX

1980–1983

A cumulative author index to the volumes of *Representative American Speeches* for the years 1937–1938 through 1959–1960 appears in the 1959–1960 volume, for the years 1960–1961 through 1969–1970 in the 1969–1970 volume, and for 1970–1971 through 1979–1980 in the 1979–1980 volume.

Anderson, W. S. 1980–81, 130–56, Meeting the Japanese economic challenge

Brink, D. R. 1981–82, 54–61, Can we avoid constitutional crisis?
Burger, W. E. 1980–81, 40–60, Address to the American Bar Association; 1981–82, 78–89, A modest proposal for prison reform

Caldicott, H. M. 1982–83, 72–80, We are the curators of life on earth
Cannon, M. W. 1981–82, 62–78, Crime and the decline of values
Carey, J. W. 1980–81, 95–110, International communications: the impact of the mass media
Carter, J. E. (Jimmy). 1980–81, 18–25, Farewell address
Cisneros, H. G. 1982–83, 24–42, A survival strategy for America's cities
Coates, J. F. 1981–82, 200–14, The future of computer data security
Cox, Archibald. 1982–83, 62–71, The best of times? The worst of times?

Ervin, S. J. Jr. 1980–81, 61–75, Judicial verbicide: an affront to the Constitution
Ewald, W. B. Jr. 1982–83, 174–9, Man of steel, velvet, and peace: Dwight D. Eisenhower

Ferraro, G. A. 1982–83, 198–207, Women in leadership can make a difference

Glenn, J. H. Jr. 1981–82, 183–94, The exploration of space: a time for decision
Gunderson, R. G. 1981–82, 172–83, Digging up Parson Weems

Harris, P. R. 1980–81, 35–48, Political pluralism and religious absolutism
Hart, Gary. 1982–83, 55–62, A time for economic reform

Ilchman, A. S. 1981–82, 102–12, The public purposes of private colleges

Jacob, J. E. 1981–82, 145–50, The state of black America

Jordan, V. D. Jr. 1980-81, 210-18. To build a more equal society

Keller, Albert Jr. 1982-83, 171-3, A memorial to American Vietnam War veterans

Kennedy, E. M. 1980-81, 25-35, The dream shall never die: speech to the Democratic National Convention

Kirkland, J. L. 1981-82, 150-60, Solidarity, indispensable key

Kirkpatrick, J. J. 1982-83, 161-70, Promoting free elections to the future

Knapp, D. C. 1980-81, 186-95, Education in the '80s

Koop, C. E. 1982-83, 207-18, Violence and public health

Laingen, L. B. 1980-81, 81-3, Welcome home

Leonard, W. A. 1981-82, 136-45, Some flaws in the golden age of journalism

Mahoney, David. 1980-81, 196-202, The new civility; the increase in defamation

Maisonrouge, J. G. 1982-83, 123-33, Some education requirements for the manager of the eighties

Mathias, C. M. Jr. 1980-81, 203-9, The state of civil liberties

McGovern, G. S. 1981-82, 25-33, The arms race vs. the human race

Newsom, D. D. 1981-82, 33-44, What Americans want in foreign policy

O'Neill, M. J. 1982-83, 97-111, The power of the press: a problem for the republic: a challenge for editors

Pepper, C. D. 1981-82, 168-72, In memory of Franklin D. Roosevelt

Quainton, A. C. E. 1980-81, 83-94, Terrorism and low-level conflict: a challenge for the 1980s

Randolph, Jennings. 1981-82, 165-8, In memory of Franklin D. Roosevelt

Reagan, R. W. 1980-81, 9-18, Inaugural address, 76-81, Welcome home; 1981-82, 9-25, The new federalism: state of the union address; 1982-83, 8-24, Staying the course: state of the union address

Rosenthal, A. M. 1981-82, 124-36, Acceptance of the Elijah Parish Lovejoy award

Rostow, W. W. 1982-83, 152-60, Foreign policy: the President, Congress, and public opinion

Saldich, A. R. 1980-81, 110-29, Electronic democracy: how television governs

Sawhill, J. C. 1980-81, 167-85, Higher education in the '80s: beyond retrenchment

Saxon, D. S. 1982-83, 112-23, The place of science and technology in the liberal arts curriculum

Schlesinger, A. M. Jr. 1981-82, 161-5, In memory of Franklin D. Roosevelt

Senese, D. J. 1981–82, 89–102, Can we have excellence in education?

Silber, J. R. 1981–82, 112–24, The gods of the copybook headings

Smith, W. F. 1981–82, 44–54, The people should govern, not the courts

Snell, G. D. 1981–82, 194–200, Technology and moral responsibility

Stevenin, T. J. 1982–83, 180–8, Now for the hard part

Stromer, W. F. 1982–83, 189–97, The future is now; a zest for living

Swearer, Howard. 1982–83, 138–43, The separation of athletics and academics in our universities

Thimmesch, N. P. 1980–81, 156–66, Organized labor in the 1980s: the push for unification

Thomas, F. A. 1982–83, 43–54, Youth, unemployment and national service

Weicker, Lowell Jr. 1982–83, 133–7, People with ideas, ideals, and the will to make them work, 144–51, Prayer in public schools

White, D. M. 1982–83, 81–97 Mass culture: can America really afford it?